GOVERNANCE IN NORTHERN ONTARIO

Economic Development and Policy Making

This book analyses economic development policy governance in northern Ontario over the past thirty years, with the goal of making practical policy recommendations for present and future government engagement with the region. It brings together scholars from several disciplines to address the policy and management challenges in various sectors of northern Ontario's economy, including the mining, pulp and paper, and tourism industries, and both small- and medium-sized businesses.

Governance in Northern Ontario assesses the role of the provincial government and its economic policy intervention in the region's economic development. The contributors evaluate the relationship between the provincial and local governments and the business sector, as well as looser structures of policy networks, such as those of First Nations and other interested community groups. Focusing on the nature of partnerships between governments and societal interests, *Governance in Northern Ontario* makes a significant contribution to the theories and practice of public policy governance in socio-economically disadvantaged regions.

CHARLES CONTEH is an associate professor in the Department of Political Science at Brock University.

BOB SEGSWORTH is a professor in the Department of Political Science at Laurentian University.

IPAC
The Institute of
Public Administration of Canada

IAPC
L'Institut d'administration
publique du Canada

The Institute of Public Administration of Canada Series
in Public Management and Governance

Editors:
Peter Aucoin, 2001–2
Donald Savoie, 2003–7
Luc Bernier, 2007–9
Patrice Dutil, 2010–

This series is sponsored by the Institute of Public Administration of Canada as part of its commitment to encourage research on issues in Canadian public administration, public sector management, and public policy. It also seeks to foster wider knowledge and understanding among practitioners, academics, and the general public.

For a list of books published in the series, see page 217.

Governance in Northern Ontario

Economic Development and Policy Making

EDITED BY CHARLES CONTEH AND
BOB SEGSWORTH

IPAC > **IAPC**

The Institute of
Public Administration of Canada

L'Institut d'administration
publique du Canada

UNIVERSITY OF TORONTO PRESS
Toronto Buffalo London

© University of Toronto Press 2013
Toronto Buffalo London
www.utppublishing.com
Printed in Canada

ISBN 978-1-4426-4547-9 (cloth)
ISBN 978-1-4426-1356-0 (paper)

Printed on acid-free, 100% post-consumer recycled paper with
vegetable-based inks.

Library and Archives Canada Cataloguing in Publication

Governance in northern Ontario : economic development and policy
making / edited by Charles Conteh and Bob Segsworth.

(Institute of Public Administration of Canada series in public management
and governance)
Includes bibliographical references.
ISBN 978-1-4426-4547-9 (bound). – ISBN 978-1-4426-1356-0 (pbk.)

1. Ontario, Northern – Economic policy.   2. Provincial-local relations –
Ontario.   3. Public-private sector cooperation – Ontario.   4. Economic
development – Ontario, Northern.   I. Segsworth, R.V., editor of
compilation   II. Conteh, Charles, 1974–, editor of compilation
III. Series: Institute of Public Administration of Canada series in public
management and governance

HC117.05G68 2013   338.9713'1   C2013-904360-8

University of Toronto Press acknowledges the financial assistance to its
publishing program of the Canada Council for the Arts and the Ontario
Arts Council.

University of Toronto Press acknowledges the financial support of the
Government of Canada through the Canada Book Fund for its publishing
activities.

Contents

Foreword

In its 2012 budget, the government of Ontario announced that it would phase out its support of the Ontario Northland Transportation Commission (ONTC), an agency that operated the Ontario Northland Railway, the Ontario Northland Motor Coach Services, and Ontera, a telecommunications company. The news barely registered in southern Ontario, but in northern Ontario the declaration resonated deeply. The potential loss of the Ontario Northland Railway, a service that was practically bred in the bone of the territory, stung particularly hard. It dated back to the earliest years of the twentieth century and had long been symbolic of the optimism and promise of the vast Ontario north. The railway had been built to develop the promising mines and lumber camps in Lake Timiskaming and Lake Nipissing, and it succeeded brilliantly. At the height of the depression of the 1930s, it was extended to practically reach James Bay. Northern Ontario's resources had not only fuelled Ontario's economic rise, giving birth to countless companies and contributing enormous wealth to the province and to Canada in general, but also spoke of unbridled faith in growth and prosperity.

The decision to close down the ONTC, in what proved to be the last months of the Dalton McGuinty government, signalled the end of an era. For the Liberal government, this was a decision that had to be made. Twenty-first-century transportation realities had to be recognized, and the reality was that the Northland was hardly used by Ontario's population. Why sink money in an agency whose usefulness simply could no longer be demonstrated? For the Liberal government's critics, the closing of the Northland demonstrated that Queen's Park had turned its back on the region and its potential. The first and most eloquent voices to react to the announcement were the mayors of the Northern

Communities Working Group (NCWG). At the core of their opposition was not only the substance of the decision, but the process. The NCWG complained bitterly that they were not consulted in advance and wanted a "new deal" for Ontario Northland. They wanted to be heard; they wanted to be involved. Their practical message is echoed in the scholarly treatments of this volume.

Indeed, the Ontario Northland episode speaks to the timeliness – in fact, the urgency – of this book. Mackenzie King famously observed that Canada had too much geography and too little history. For decision makers in the government of Ontario, this has long seemed to be a reality that bedevils policy making. Like all provinces (save perhaps for the Maritimes) and the government of Canada, the "problem" of hinterland development has been difficult to resolve. On one hand, the merits of development have been self-evident: the rich natural resources were mostly accessible and usually command rewarding prices on the national and international commodity markets. It has been a classic application of the "staples" theory of development whereby Canada's urban centres promoted hinterland exploitation as a means to enrich themselves. For the government, it made sense for its policies to invest a part of its treasure in developing infrastructures that would make possible the transportation of raw materials over vast distances and attract a workforce that, in turn, would make such development possible.

But while geography quietly lent itself to utilization, human history made more noise. Through the years, the dream of an Ontario north had grown from a business community's notion to the reality that the region was home to generations of Canadians, as well as the many indigenous communities that had walked these lands since time immemorial. Over time, Canadian values instructed governments to ensure that the services in those areas be at least comparable to those in southern, urban Ontario. The idea that northern development could be done inexpensively rapidly eroded in the 1980s and into our new century. The hinterland remained rich and full of promise, but global commodity markets now dictated the rate of growth, and declining prices guaranteed relatively lower tax revenues for the state. The policy problem became acutely pointed as governments slashed budgets and coped with rising costs of servicing the northern population with health care, education, and social services.

What could be done to guarantee the sustainability of these communities and ensure that they had the tools and means to govern themselves successfully with minimal intervention from the metropolis? To fail in this concern is simply to prolong a colonial relationship – one that satisfies neither the northerners nor the policy makers in Queen's Park. As the mayors of northern Ontario showed in the drama of the closing down of the ONTC, the governance of the north had to be changed to include more intergovernmental collaboration and bold new thinking.

This book's originality rests on the treatment the editors and contributors give to the policy development as public servants and politicians struggle to reconcile the burdens of responsibility with the requirements of northern development. The issue has been as simple as it has been difficult: how can Ontario (or any other province, for that matter) develop the hinterlands as sources of revenue and employment while at the same time limiting the costs of servicing small populations spread out over a territory of almost 800,000 square kilometres, roughly the size of Western Europe? The only answer is better knowledge, better understanding, and better planning, and that can only happen with a revamped governance that gives primacy to intergovernmental collaboration.

This book will be valuable for policy makers and students of policy in Ontario but also far beyond the borders because it examines the knotty problem of hinterland development from illustrative vantage points. It is rich in background information and stimulating insights on what policy directions might want to explore. Anchored in the experience of the twentieth century, it speaks to the realities of our day with a clear and eloquent voice.

Patrice Dutil
Editor, IPAC Series in Public Management
Ryerson University
August 2013

Acknowledgments

We are indebted to several organizations and individuals for their support in the development of this book. The Institute of Public Administration of Canada (IPAC) responded positively to our request for funding in August 2008. Wendy Feldman, the IPAC director of research, has provided encouragement and support since that time. As part of the process of preparing the chapters, prospective authors were invited to present papers at a workshop held at Laurentian University in the fall of 2009. A workshop grant from the Social Sciences and Humanities Research Council of Canada, a travel grant from the Ontario Ministry of Northern Development, Mines and Forests, and financial support from Laurentian University allowed us to bring delegates from the Atlantic Canada Opportunities Agency, the Federal Economic Development Initiative in Northern Ontario, the Ministry of Northern Development, Mines and Forests, First Nations communities, and chambers of commerce, as well as economic development officials from several municipalities, to comment on and offer constructive criticism of many of the chapters. To them we owe a considerable debt. France Girard, Laura Sanche, and Sarah Nixon provided invaluable administrative support for the workshop. The contributions of Dr Tim Nieguth, Dr Claude Vincent, and Dr Ray Bollman provided a deeper appreciation of the current economic and political context of northern Ontario. Nick Swift provided editorial service beyond the call of duty. Léo Larivière responded to our pleas for help and recreated the figures to meet the publication requirements of the University of Toronto Press. Daniel Quinlan, our acquisitions editor; Wayne Herrington, managing editor; other staff at the University of Toronto Press; and freelance copy editor Barry Norris provided encouragement, support, and professional advice that improved the quality of the book immensely.

The most serious expression of gratitude is reserved for the contributors to this book. They endured the harassment, erratic behaviour, and peculiar work schedules of the editors with good humour, patience, and a willingness to respond quickly to questions and comments. Without their expertise and support, this book would not have been possible.

GOVERNANCE IN NORTHERN ONTARIO

Economic Development and Policy Making

1 Introduction

CHARLES CONTEH AND BOB SEGSWORTH

Regional economic development policy is an intrinsically multidimensional field of study. Comprehensive research into it inevitably will include consideration of certain political and institutional facts. The chapters in this volume, therefore, seek to highlight and examine the political and institutional dimensions of regional economic development policy governance in northern Ontario. For the purposes of the discussions in this volume, the distinction between economic growth and economic development is worth noting. Economic growth focuses on macroeconomic indicators of how well an economy is doing, as often measured by the expansion (or contraction) of its gross domestic product. Economic development, however, shifts the focus of well-being from the economy to the people. Although economic growth is important, the more relevant consideration becomes how its translates into human welfare, measured by factors such as the creation of sustainable jobs, the number of people earning a decent wage, and improvements in general living standards.

The goal of this introductory chapter is to provide a framework for the two major themes that bind the chapters together – namely, governance and sustainability. But before elaborating on these two themes, we offer a cursory overview of the evolution of approaches to economic development. Although the intention of this volume is not to test or analyse theories of economic development, nevertheless, a brief mention of these various approaches serves to provide background context for the reader. A wide range of theories frames the field of economic development, including staples theory, dependency theory, geographical pyramid of control, centre-periphery theory, export-base theory, import-substitution, and more recently, community economic development. Elaborating on all of these theories would require a separate project, but here we briefly overview of some of the major theoretical frameworks that have influenced regional economic development in Canada dating back to the "growth pole" concept of the 1960s.[1]

The growth pole approach views regional development from a broad perspective, and calls for a number of interventionist measures designed to stimulate growth within a particular geographical space. This space – often a particular city chosen for its location and/or size – in turn is expected to act as the engine of growth and development for the surrounding region. The growth pole approach characterized Canada's early model of regional economic development,[2] but fell into disuse in the 1970s as students of regional economic development in member countries of the Organisation for Economic Co-operation and Development joined a wider international school of thinking on economic development known as the "development approach."[3] This approach was limited, however, inasmuch as it was inspired by the study of underdeveloped countries, and thus made certain theoretical assumptions about institutional and societal capacity that did not fit advanced, industrialized polities such as Canada.[4] Even though Atlantic Canada was considered "underdeveloped,"[5] such a description was based on comparisons with other provinces in Canada and could not refer to the dismal realities of extreme poverty and underdevelopment in most developing countries.

The emergence in the early 1970s of "trade theory" effectively discredited and displaced the interventionist impulse of the development approach.[6] Trade theory was marked by the ascendance of neo-classical economics and its focus on free markets and the principle of comparative advantage. This approach is fundamentally opposed to most forms of state intervention to foster economic growth and development, and instead insists on the invisible hand of economic restructuring, whereby any attempt by the state to support less competitive regions and sectors is inevitably inefficient. A major ideational shift during this time, therefore, was the resurgence of ideological displeasure with market-intrusive policy interventions.[7] Regional economic development aimed at easing disparities, for instance, was viewed as bound to distort natural market forces and potentially damaging to full economic growth.

By the latter part of the 1990s, however, the assumptions of neo-classical trade theory were increasingly questioned as seismic shifts in balance of trade brought on by the emerging global economy lent credibility to more "developmental" or "mixed economy" approaches employed by countries such as China and India. Along with these shifts came not only a focus on the knowledge economy, but also strategic means by which state intervention could nurture sectoral and regional competitiveness in a country's domestic economy.[8]

Moreover, shifts in thinking about the governance of regional economies were changing policy perspectives on regional development in Canada and around the world. By the close of the 1990s, global trends had moved towards an almost complete integration of economies around the world.[9] These trends created certain apparent contradictions or paradoxes, wherein a globalized world with integrated markets witnessed the emergence of a greater desire on the part of subnational governments – and even local communities – to exercise more control over their socio-economic destinies. Regional development policy in Canada was affected by these trends, as discussions metamorphosed into a preoccupation with local development. These emergent ideas about economic development emphasized approaches that favour the systematic use by states of policy instruments to encourage the development of critical sectors of a regional economy.[10] As a consequence, subnational jurisdictions arose as centres of economic policy intervention.

With these shifts in theory in mind, the contributors to this volume offer their critiques of the capacity and integrity of the political and institutional framework of regional economic development policy governance in northern Ontario. Particularly since the turn of the millennium, the Ontario provincial government has been increasingly willing to direct the course of regional economies as components of the provincial economy, and has defined its policy vision for its northern region in bolder terms, with longer-range planning. The predominant policy framework suggests that, with the right mix of strategic intervention and market rationality, northern Ontario could become a productive centre, cluster, or node within the national and global economies, although the proposed strategies are usually confined to creating a locally driven regional economy.[11]

More broadly, the economic history of Canada as that of a staples system has led to a strong tendency to interventionism in approaches to national development.[12] In social policy, such interventionism has crystallized in a gradual transition to collectivism, manifested over the past five decades as a developed welfare state.[13] In economic development policy, a key example of active policy intervention in society has been the federal government's efforts to correct structural imbalances in industrial diversity and growth among the regions.[14] From its humble beginnings in the early 1960s, regional economic development policy has become an enduring feature of public policy and governance at both the national and provincial levels.

Although much of the Canadian literature on regional economic development has focused on the federal government's activities in Atlantic Canada, provincial governments across the country have engaged in similar activities to correct perceived regional imbalances. This volume thus attempts to fill a gap in the Canadian literature by examining economic development policy governance in northern Ontario, a region in the midst of economic and social change, crisis, and transition. Issues affecting its economic performance include the presence of a declining sector linked to older industry, an aging population, out-migration of the younger population, persistent poverty in First Nations communities, and the absence of coherent strategies to drive economic growth.

Northern Ontario has a vast land mass of approximately 800,000 square kilometres – almost 90 per cent of Ontario – yet its population of 786,500 is less than that of Ottawa.[15] The economy of the region is dominated by five large population centres: Greater Sudbury, Thunder Bay, Sault Ste Marie, North Bay, and Timmins. The history and structure of industry in northern Ontario confirm a trend of persistent decline in primary resource industries (traditionally the mainstay of the economy), as well as weakness in secondary manufacturing – despite the presence of numerous pulp and paper mills[16] – and in the services industries. The share of employment in primary and manufacturing industries declined from 28 per cent in 1981 to 16 per cent in 2001.

The politics of socio-economic development in northern Ontario thus has been shaped by a desire to eliminate the lingering features of underdevelopment. Calls are growing for a transformation in attitude and culture from one of dependency to a "fearless, creative, resourceful and confident society that takes responsibility for itself."[17] Although progress has been made in many aspects of governance in northern Ontario, especially in contrast to the hinterland politics of the past, underdevelopment remains dangerously persistent. At the same time, an important political and policy context is evolving. One element involves changing provincial policy on northern development. A second is about the range of programs and initiatives that provide support for and guide adjustments to the northern Ontario economy, as well as issues of overlap and duplication and the need for better policy and program coordination.

In 2004 Ontario's minister for Northern Development and Mines introduced the "Northern Prosperity Plan."[18] In the same year the Panel on the Role of Government in Ontario issued its report, "Investing in People: Creating a Human Capital Society for Ontario," which recommended that the province "phase out regional economic development programs, such as the provision of subsidies and tax incentives to businesses, which risk promoting permanent government-induced dependency."[19] In part this recommendation reflected the perspective of a research report prepared for the panel by Enid Slack, Larry Bourne, and Meric Gertler,[20] who argued that the provincial government, local governments, and regional authorities should recognize the "inevitability of decline" of small and remote communities, and develop strategies to deal with it. They went on to say that the province "should also consider restricting further settlement expansion in the north by drawing firm lines indicating where it would and would not guarantee access to public services."[21]

A concern about the 2004 Prosperity Plan was that it displayed a hierarchical approach by the Ontario government – indeed, the Northern Ontario Large Urban Mayors (NOLUM) later protested that "[w]e were not widely consulted in the 'Plan-making' process."[22] In 2005 NOLUM, the Northwestern Ontario Municipal Association (NOMA), and the Federation of Northern Ontario Municipalities (FONOM) called for extensive consultation on regional economic development in the north. Their report, "Creating Our Future: A New Vision for Northern Ontario," argued that "the current approach to regional economic development in Northern Ontario is not producing the desired results," and called for a more collaborative approach involving "all orders of government to pursue a new vision for Northern Ontario through coordinated strategies and actions."[23] At the end of the consultation process, a Northern Ontario Summit was proposed.

By 2007 the Ontario government had responded to these concerns and challenges by establishing a process under the 2005 Places to Grow Act to produce a new plan for the development of northern Ontario. Over the course of the next three years, the government received input from "more than 2,500 northerners ... in over 80 events across the north including 13 regional forums, 13 technical tables, a Think North Summit, 20 meetings with Aboriginal communities and organizations and workshops engaging more than 200 youth."[24] The result of this process, *Places to Grow – Better Choices, Brighter Futures: Proposed Growth Plan for Northern Ontario*, was announced as open for comment in fall

2009, and a final revised plan was to have been released by the end of 2010.

In the meantime, in a 2008 report, Industry Canada noted a somewhat lengthy list of economic development programs for northern Ontario that included the Northern Ontario Development Program, the Northern Ontario Heritage Fund, the Ontario Trillium Foundation, the Rural Economic Development Program of the Ontario Ministry of Agriculture, Food and Rural Affairs, the Ontario Job Creation Partnerships, and programs offered by Human Resources and Social Development Canada, the National Research Council, Indian and Northern Affairs Canada, and various municipalities. The report acknowledged overlaps among these programs, but concluded, "there are mechanisms in place to ensure collaboration occurs and to avoid duplication across funding sources."[25] Slack, Bourne, and Gertler, however, did not agree, claiming "there is ... a clear need for much better coordination of these government programs and policy initiatives."[26] They went on to suggest that an interdepartmental committee of cabinet with representatives from relevant provincial departments and agencies might be useful. NOLUM, NOMA, and FONOM argued that federal and provincial programs and initiatives required coordination. They also made the point that such programs and initiatives must be sufficiently flexible to accommodate northern Ontario communities' development strategies.

The Proposed Growth Plan was in some measure an attempt to respond to the perceived need for better coordination in the development of policy. Two lead ministries, Northern Development, Mines and Forestry, and Energy and Infrastructure, worked with fifteen other provincial ministries to develop the plan. In a local television interview on the day the proposed plan was announced, the current director of the Institute for Northern Ontario Research and Development, Dr David Robinson, suggested that its most impressive feature was the fact that representatives of seventeen provincial ministries actually had worked together to produce it. What is interesting, however, is that the proposal appeared not to include all three levels of government as partners; consequently, concerns about duplication, overlap, and a lack of coordination and responsiveness to local development planning continued.

It is against this policy background that we hope to evaluate the capacity, relevance, and integrity of the existing environment, institutions, and processes of regional economic development in northern Ontario at a time when the region faces strategic challenges marked by a radical reconfiguration of markets and communities, as well as by changing contours of political awareness and engagement. The contributors to this volume cover major sectors of the region's economy, including mining, forestry, agriculture, tourism, manufacturing, small- and medium-size business development, and the information and cultural industries. Using various analytical frameworks, the contributors assess the role of the federal, provincial, and municipal governments in the region's economic development (or underdevelopment). A central question is whether certain regions can be shown to score less than other regions in the same jurisdiction on objective socio-economic indicators, a question two chapters attempt to answer by providing various measures of economic activities that juxtapose northern and southern Ontario. But the book also moves the discussion beyond objective measures of relative deprivation by identifying the causes of underdevelopment and what should be done about it.

The first of the two central themes that emerge in the volume is *governance* – the institutions and processes that determine how policies are made. The contributors argue from various perspectives that a fundamental limitation of economic development in northern Ontario is the lack of a forum for making regional policy that reflects regional interests. In particular, there has been a systematic lack of cooperation or coordination between the federal and Ontario governments. Moreover, local jurisdictions such as municipalities lack the authority and resources to pursue sustained local economic development, as well as effective agency to make systemic policy changes that affect the socio-economic conditions of the region.

But beyond deficiencies in the institutional infrastructure of vertical intergovernmental relations, there are horizontal weaknesses within northern Ontario itself. In particular, there is a systemic lack of policy cooperation among the public, private, and community or non-profit sectors in a number of fields. For instance, the importance of addressing the tensions and fissures between the growing First Nations communities and the rest of the northern population can hardly be overstated. Other horizontal challenges include infrastructural problems such as transportation and communications in this geographically vast yet sparsely populated region.

The other thread that weaves through the volume is *sustainability* – in particular, the absence of sustainable development in northern Ontario. The theme of economic sustainability cuts across constitutional, political, institutional, and policy lines, touching on issues such as the treaty rights of First Nations and the autonomy of local regions to manage their own resources. A perennial challenge of economic development in the region has been the structure and character of its resource-based economy – indeed, the nature of wealth-extraction policies is a lightning rod for resentment about northern Ontario's underdevelopment. The substance of the controversy is that the nature of resource extraction perpetuates economic dependency, stifles economic diversification, and demoralizes community agency. Some of the contributors to the volume raise such uncomfortable questions as who really benefits from current policies, and whether northern Ontario can be rightly viewed as a periphery or hinterland region. The salience of these questions is made even more poignant by the fact that, although it located in one of the wealthiest provinces, northern Ontario increasingly is considered as a have-not region.

In Chapter 2, Chris Southcott highlights major socio-economic changes in northern Ontario, including those of a demographic, social, and economic nature. He also analyses the relationships between these broad changes and the policy of regional economic development, and how a deeper understanding of these changes could usefully inform economic policy development in the region.

In Chapter 3, Charles Conteh looks at the relationship between the three levels of government and their interaction with non-state actors. A recurrent theme of regional economic development policy governance in northern Ontario has been the need to integrate development policy interventions of the various levels of government to eliminate fragmentation, duplication, and waste. An example of this, as Conteh discusses, is the institutional relationships among Industry Canada's Federal Economic Development Initiative in Northern Ontario, the provincial Ministry of Northern Development, Mines and Forestry, and the municipalities. He thus recommends ways they could better coordinate their activities, since economic development programs and projects are often funded by more than one agency.

Bob Segsworth discusses results measurement and economic development in northern Ontario in Chapter 4. The discussion here links well with that in Chapter 3 since it examines the validity and utility of instruments to evaluate policy interventions of the provincial and federal governments. The main thrust of Segsworth's argument is that, although such performance indicators reflect contemporary public sector management commitments that have been implemented elsewhere, they provide evidence of policy that is not meeting publicly stated goals or objectives. He also offers recommendations for improving the quality of policy and program evaluation in ways that are regionally relevant and that could improve the quality of research information designed to enrich the discussion about the success of economic development policies and programs in the region.

In Chapter 5, Dawn Madahbee attempts to correct some of the oversights of standard textbook narratives about the economic development endeavours of First Nations people in Canada. Although much of her analysis is contextualized within northern Ontario, the discussion holds important implications for our understanding of the foundations and existing institutional and policy features of First Nations economic challenges, successes, and failures. Madahbee also looks at mechanisms by which First Nations can tap their entrepreneurial spirits, become business and community leaders, and influence the nature and direction of policy governance to eliminate poverty and create community wellness.

In Chapter 6, Michel Beaulieu provides a historical narrative of regional economic development at the municipal level, with a focus on Thunder Bay. He examines economic development policies in the city over a period of three decades starting in the late 1960s, and evaluates the complexities of its engagement with higher levels of government. He identifies the main actors, institutions, and policies, and the extent to which provincial and federal considerations have facilitated or impeded local economic development policies.

David Robinson offers an insightful and thought-provoking reconsideration of mineral wealth management in the north of the province in Chapter 7. Along with a description of the main features of the economic policies that govern mineral wealth management, Robinson offers a defensible and useful interpretation of the administrative and institutional challenges surrounding the limited success of existing mineral and mining policies in the region. He also identifies necessary features of a sustainable development strategy for the mineral and mining sector.

In Chapter 8, Doug West examines the provincial and federal governments' policy responses to the decline of agricultural activity in northern Ontario. In particular, he focuses on steps the two levels of government have taken to encourage new farms and farmers. He also provides an overview of the historical and current institutional infrastructure of agri-food policy in the region, and looks at the local food movement. He also examines alternative policy options to encourage and stimulate localized farming activities.

Chapter 9, on regional tourism approaches in northern Ontario, is a collaborative work by R. Harvey Lemelin and Rhonda Koster. The authors address the institutional deficiencies of tourism in the region by examining the concept of "region" in the rural tourism development of resource-based communities. Their objectives are to examine the various influences of power structures in the region; to understand more fully how residents of rural communities and regional stakeholders define region and their relationship to it; to determine the various scales at which they employ the concept of region in their planning, development, and implementation of tourism strategies; and to examine how communities that comprise a region interact with one another socially, economically, and politically. Determining how interactions in regional tourism strategies can contribute to and impede development strategies is essential to our understanding of the newly emerging economies of northern Ontario.

In Chapter 10, David Robinson looks conceptually and empirically at forest tenure systems and their implications for understanding the economic development of northern Ontario and the constraints they impose on community-driven development and change. A central theme that emerges from the chapter is the need for a stronger legal and institutional infrastructure of forest tenure, one that empowers and encourages community self-governance conducive to the adaptive and absorptive capacity of innovative policies to encourage economic diversification. This is an issue that divides stakeholders at the time of writing: the Ontario government wishes to move forward quickly with a revised land tenure policy, while others are calling for more consultation, discussion, and revision of what the government is proposing.[27]

The concluding chapter, by the editors of this volume, offers some final thoughts on the two themes of governance and sustainability in northern Ontario. The integration of the two themes brings into focus the lack of policy infrastructure to enhance the relevance, coherence, and legitimacy of development policy interventions in the region.

Together, the contributions to this volume provide a variety of compelling critiques of the existing infrastructure of policy formulation and implementation in northern Ontario that renders it almost impossible to envisage the development of a self-sustaining diversified economy in the region, especially in light of the exogenous and strategic challenges it faces. The authors forcefully make the point that northern Ontario is no more than a geographical construct unless the region's blatant institutional lacuna is addressed. It is also worth reiterating that these institutional limitations extend beyond the vertical dimensions of intergovernmental relations to include the horizontal relations among the public, private, and community sectors in the region.

NOTES

1 Economic Council of Canada, *Living Together: Regional Disparities in Canada* (Ottawa: Minister of Supply and Services, 1977); A.O. Hirshman, *The Strategy of Economic Development* (New Haven, CT: Yale University Press, 1965); and M.P. Todaro, *Economic Development* (New York: Longman, 2001).

2 M. Bradfield, *Regional Economic Analysis and Policies in Canada* (Toronto: McGraw-Hill Ryerson, 1988); and R.D. Howland, *Some Regional Aspects of Canada's Economic Development* (Ottawa: Royal Commission on Canada's Economic Prospects, 1957).

3 G.J. Benedetti and R.H. Lamarche, *Shockwaves: The Maritime Urban System in the New Economy* (Moncton, NB: Canadian Institute for Research on Regional Development, 1994); and D.J. Savoie, *Regional Economic Development: Canada's Search for Solutions* (Toronto: University of Toronto Press, 1986).

4 F.J. Anderson, *Regional Economic Analysis: A Canadian Perspective* (Toronto: Harcourt Brace Jovanovich Canada, 1988); and J.R. Melvin, "Regional Inequalities in Canada: Underlying Causes and Policy Implications," *Canadian Public Policy* 13 (3): 304–17.

5 D.J. Savoie, *Rethinking Canada's Regional Development Policy: An Atlantic Perspective* (Moncton, NB: Canadian Institute for Research on Regional Development, 1997).

6 See J.N. Bhagwati, *In Defense of Globalization* (New York: Oxford University Press, 2004).

7 J.M. Mintz and M. Smart, *Brooking No Favorites: A New Approach to Regional Development in Atlantic Canada*, C.D. Howe Institute Commentary 192 (Toronto: C.D. Howe Institute, 2003).

8 L. Di Matteo, "Strategies for Developing a Broadly Based Regional Knowledge Economy in Northwestern Ontario" (Thunder Bay, ON: North Superior Training Board, 2006); M. Goldenberg, *Review of Rural and Regional Development Policies and Programs* (Ottawa: Canadian Policy Research Networks, 2008); and W.S. Prudham, *Knock on Wood: Nature as Commodity in Douglas-Fir Country* (New York: Routledge, 2005).

9 See Organisation for Economic Co-operation and Development, "Investing for Growth: Building Innovation Regions" (Paris: OECD, 2009); available online at http://www.oecd.org/document/27/0,3343, en_2649_33735_33711480_1_1_1_1,00.html.

10 A. Holbrook and D.A. Wolfe, *Knowledge, Clusters, and Regional Innovation: Economic Development in Canada* (Montreal; Kingston, ON: McGill-Queen's University Press, 2002).

11 Di Matteo, "Strategies for Developing a Broadly Based Regional Knowledge Economy in Northwestern Ontario"; Organisation for Economic Co-operation and Development, *Regional Problems and Policies in Canada* (Paris: OECD, 1994); and M.G. Reed, *Taking Stands: Gender and the Sustainability of Rural Communities* (Vancouver: UBC Press, 2003).

12 H.V. Nelles, *The Politics of Development: Forests, Mines & Hydro-electric Power in Ontario, 1849–1941* (1974; repr., Montreal; Kingston, ON: McGill-Queen's University Press, 2005).

13 S. Brooks and L. Miljan, *Public Policy in Canada: An Introduction* (Don Mills, ON: Oxford University Press, 2003).

14 A. Careless, *Initiative and Response: The Adaptation of Canadian Federalism to Regional Economic Development*, Canadian Public Administration Series (Montreal; Kingston, ON: McGill-Queen's University Press, 1977).

15 R. Bollman, R. Beshiri, and V. Mitura, "Northern Ontario's Communities: Economic Diversification, Specialization and Growth," Agriculture and Rural Working Paper 82 (Ottawa: Statistics Canada, 2006), 7.

16 See Di Matteo, "Strategies for Developing a Broadly Based Regional Knowledge Economy in Northwestern Ontario"; and Chris Southcott, *The North in Numbers: A Demographic Analysis of Social and Economic Change in Northern Ontario* (Thunder Bay, ON: Lakehead University, Centre for Northern Studies, 2006).

17 M. Atkins, "Getting It Done: Creating a New Northern Ontario Regional Government" (presentation to the Federation of Northern Ontario Municipalities Leaders Summit, Timmins, ON, 2007), 2.

18 Ontario, "Northern Prosperity Plan" (Toronto: Ministry of Northern Development and Mines, 2004).

19 Panel on the Role of Government in Ontario, "Investing in People: Creating a Human Capital Society for Ontario" (Toronto: Queen's Printer, 2004), 81.

20 E. Slack, L.S. Bourne, and M.S. Gertler, "Small, Rural and Remote Communities: The Anatomy of Risk" (paper prepared for the Panel on the Role of Government in Ontario, Toronto, 2003); available online at http://www.law-lib.utoronto.ca/investing/reports/rp18.pdf.

21 Ibid., 32.

22 Northern Ontario Large Urban Mayors, "Northern Lights: Strategic Investments in Ontario's Greatest Asset" (n.p., 2007), 6; available online at http://www.cityofnorthbay.ca/cityhall/otm/photos/nolum.pdf.

23 Northern Ontario Large Urban Mayors, Northwestern Ontario Municipal Association, and Federation of Northern Ontario Municipalities, "Creating Our Future: A New Vision for Northern Ontario" (n.p., 2005), i; available

online at http://www.city.greatersudbury.on.ca/content/div_mayor/documents/CreatingOurFuture_march29-05.pdf.

24 Ontario, Ministry of Energy and Infrastructure and Ministry of Northern Development, Mines and Forestry, *Places to Grow – Better Choices, Brighter Future: Proposed Growth Plan for Northern Ontario* ([Toronto]: Queen's Printer for Ontario, 2009), 6.

25 Canada, Industry Canada, Audit and Evaluation Branch, "Mid-Term Evaluation of the Northern Ontario Development Program (NODP)" (Ottawa: Industry Canada, 2008), i.

26 Slack, Bourne, and Gertler, "Small, Rural and Remote Communities," 32.

27 See, for example, Timmins Economic Development Corporation, Corporation of the City of Timmins, and Timmins Chamber of Commerce, "Position on the Proposed Framework to Modernize Ontario's Forest Tenure and Pricing System" (Timmins, ON, 2 June 2010); available online at http://www.timminschamber.on.ca/documents/tenure_reform.pdf.

2 Regional Economic Development and Socio-economic Change in Northern Ontario

CHRIS SOUTHCOTT

Northern Ontario has an economy that is unique in contemporary economic terms. Its development was based almost entirely on the resource needs of twentieth-century industrialism.[1] Unlike other regions, it had no real experience with nineteenth-century forms of agricultural development or "competitive" capitalism. Apart from the region's Aboriginal communities, almost all of northern Ontario's communities were created by large resource- or transportation-based corporations, often in partnership with the provincial government, to extract natural resources for use elsewhere.[2] Unfortunately for northern Ontario, twentieth-century industrialism is becoming more and more imperilled as a sustainable form of economic development. Yet the absence of experience of other economic systems and the legacy of industrialism present problems for any attempt the region might make to create new economic alternatives. New policies of economic development thus must be formulated with a clear understanding of the effects of previous developments and the barriers these effects present. In this chapter, I outline the current demographic and economic situation in northern Ontario, and I identify those trends that present problems for the development of new economic policies for the region. I also try to identify several socio-economic trends that policy makers might find it useful to focus on in their attempts to develop policies to assist communities that are in economic difficulty.

Throughout the twentieth century northern Ontario was different from other regions of the province.[3] To a much greater extent than in the south, towns in northern Ontario were ethnically diverse, blue-collar, union-loyal, single-industry communities in which most women stayed in the home. Moreover, northern Ontarians believed that their communities had not shared equally in the wealth their region had produced – indeed, until the 1980s, the region saw itself as playing a major part in making Ontario a wealthy and economically dynamic province.[4] Yet a large part of the capital produced in northern Ontario left the region without providing the multiplier effects that were evident elsewhere.

This perception started to change in the late 1980s, when people in the north became less concerned about wealth leaving the region than they were about jobs leaving.[5] There was increasing awareness that the forestry and mining industries – the region's economic base – were no longer major producers of prosperity but instead were concentrating on labour-saving technologies to lower production costs in attempting to compete in an increasingly globalized marketplace. In the forestry industry, labour downsizing accompanied the decline of chainsaw/skidder harvesting, while pulp and paper mills stopped hiring new workers and either closed down or bought new machines that required fewer workers. The railroads – the earliest major industrial activity of the region – were also reducing their workforces in an attempt to stay profitable, the effect of which was devastating on communities previously dependent upon them. The industrial era that had given birth to most of northern Ontario's communities and that had valued the pulp, wood, and minerals these communities produced was coming to an end, and northern Ontarians began to worry about the long-term future of their region.

An Introduction to Northern Ontario

Northern Ontario contains almost 89 per cent of the land mass of Ontario, but only 6.5 per cent of the province's population. As the region has no legislated boundaries, its definition varies. For example, for the purpose of programming and statistical analysis, the provincial government defines northern Ontario as comprising the City of Greater Sudbury and the districts of Kenora, Rainy River, Thunder Bay, Algoma, Cochrane, Manitoulin, Sudbury, Timiskaming, Nipissing, and Parry Sound. In 2000 it added the Muskoka District Municipality to the definition, a somewhat problematic move given that the socio-economic characteristics of that district differ so much from those of the rest of northern Ontario, and indeed, the provincial government removed Muskoka from the definition in 2004, although the federal government continues to include it in its operational definition of the region for the purposes of programming under its Federal Economic Development Initiative in Northern Ontario.

Continuous settlement by non-natives in northern Ontario is more recent than in the rest of the province.[6] Settlement started in earnest with the construction of the Canadian Pacific Railway in the late 1870s and 1880s, soon followed by the construction of the Canadian Northern Railway and the Grand Trunk and National Transcontinental railways. Indeed, most non-Aboriginal communities in the region began as railway towns. Since the building of the railways, the region's growth has been driven primarily by the forestry and mining industries. The development of communities was undertaken, for the most part, by large resource-extraction corporations based outside the region, rather than by local entrepreneurs.

Lack of local control of its development has meant that the social and economic structure of northern Ontario exhibits several unique characteristics.[7] The first relates to an overdependence on natural resource exploitation, which has meant a high degree of vulnerability to resource depletion, world commodity price changes, corporate policy changes, the boom and bust cycles of the resource industries, changes in the Canadian dollar exchange rate, and changes in government policies regarding northern Ontario.[8] The second characteristic is a high degree of dependence on external forces. That most communities were developed by outside interests means that local entrepreneurship has been more limited than in other regions, which has acted as a barrier to the development of an entrepreneurial culture in these communities. This dependence is also seen in the area of political decision making. Unlike most areas of the province, northern Ontario is made up of districts, instead of counties, and unlike counties, districts do not have regional governments. Thus, northern Ontario has no regional government that can act as an intermediary between the provincial government and the municipalities.[9]

Although all communities in the region share some characteristics, they can be differentiated into three types. The most diversified are its small and medium-sized cities, of which five had more than 40,000 inhabitants according to the 2006 census: Sudbury (157,857), Thunder Bay (109,140), Sault Ste Marie (74,948), North Bay (53,966), and Timmins (42,997). Like almost all communities in northern Ontario, these cities are heavily dependent on resource industries, but they are also relatively diversified in that they tend to be important centres for health, education, and other services for the outlying regions. Other than these cities, the vast majority of the region's non-Aboriginal communities are resource-dependent, single-industry towns that share many distinct characteristics.[10] Finally, northern Ontario is unique in having a large number of Aboriginal communities, reflecting the size of the region's Aboriginal population (almost 12.6 per cent of the total).[11] Indeed, Aboriginals are the fastest-growing segment of northern Ontario's population, and the population in the area north of the 50th parallel is made up almost entirely of these communities. Of all the communities in the region, Aboriginal communities face the greatest number of social and economic challenges.

Population Trends in Northern Ontario

Population Growth and Decline, 1871–2001

One of the most frequently cited indicators of the general prospects of a region or community is its rate of population growth.[12] As long as growth is not too rapid, a community's increasing population is generally considered to be a positive sign:[13] it often means that house prices are increasing, along with the equity people have in their homes, and so are employment opportunities. Although there are costs to municipalities and public service providers associated with population growth, they are generally seen as less problematic than those associated with population decline. In cultural terms, moderate population growth is often linked to an increase in the overall level of confidence and pride people have in their communities. Population decline, however, generally indicates economic and social problems. It often means a decrease in housing prices, which, while making things easier for some, is a loss of equity for homeowners. A declining population also usually means an unhealthy employment situation and the flight of youth from the community.

In 1871 the population of northern Ontario was listed as 9,390 (see Table 2.1) – although this figure is problematic, as census officials have often improperly counted the Aboriginal population.[14] The area with the largest population was Algoma (Centre), with 2,177 people, most of whom lived in Sault Ste Marie, then the largest community in northern Ontario. Algoma (West), the southern area of what is now northwestern Ontario, had a population of 1,858, Manitoulin 2,011, and Parry Sound 1,519. As Table 2.1 shows, the region reached its maximum population of 822,450 in 1991.

Table 2.1. Population Change, Northern Ontario, 1871–2001

Census Year	Population	Census Year	Population
1871	9,390	1941	484,064
1881	32,236	1951	563,765
1891	74,656	1961	751,806
1901	125,337	1971	806,749
1911	245,323	1981	819,576
1921	294,410	1991	822,450
1931	384,019	2001	786,443

Source: Statistics Canada, Census of Canada, 1871–2001.

The pattern of population growth for northern Ontario has always been quite different from that of Ontario as a whole, as Figure 2.1 shows: until 1951 the growth rate was higher than that of the rest of the province, but since 1971 it has been substantially lower; only in the 1951 and 1961 censuses were growth rates similar across Ontario. Then, from 1966 to 1996, while the population of the province as a whole continued to grow, that of northern Ontario remained more or less stable. The 2001 census, however, showed a significant decline in all districts except for Manitoulin.

Population Change, 2001–06

Between 2001 and 2006 Canada's population grew by 5.4 per cent, the highest of the Group of Eight major industrialized countries; from 1996 to 2001, in contrast, the population grew by only 4 per cent.[15] Fully two-thirds of the increase was due to immigration, unlike in the United States, where 60 per cent of the population growth over the same period was the result of natural increase. More than two-thirds of Canada's population growth occurred in Alberta (with a growth rate of 10.6 per cent) and Ontario (6.6 per cent). Over the past fifteen years, in fact, Ontarios' population growth rate has been fairly steady, at just over 6 per cent.

Most of the population growth occurred in the largest urban areas, with growth rates higher than the national average in the major metropolitan centres of southern Ontario, Quebec, and British Columbia, and in the Calgary–Red Deer–Edmonton corridor of Alberta. Rural areas

Figure 2.1. Population Growth Rate, Ontario and Northern Ontario, 1891–2001

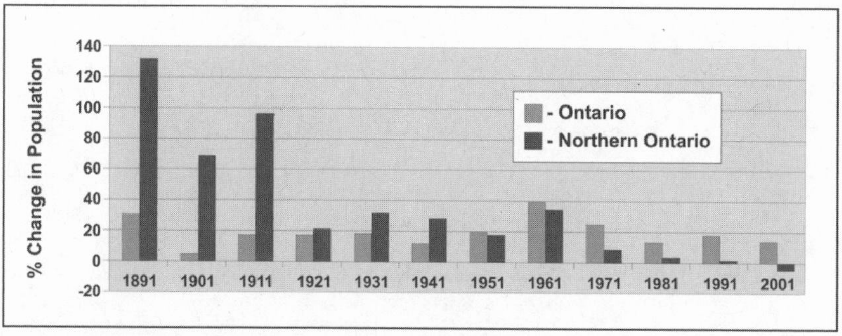

Source: Statistics Canada, Census of Canada, 1891–2001.

continued to see lower-than-average rates of growth or even decline. According to Statistics Canada, "[s]ince 2001, most rural areas grew at a slower pace than the country as a whole or, in some cases, suffered a population decline. In general, these areas are located far from the country's large urban centres. In most cases, they have natural resource-based economies, such as fishing, agriculture, forestry and mining."[16]

Between 2001 and 2006 Ontario's population grew by over 750,000, representing fully half of all the population growth in Canada over that period. Immigration from abroad accounted for more than 600,000 of Ontario's population growth during that time. Over 84 per cent of Ontario's growth occurred in the Golden Horseshoe around the western end of Lake Ontario. The population of northern Ontario, in contrast, grew by a barely perceptible 0.025 per cent from 2001 to 2006. The highest population growth occurred in the district of Kenora, at 4.2 per cent, followed by the districts of Manitoulin and Parry Sound at 3.2 per cent each. The district of Sudbury had the largest decline, at 6.6 per cent, followed by Timiskaming at 3.4 per cent. Of the fifty fastest-growing census subdivisions from 2001 to 2006, thirty-six were those in which Aboriginal communities are located; the average growth rate for Aboriginal communities over the period was 16.5 per cent.

As Figure 2.2 indicates, there has been considerable variation in population growth rates in northern, resource-dependent regions in Canada in recent censuses. Northern Ontario and northern Manitoba saw the lowest rates of increase, while the Yukon and Northwest Territories had rates of growth higher than that of Canada as a whole.

Figure 2.2. Population Change, Northern Canada, 1996–2006

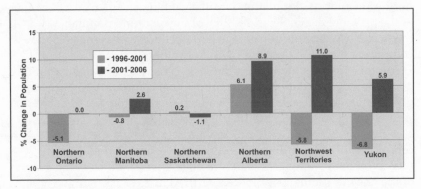

Source: Statistics Canada, Census of Canada, 1996, 2001, and 2006.
Note: Northern Manitoba is defined as census divisions 19, 21, 22, and 23; northern Saskatchewan as census divisions 14, 15, 16, 17, and 18; and northern Alberta as census divisions 12, 13, 16, 17, 18, and 19.

Looking at the region's cities, the two Census Metropolitan Areas (CMAs) in northern Ontario, Sudbury and Thunder Bay, had population increases of 1.7 per cent and 0.8 per cent, respectively, but well below the 6.9 per cent average for all CMAs in Canada; in contrast, both cities experienced a population decline between 1996 and 2001. Most other cities in the region also grew from 2001 to 2006 (North Bay by 2.3 per cent), but Kenora declined by 3.4 per cent and Elliot Lake by 1.6 per cent. In 2006, the fastest-growing of the 94 townships and villages in northern Ontario tended to be either in the southern areas of the region or in close proximity to a larger urban area: of the thirty that showed a growth in population between 2001 and 2006, nine were in the district of Parry Sound, four in the district of Nipissing, four in the district of Algoma (all near Sault Ste Marie and with substantial lakeshore areas), and two in the district of Thunder Bay (both close to that city).

Recent Trends

The 2006 census data show several population trends in the region. One is that the population has stabilized. As noted above, northern Ontario's population increased very slightly from 2001 to 2006, indicating that the socio-economic situation had improved somewhat since 1996, when most communities experienced decline. Nonetheless, northern Ontario's population is still shrinking as a percentage of that of the province as whole: in 2001 6.9 of the Ontario's population was in the north; by 2006 this percentage had declined to less than 6.5, due to continuing high population growth in southern Ontario.

Another trend evident from the 2006 census data is the continuing growth in the population of most Aboriginal communities: the average growth rate for these communities increased to 16.5 per cent in 2006 from 5.9 per cent during the 1996–2001 period.

A third noticeable trend is population growth of the largest urban centres. North Bay, Sudbury, Sault Ste Marie, and Thunder Bay all saw their populations grow from 2001 to 2006. Indeed, much of the growth of the non-Aboriginal population occurred in these cities. It thus might be true, as several reports maintain, that the largest urban centres are best placed to adapt away from the traditional resource industry economy and towards a knowledge-based economy.[17] As well, according to the 2006 census, mining-dependent communities were better off than forestry-dependent ones, with mining communities such as Sudbury, Pickle Lake, and Red Lake all seeing growth from 2001 to 2006 while many forest-dependent communities continued to experience declines similar to those they experienced from 1996 to 2001. Finally, communities closest to the urban centres of southern Ontario tended to grow, rather than decline, particularly in the traditional cottage country areas of Muskoka and Parry Sound but also creeping into more northern areas of the district of Parry Sound and into certain areas of the district of Nipissing.

Youth Out-migration

Problems generally develop when the number of young people leaving communities is greater than the number coming in,[18] a demographic imbalance that can have important implications for such things as the provision of services, housing prices, political influence, and credit ratings. Most of all, however, youth out-migration has a negative psychological impact on a community and on its prospects for future growth. Moreover, studies of youth out-migration note that, generally speaking, rural areas have higher rates of youth out-migration than urban areas.[19]

Youth outmigration is not a new problem for northern Ontario. Following the Second World War, resource-dependent regions such as northern Ontario experienced labour-retention problems that were often costly for resource companies. Small, one-industry towns found it hard to keep young male workers in their communities for long periods. They would come, work for a while, and then move on, requiring the industry to find and train new workers; companies thus went to considerable effort to find ways of keeping young male workers in the community.[20] In the early 1960s, there was a great deal of concern in the region that the brightest youth had to leave to get a university education, and that once they left they probably would not return, causing the region to lose its future leaders.[21] This was one of the reasons cited for establishing and expanding both Lakehead University in Thunder Bay and Laurentian University in Sudbury. Still, it was not until the 1980s that people started to be concerned in earnest about the decline in the total number of youth in the region.

Youth out-migration was one of the major problems dealt with by the Northern Development Councils, a series of local advisory groups set up in the late 1980s. In 1991 these councils produced a report that outlined the extent of the problem and examined several reasons for it.[22] The issue seemed to decline in importance in the early 1990s as unemployment rates in metropolitan Toronto were close to or higher than those in northern Ontario, and northern Ontario's youth seemed less inclined to leave for the south, but youth out-migration increased substantially again in the latter part of the decade.

Data from the 2006 census indicate that youth out-migration remains a problem. When the cohort of those in northern Ontario who were between fifteen and twenty-nine years of age in 2001 reached the ages of twenty and thirty-four in 2006, their number had declined by 10.5 per cent. This is quite different from the situation in both Canada and Ontario. In Canada as whole, in contrast, this age cohort had increased by 3 per cent, and in Ontario as a whole the increase was 5.2 per cent. Nonetheless, despite the high rate of youth out-migration reported in the 2006 census, it was still less than that for the period 1996 to 2001, when it was 18.3 per cent (see Figure 2.3).

An interesting aspect of youth out-migration in northern Ontario is that rates for females are lower than those for males: for the 1996–2001 period, the rate was 16.1 per cent for females in the fifteen-to-twenty-nine-year age cohort and 20.5 per cent for males; from 2001 to 2006, the rate was 8.8 per cent for females and 12.3 per cent for males.

Looking at youth out-migration rates for specific types of communities in northern Ontario, we see that Aboriginal communities continue

Figure 2.3. Changes in the 15-to-29-Year-Old Age Cohort, Northern Ontario, 1976–2006

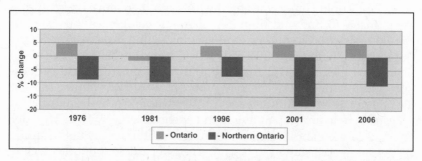

Note: The published census data for 1981 and 1986 include only those for the 25-to-34 age group, making it impossible to measure changes in the 15-to-29 age cohort using my method for 1981–86 and 1986–91; data prior to 2006 include the Muskoka District Municipality.
Source: Statistics Canada, Census of Canada, 1971, 1976, 1981, 1991, 1996, 2001, and 2006.

to have a lower overall rate than other communities, and the rate is also substantially lower in the largest urban centres. The data also reveal that many mining-dependent communities either substantially reduced their rates of youth out-migration or actually experienced an in-migration of youth. The areas with the highest rates of youth out-migration were smaller communities, unorganized areas, and forestry-dependent communities.

Lower Migration Levels and Few Immigrants

For most of its history, northern Ontario's population has been highly mobile.[23] Starting in the 1880s and lasting until the beginning of the First World War, in-migration rates were very high. Then, from 1919 until the late 1930s, the region saw both in- and out-migration as the resource sector experienced boom and bust periods. From the end of the Second World War until the 1960s, there were high rates of in-migration, including by large numbers of immigrants from outside Canada, although, as noted earlier, resource-dependent communities experienced labour-retention problems that were often costly to

Figure 2.4. In-migration from Abroad, Canada, Ontario, and Northern Ontario, 1996–2001 and 2001–06

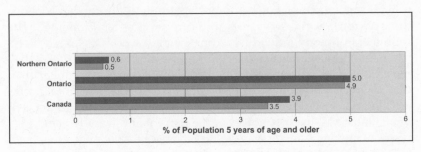

Source: Statistics Canada, Census of Canada, 2001 and 2006.

resource companies, as migrant male workers would come, work for a while, and then move on.

Since the 1960s, however, there has been a noticeable change in migration patterns in northern Ontario. For one thing, if one looks at the percentage moving to a different community over the 2001–06 period, the region's population has become considerably more stable than that of either the province or Canada as a whole, with only 13.2 per cent of northern Ontarians changing community, compared with 18.9 per cent of all Ontarians and Canadians. As well, a higher percentage of northern Ontario's migrants move from one community to another within the province – 80.9 per cent in the 2006 census; the corresponding figures for Ontario and Canada as a whole were 65 per cent and 63.9 per cent, respectively. Thus, it is likely that a large percentage of northern Ontario's migrants are not in-migrants from the point of view of the region, but residents of northern Ontario who are simply moving to another location in the same region.

Another important aspect of migration in northern Ontario, especially considering the region's past, is the very small number of migrants who now come from outside the country. As Figure 2.4 shows, of all Ontarians who were five years of age or older in 2006, more than 5 per cent had come to the province from outside the country since 2001; the corresponding figure for Canada was 3.9 per cent, and for northern Ontario just 0.6 per cent, or 4,775 people. The latter number is, however, an increase from the 3,555 newcomers reported in the 2001 census, so this trend might be starting to change.

A Rapidly Aging Population

Canada's aging population has important implications for the economy, the workforce, social services, health care services, and training.[24] The retirement of many individuals from the paid workforce at age sixty-five has a serious impact on the communities and regions in which they live. Until recently northern Ontario's population was younger than that of Ontario as a whole. In 1986, for example, 10.3 per cent of northern Ontarians were age sixty-five or older, compared with 10.9 per cent of all Ontarians. In 2006, however, the percentages were 15.8 and 13.6, respectively; for Canada as a whole, it was 13.7 per cent. Moreover, northern Ontario's population is aging at a more rapid rate than that of the province as a whole, with those age sixty-five and older having increased by 10 per cent from 2001 to 2006 in northern Ontario but by 5.4 per cent for all of Ontario.

These trends have important implications for policy decisions. The infrastructure of most communities in northern Ontario was based on a population dominated by young families.[25] Expenditures were often based on the desire to create a community that would meet the needs of these families so that labour-retention rates would increase. As the populations of these communities are made up of an increasing number of elderly, attention must shift to finding ways to retain greater numbers of this sector of the population.

A Declining Resource-based Industrial Structure

The industrial structure of northern Ontario traditionally has been quite simple. The railways, forestry, and mining industries were the most important sectors, starting in the 1870s, and jobs in these blue-collar industries were the largest single source of employment in the regional economy, a factor that differentiated northern Ontario from other regions of the province that depended more heavily on the manufacturing sector.[26] Employment in traditional blue-collar industries, however, has been declining.[27] As Figure 2.5 shows, employment in Ontario's goods-producing industries decreased substantially in the early 1990s, although it has shown fairly slow but constant growth since 1994; northern Ontario experienced an even greater decline in that sector during the 1990s, but, unlike the rest of the province, it has not seen a recovery of those losses since that time. Moreover, as Figure 2.6 shows, the loss of employment in northern Ontario's forestry,

Figure 2.5. Employment in the Goods-producing and Services-producing Sectors, Ontario and Northern Ontario, 1987–2004

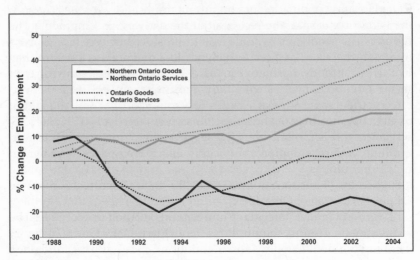

Source: Statistics Canada, *Labour Force Historical Review*, 2005.

Figure 2.6. Employment by Goods-producing Industry, Northern Ontario, 1987–2004

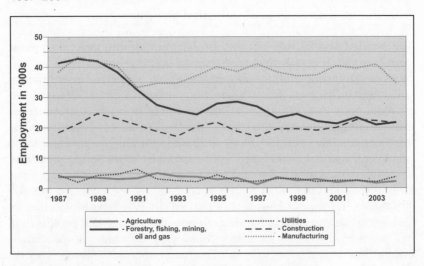

Source: Statistics Canada, *Labour Force Historical Review*, 2005.

fishing, mining, and oil and gas industries has been particularly severe, with jobs in those sectors declining from an estimated 41,400 in 1987 to 21,800 in 2004.

In contrast, despite the recession of the early 1990s, employment in the services-producing sector has shown slow but constant growth, although the rate has been somewhat less in northern Ontario than in the province as a whole. As Table 2.2 shows, employment trends in the services industries were fairly constant from 1987 to 2004, with few rapid increases or decreases.[28] The subsector that saw the largest growth was health care and social assistance, which added 12,800 jobs, while the subsector with the largest percentage growth was business, building, and other support services, which increased its employment by 125 per cent.

Figure 2.7, which compares the industrial structure of northern Ontario with that of the province as a whole, shows that northern Ontario has a higher percentage of what can be called primary resource industry jobs. Despite the importance of agriculture in areas of southern Ontario, in 2006 only 1.8 per cent of all industry jobs in Ontario were in this sector, but although northern Ontario's agricultural sector is relatively small, 2.8 of the jobs in the region were in this sector. The mining and oil and gas extraction industries accounted for 3.5 per cent of the jobs in northern Ontario but only for 0.4 per cent of the jobs in the province as a whole.

The next most important difference between the north and the province as a whole is that northern Ontario's economy has a lower percentage of jobs associated with what some call the new economy, or knowledge economy, but that I refer to in a more general sense as professional services industries[29] – the knowledge-intensive industries that are replacing traditional manufacturing industries as engines of growth.[30] In each of these categories, northern Ontario's percentage of workers is lower than in Ontario as a whole: in 2006, professional service industries accounted for 17 per cent of all jobs in Ontario but for only 8.5 per cent of jobs in northern Ontario. Northern Ontario also continues to depend more highly on public sector services – health, education, social assistance, and public administration – for jobs (28.7 per cent of the total) than does the province as a whole (21.5 per cent).

One of the main characteristics of northern Ontario's traditional industrial structure was a lower percentage of manufacturing jobs than the provincial average – resources harvested in the region were transformed in factories outside it. Data from the 2006 census confirm that, despite a general lessening of the importance of manufacturing

Table 2.2. Employment in Services Industries, Northern Ontario, 1987 and 2004

Subsector	1987	2004	Total change	Change
Trade		(thousands of jobs)		(per cent)
Transportation and warehousing	52.2	59.2	7.0	13.41
Finance, insurance, real estate, and leasing	19.9	19.8	-0.1	-0.50
Professional, scientific, and technical services	14.6	15.2	0.6	4.11
Business, building, and other support services	6.8	12.8	6.0	88.24
Educational services	21.3	27.5	6.2	29.11
Health care and social assistance	38.9	51.7	12.8	32.90
Information, culture, and recreation	8.8	14.1	5.3	60.23
Accommodation and food services	23.5	28.9	5.4	22.98
Other services	20.5	14.1	-6.4	-31.22
Public administration	23.3	22.9	-0.4	-1.72

Source: Statistics Canada, Labour Force Historical Review, 2005.

industry employment, disparities between the north and the province as a whole continue: jobs in manufacturing industries in 2006 were 13.9 per cent of the province's total employment, but they accounted for only 8.9 per cent of the total in northern Ontario. The north also had a lower percentage of employment in the wholesale trade industries. At the same time, northern Ontario is more dependent than the province as a whole on employment in the utilities industries, accommodation and food service, transportation, warehousing, and the retail industries.

Northern Ontario, then, continues to be heavily dependent on the resource-extraction industries for jobs, but these are declining in number. The region has seen increases in services sector employment, but these are mostly in lower-paying, less knowledge-intensive, categories; there has not been a significant increase in the number of jobs in the higher-paying professions of the sector. Northern Ontario is also highly dependent upon public sector services, such as health, education, and social assistance.

Gender Differences in the Workforce

Northern Ontario's wage economy traditionally has excluded women to a greater extent than in most other regions of the province.[31] The

Figure 2.7. The Industrial Structure of the Economy, Ontario and Northern Ontario, 2006

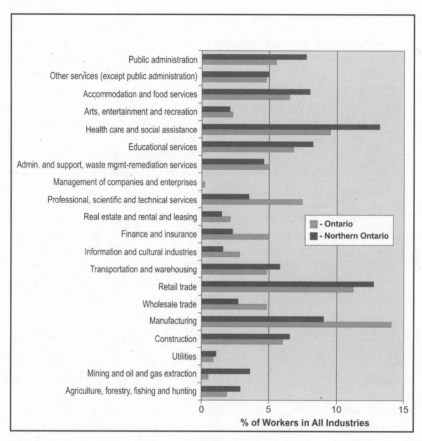

Source: Statistics Canada, Census of Canada, 2006.

resource industries that dominate the regional economy overwhelmingly employ males. In the past this also resulted in a gender imbalance in the population as a whole, as the region had a lower ratio of females to males than did the province or the nation. Resource-dependent communities have often been labelled "no place for a woman."[32] Research on such communities conducted in the 1970s indicated that the job market was characterized by a rigid sexual division of labour.[33] The inability of women to get jobs in the resource industries and the under-development of secondary industry and services meant there were few employment opportunities for women. Recent studies have indicated some change in these conditions,[34] yet important differences between men and women in the region persist. Figure 2.8 shows that women in Northern Ontario have a significantly lower labour force participation rate (56.3 per cent) than men (66.8 per cent), and rates for both are well below the rate for Ontario as a whole (73.4 per cent). Interestingly, however, in 2006 participation rates were identical for males and females ages fifteen to twenty-four. In fact, the gap between the two participation rates is closing: in 1986 the difference was 23.3 percentage points; by 2006 it had fallen to 8.3 percentage points, although it is important to note that the main reason for the narrowing gap is the declining participation rate of men.

Where men and women work in northern Ontario differs significantly than where they do in Ontario as a whole.[35] Far more women work in the health and social assistance services industries (22.5 per cent of all female employment) than do men 4.2 per cent), while the educational service industries employ 11.9 per cent of all female workers and only 4.6 per cent of all male workers. Females also have a substantially larger

Figure 2.8. Labour Force Participation Rates, Ontario and Northern Ontario, 1986–2006

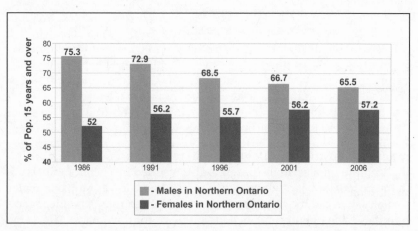

Source: Statistics Canada, Census of Canada, 1986, 1991, 1996, 2001, and 2006.

presence (11.0 per cent) in accommodation and food services than males (5.1 per cent). Women in Northern Ontario are underrepresented in all the traditional blue-collar industries. Manufacturing accounts for 14.5 per cent of all male employment in northern Ontario, but only 2.9 per cent of female employment. The situation is similar in construction, mining, transportation and warehousing, and agriculture, forestry, fishing, and hunting.

Lower Levels of Education

For many social scientists, one of the most important recent changes for the "new economy" is the rise of the knowledge society.[36] To an ever greater extent, knowledge is the driving force of national and regional economies. Economic and social development increasingly depends on levels of education. This represents a change from the industrial era of the nineteenth and early twentieth centuries, when the most important criterion for a region's or a country's economic success was access to capital to invest in industrial development. "Fordist" industrialism meant that one's income and ability to find a job were not necessarily directly related to one's level of education. Unionized blue-collar jobs could supply workers with fairly stable and relatively well-paid employment without the need for high levels of formal education.

That situation persisted in northern Ontario for most of the twentieth century. Historically, levels of education have been lower in the region than in the province as a whole. The region's single-industry resource-dependent communities provided jobs at fairly good wages for males with little formal education.[37] The norm was for males to leave high school as soon as they reached the age when they could find employment in the mills or mines that served as the main employers in these communities. Since formal education was not that important for the regional economy, the lower levels were not a great concern.

Alarmingly, however, not only are many of the traditional disparities in levels of education still in place; they are intensifying. In 2006, as Figure 2.9 shows, among those twenty-five years of age or over, 25.9 per cent of northern Ontarians had less than a high school diploma, compared with 18.7 per cent for Ontario as a whole. The most important determinant of higher income is possession of a university degree,[38] and 23.1 per cent of Ontarians twenty-five or older have one, but only half as many (12.6 per cent) of northern Ontarians do. In the province as a whole, 9.1 per cent had a post-graduate degree, but the figure for

Figure 2.9. Highest Level of Education Achieved, Population Age 25 and Over, Ontario and Northern Ontario, 2006

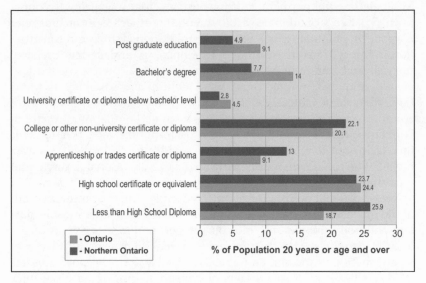

Source: Statistics Canada, Census of Canada, 2006.

northern Ontario was only 4.9 per cent. These differences, moreover, are increasing. In 1986, the percentage of people in northern Ontario fifteen years and over with less than a high school diploma was only 16.2 per cent higher than the average for the province; by 2006 this difference had risen to 31.5 per cent. Seen from another perspective, in Ontario from 1986 to 2006 the percentage of people age fifteen and over with less than a high school education decreased by 48.5 per cent, while in northern Ontario, the decrease was 41.7 per cent.

The Increasing Importance of the Aboriginal Population

Many of the socio-economic trends in northern Ontario are problematic for policy makers, but some might be seen as generally positive for the future of the region. The most important of these is the increasing importance of the region's Aboriginal population,[39] the proportion of which is much higher than in the rest of the province. Over the past thirty years, this population has become more visible in the social, cultural, and political affairs of the region, and the most important force for change in northern Ontario.

The Aboriginal population of the region is increasing rapidly, rising from 64,370 in 1996 to 97,935 in 2006, and increasing as a percentage of the total population from 7.9 per cent in 1996 to 12.6 per cent in 2006. If this trend were to continue, Aboriginals would be the majority population of the region by 2086. Much of the growth over the ten-year period was among those who identified themselves as Métis (a 204 per cent increase): those who identified themselves as North American Indian increased by 28 per cent. Population growth in reserve-based communities averaged 5.9 per cent from 1996 to 2001, then increased to 19.6 per cent between 2001 and 2006, a surprisingly high figure given constraints such as limited on-reserve housing and infrastructure.

The Aboriginal population is much younger than the rest of the population of northern Ontario and the province. Almost 28.9 per cent of the total Aboriginal identity population was under fifteen years of age in 2006, compared with 18.2 per cent for all of Ontario, and 17.1 per cent for northern Ontario. There were fewer young among urban Aboriginals (26 per cent) than among reserve-based Aboriginals (33.2 per cent), and far fewer older people among all Aboriginal populations (8.6 per cent over age sixty) than in the provincial (18.3 per cent) and regional (21.4 per cent) populations.

The Aboriginal population of the region continues to face difficulties in terms of education and employment. Aboriginals have lower levels of formal education and a lower labour force participation rate than other northern Ontarians. Few Aboriginals are employed in business-oriented industries such as retail trade, finance, and business services or in the higher-paying professional occupations. More find work in the trades and blue-collar occupations, although Aboriginals experienced a significant decline in blue-collar jobs between 2001 and 2006, indicating that they are often the most vulnerable Ontarians to changes in the economic climate.

Conclusions

Northern Ontario remains heavily dependent on the traditional industrial economy that gave birth to most of its communities. Indeed, differences between the region and the province are increasing, as Ontario as a whole increasingly becomes part of the new economy.

Although Ontario's population continues to experience high levels of growth, northern Ontario's population is either stagnating or in decline, not only in the major urban areas of the region, but also in non-Aboriginal, resource-dependent communities. Youth in-migration is the norm for the province as a whole, but northern Ontario is experiencing high levels of out-migration. The population is now older than the provincial norm. Ontario as a whole is becoming increasingly diverse and globalized by attracting increasing numbers of immigrants from outside Canada, while the north is increasingly ethnically homogenized.

Differences in the industrial structures of Ontario and northern Ontario are increasing. Northern Ontario has a higher percentage of jobs in primary resource industries, a lower percentage in manufacturing industries, a higher dependence on public sector services industries, and a lower percentage in professional services industries. Compared to the rest of Ontario, women in the region are overrepresented in the health and social assistance service industries and in the accommodation and food service industries, and continue to be markedly underrepresented in the manufacturing, construction, mining, and transportation industries. This high level of occupational gender segregation is present in all districts of the region.

Education differences between the north and the rest of the province remain strong. Education levels in northern Ontario continue to be lower than the average for Ontario. Northern Ontario has a higher percentage of people with less than a high school diploma, and a lower percentage of people with a university degree.

These indicators show that the region continues to depend strongly on the "old" industrial economy dominant in the twentieth century and that, although the new economy has had an impact, its growth in the region is much less than that for the province as a whole. This does make it appear that the region is being increasingly left behind. Some might project that most communities in the region will continue to decline until they disappear. In the mind of this researcher, however, this is extremely unlikely, for several reasons. First, there will always be a demand for the products produced by the resource industries of northern Ontario. Technological change has meant a decline in traditional blue-collar industrial jobs, but new jobs are arising to service the new technologies.

The Aboriginal population represents a new force for development in the region. Aboriginals are increasing in number and are younger than Ontarians as a whole. They are demanding more of a say in the political and economic affairs of the region, and have both social and political capital that could be used to deal with future problems the region might face.

Northern Ontario has also shown an extremely strong desire to maintain its communities. The social capital necessary to allow it to do so is only now starting to emerge. As companies close down operations and leave the region, and as governments follow neo-liberal economic strategies, communities are starting to realize that they are on their own, and that there is no one there to take care of them. This adjustment has been difficult, and attitudes are only now starting to change, but it is increasingly a force that policy makers need to keep in mind.

There are, therefore, key forces that could be mobilized to ensure a sustainable future for communities in the north. Yet these forces need the appropriate tools to accomplish this goal. Recent trends towards greater local control of the economy, new ways of ensuring that a greater share of resource rents stay in the region, new partnerships between non-Aboriginal and Aboriginal communities, and a greater commitment to reducing educational inequalities are all important policy objectives that could help northern Ontario achieve a greater degree of economic sustainability.[40]

NOTES

1 R. Rosehart, *Northwestern Ontario: Preparing for Change*, Northwestern Ontario Economic Facilitator Report (n.p., 2008), available online at http://www.mndm.gov.on.ca/nordev/documents/noef/REPORT_FEB2008; C. Southcott, *The North in Numbers: A Demographic Analysis of Social and Economic Change in Northern Ontario* (Thunder Bay, ON: Lakehead University, Centre for Northern Studies, 2006).
2 H.V. Nelles, *The Politics of Development: Forests, Mines & Hydro-electric Power in Ontario, 1849–1941* (1974; repr., Montreal; Kingston, ON: McGill-Queen's University Press, 2005).
3 Ibid.
4 See Rosehart, *Northwestern Ontario*; and M. Goldenberg, *Review of Rural and Regional Development Policies and Programs* (Ottawa: Canadian Policy Research Networks, 2008).
5 See Southcott, *North in Numbers*.
6 See ibid.; and R. Bollman, R. Beshiri, and V. Mitura, "Northern Ontario's Communities: Economic Diversification, Specialization and Growth," Agriculture and Rural Working Paper 82 (Ottawa: Statistics Canada, 2006).

7 This has been pointed out by several government studies undertaken over the past thirty years; see, for example, Ontario, Royal Commission on the Northern Environment (Fahlgren Commission), *Final Report* (Toronto: Ministry of the Attorney General, 1985); and Ontario, Advisory Committee on Resource Dependent Communities in Northern Ontario (Rosehart Report), *Final Report and Recommendations* (Toronto: Ministry of Northern Development and Mines, 1986).

8 For an elaboration on these points, see B. Dadgostar, W.B. Jankowski, and B. Moazzami, *The Economy of Northwestern Ontario: Structure, Performance and Future Challenges*, Research Report 31 (Thunder Bay, ON: Lakehead University, Centre for Northern Studies, 1992).

9 For a detailed discussion of this aspect of northern Ontario, see S. McBride, S. McKay, and M.E. Hill, "Unemployment in a Northern Hinterland: The Social Impact of Political Neglect," in *A Provincial Hinterland: Social Inequality in Northwestern Ontario*, ed. C. Southcott (Halifax, NS: Fernwood, 1993).

10 See J. Randall, and R.G. Ironside, "Communities on the Edge: An Economic Geography of Resource-Dependent Communities in Canada," *Canadian Geographer* 40 (10, 1996): 17–35.

11 The 2006 census uses various indicators of Aboriginal status. The figure of 12.6 per cent refers to those who have indicated an Aboriginal identity; if "Aboriginal origins" is used, the figure increases to 14.8 per cent; if status as Registered Indian is used, the figure is 8.3 per cent.

12 For a more elaborate description of northern Ontario's population trends, see C. Southcott, "The Changing Population of Northern Ontario," 2006 Census Research Paper Series Report 1 (Thunder Bay, ON: Local Boards of Northern Ontario, May 2007).

13 Interpretation of the consequences of population change is a standard feature of textbooks on demography. An excellent example is J. Weeks, "Demographic Perspectives," in *Population: An Introduction to Concepts and Issues*, 8th ed. (Belmont, CA: Wadsworth/Thomson Learning, 2002).

14 Population figures for the census divisions in northern Ontario are not as reliable as for those in the rest of the province, due in mostly to the large number of Aboriginal communities that, for various reasons, are improperly counted. If Statistics Canada cannot count a community properly, it does not include the community's population in the totals for the census division. As a result, population figures for almost all the census divisions in northern Ontario are incomplete, making it difficult to compare figures from one census to another. Accordingly, I have adjusted the population

figures for northern Ontario to try to deal with these inconsistencies. For communities whose populations were excluded from the 2001 census, I added an estimated population to the total for northern Ontario that is based on the average change in the population of all Aboriginal communities that were included in both the 2001 and 2006 census (16.5 per cent). If a community was included in 2006 but not in 2001, I estimated the population in 2001 by multiplying the 2001 figure by .835; for those few communities that were included in 2001 but excluded in 2006, I multiplied the 2001 population by 1.165.

15 Most of the information in this section is from Statistics Canada, "Portrait of the Canadian Population in 2006, 2006 Census," 2006 Census Analysis Series, Cat. no. 97-550-XIE (Ottawa, March 2007).

16 Ibid., 21.

17 See, for example, Sudbury and Manitoulin Workforce Partnership Board, "Trends, Opportunities, and Priorities Report 2006" (Sudbury, 2006); and North Superior Training Board, "Trends, Opportunities, and Priorities Report 2007" (Thunder Bay, 2007).

18 For a more elaborate description of youth out-migration, see C. Southcott, "Youth Out-migration Trends in Northern Ontario," Census Research Paper Series Report 2 (Thunder Bay, ON: Local Boards of Northern Ontario, September 2007).

19 See, for example, J. Tremblay, "Rural Youth Migration between 1971 and 1996," Agriculture and Rural Working Paper 44 (Ottawa: Statistics Canada, Agriculture Division, 2001); N. Rothwell, R.D. Bollman, J. Tremblay, and J. Marshall, "Recent Migration Patterns in Rural and Small Town Canada," Agriculture and Rural Working Paper 55 (Ottawa: Statistics Canada, Agriculture Division, 2002); and R.A. Malatest & Associates, "Rural Youth Migration: Exploring the Reality Behind the Myths" (Ottawa: Agriculture and Agri-Food Canada, 2002).

20 See A. Himelfarb, "The Social Characteristics of Single Industry Towns," in *Little Communities and Big Industry*, ed. R.T. Bowles (Toronto: Butterworths, 1982).

21 See G. Weller, "Hinterland Politics: The Case of Northwestern Ontario," *Canadian Journal of Political Science* 10 (4, 1977): 444–70.

22 Ontario, Ministry of Northern Development and Mines, "Youth Migration: Northern Perspectives" (Thunder Bay, ON, 1991).

23 For more elaborate descriptions of these trends, see C. Southcott, "Ethnicity and Community in Thunder Bay," *Polyphony* (1987): 10–20; and idem, "Migration and Mobility Trends in Northern Ontario," Census

Research Paper Series Report 4 (Thunder Bay, ON: Local Boards of Northern Ontario, December 2007).

24 For more on this trend, see C. Southcott, "Aging Population Trends in Northern Ontario," Census Research Paper Series Report 3 (Thunder Bay, ON: Local Boards of Northern Ontario, September 2007). See also Statistics Canada. "Portrait of the Canadian Population in 2006, by Age and Sex, 2006 Census," Cat. no. 97-551-XIE (Ottawa, 2007).

25 Himmelfarb, "Social Characteristics of Single Industry Towns."

26 For a more in-depth look at the industrial structure of northern Ontario, see C. Southcott, "Labour Force Participation Trends in Northern Ontario," Census Research Paper Series Report 5 (Thunder Bay, ON: Local Boards of Northern Ontario, April 2008); and idem, "The Changing Industrial Structure of Northern Ontario," Census Research Paper Series Report 6 (Thunder Bay, ON: Local Boards of Northern Ontario, April 2008). See also idem, "A Regional Outlook for Northern Boards: A Northern Approach to Regional Labour Force Development" (Dryden, ON: Training Boards of Northern Ontario, 2000), 5–6. Blue-collar industrial employment includes the following census categories as contained in the 1980 Standard Industrial Categories: Logging and Forestry, Mining and Quarrying, Manufacturing, Construction, Transportation and Storage, and Communication and Utilities. Longitudinal consistency requires that the categories of Agriculture and Trapping and Fishing also be included in this definition, as the 1986 public profile categories did not separate these categories from Mining and Primary Forestry employment.

27 See Southcott, "Regional Outlook for Northern Boards," 6.

28 One important exception was a rapid decline in public administration jobs from 27,500 in 1996 to 20,300 in 1998.

29 See Ontario, Task Force to Review the Ontario Technology Fund in the Context of an Innovation-Based Society, Ontario 2002 (Toronto: Premier's Council on Economic Renewal, 1993), 54–5. The concept is also noted in other popular economic works, such as A. Carnevale, America and the New Economy (San Francisco: Jossey-Bass, 1991); and P.F. Drucker, Post-Capitalist Society (New York: Harper Business, 1993).

30 These industries are often those placed in the following categories of the 1997 North American Industrial Classification System: information and cultural industries; finance and insurance; real estate and rental and leasing; professional, scientific, and technical services; industries involved in the management of companies and enterprises; administrative and support industries; and waste management and remediation services.

31 For a more in-depth elaboration of methodologies used and more
    discussion of women in the workforce, see C. Southcott, "Women and
    the Economy of Northern Ontario," Census Research Paper Series
    Report 10 (Thunder Bay, ON: Local Boards of Northern Ontario, July
    2008).
32 This was the title of a 1979 National Film Board production on resource-
    dependent communities.
33 M. Luxton, *More than a Labour of Love* (Toronto: Women's Press, 1980).
34 A. Gill, "Women in Isolated Resource Towns: An Examination of Gender
    Differences in Cognitive Structures," *Geoforum* 21 (3, 1990): 347–58; and
    Randall and Ironside, "Communities on the Edge."
35 To compare differences in industrial structures, I calculated the total
    variance between the percentage of male workers and the percentage of
    female workers for each category of the above-listed industrial categories.
    I then squared these differences, and calculated the square root of each.
    I then added these answers together to obtain a figure for total variance.
    In 2001 the total variance between the industrial structure of male
    workers and that of female workers in northern Ontario was 80.8; for
    Ontario as a whole the number was a significantly lower 56.4. In 2006
    the numbers were almost identical (80.4 for northern Ontario, 57.3 for
    Ontario).
36 For a more in-depth elaboration of methodologies and more discussion
    of levels of education, see C. Southcott, "Trends in Northern Ontario's
    Education Levels," Census Research Paper Series Report 8 (Thunder
    Bay, ON: Local Boards of Northern Ontario, April 2008). On the knowl-
    edge economy, see, for example, P.F. Drucker, "Knowledge Work and
    Knowledge Society: The Social Transformations of This Century," The
    1994 Edwin L. Godkin Lecture, Harvard University, 4 May 1994; available
    online at http://www.ksg.harvard.edu/ifactory/ksgpress/www/ksg_news/
    transcripts/drucklec.htm; accessed 16 January 2006; see also J. Bindé,
    Towards Knowledge Societies, UNESCO World Report 1 (Paris: UNESCO,
    2005).
37 See R. Lucas, *Minetown, Milltown, Railtown: Life in Canadian Communities
    of Single Industry* (Toronto: University of Toronto Press, 1971).
38 See, for example, Statistics Canada, "Earnings of Canadians: Making
    a Living in the New Economy," 2001 Census Analysis Series, Cat. no.
    96F0030XIE2001013 (Ottawa, 2003), 5.
39 For a more in-depth elaboration of methodologies and more discussion of
    this issue, see C. Southcott, "The Aboriginal Population and the Economy

of Northern Ontario," Census Research Paper Series Report 12 (Thunder Bay, ON: Local Boards of Northern Ontario, April 2009).
40 For a summary of these policy objectives, see C. Southcott and S. Irlbacher-Fox, "Changing Northern Economies: Helping Northern Communities Build a Sustainable Future" (Victoria, BC: Northern Development Ministers Forum, April 2009).

3 Administering Regional Development Policy in Socio-economically Disadvantaged Regions

CHARLES CONTEH

Introduction

This chapter focuses on evaluating the capacity, relevance, and integrity of existing institutions of economic development policy governance in northern Ontario in the light of exogenous and strategic challenges confronting the region. I address two main questions. First, what is the nature of the existing institutional infrastructure of regional economic development policy implementation in northern Ontario? Second, how can these mechanisms be altered to improve coordination and partnerships between the various levels of governments and organized community interests in the region?

I begin by sketching the background of regional economic development policies and programs in the northwestern region of northern Ontario, to create a context for the rest of the discussion. Then, I examine the current administrative and institutional mechanisms of regional economic development policy implementation, drawing attention to their strengths and limitations. Finally, I assess alternative institutional infrastructures in the context of emerging forces of change in northwestern Ontario.

Regional Economic Development in Northwestern Ontario

The challenge of economic development is a worldwide one, as even resource-rich regions in developed and developing countries fail to reach a sustainable level of it. Canada is surely one of the most regionalized industrial countries and, accordingly, is very fragmented. In such an economy the so-called free market does not function well for all regions simultaneously, so that macroeconomic policies tend to be insufficient. Regionally targeted economic development policies, therefore, have become a key feature of Canada's policy landscape. Regional economic development could be defined as a general effort by governments to support economic activities in less developed regions. Its policy instruments often include employment and wealth-generating activities, and involve related fields such as rural development, industrial and commercial competitiveness, and urban policy.

Despite its troubled legitimacy and the debates surrounding its place in Canada's economic policy, regional economic development has features and salience as enduring as the realities of Canadian federalism.[1] Discussions about regional economic development policy in Canada have often focused on the challenges of relations between the federal and provincial governments, implicitly discounting the role of municipal governments.[2] The omission is significant given the spatial aspect of regional economic development and that local governments have been known to be involved in efforts to attract new businesses, enhance the capacity of existing local enterprises, and strengthen the competitiveness of their local economies.

Nor is the role of municipal government the only oversight in policy research on regional economic development in Canada. Scholars pay much attention to intra- and interorganizational challenges within the public sector, and are uninterested in the nature of interactions between state and societal interests in disadvantaged regions. This chapter seeks to remedy the gap in the research on regional economic development policy in Canada, first by highlighting the roles municipalities increasingly play in regional economic development, and, second, by incorporating the state-society relations perspective.

The Region of Northwestern Ontario

Northwestern Ontario is a vast region of many diverse communities with a total population of approximately 240,000. It is currently in the midst of economic change, crisis, and transition. Issues undermining its performance include a declining sector linked to older industry, aging populations, out-migration of the younger population, and the absence of coherent strategies to drive economic growth.[3] The only significant population growth is in Aboriginal communities.

The traditional economy of northwestern Ontario has been dominated by a small number of larger companies with relatively high employment levels, as well as services industries dependent on larger employers or communities. The past two decades in particular have seen significant layoffs in the forest industry; these job losses likely will be permanent.[4] The closures of several pulp and paper and lumber mills have been driven by factors largely outside the influence of Ontario, including the rising Canadian dollar, the declining housing market in the United States, strong international competition, increasing energy prices, environmental pressures, and climate change. Clearly, northwestern Ontario's economy is vulnerable while it is in transition.

The history and current structure of industry in the region confirms a trend of persistent decline in the mainstays of the economy – mostly primary resource industries. There is a general decline in industrial activity and a growing weakness in secondary manufacturing and services industries, even with the presence of pulp and paper mills.[5] The share of employment in primary and manufacturing industries declined from 28 per cent in 1981 to 16 per cent in 2001. The picture of industrial stagnation and even decline gives the impression of developing-country conditions in northern Ontario, with socio-economic underdevelopment by most indicators.

The region is also facing a demographic quagmire of population decline, mostly due to out-migration of the young and the unemployed and an increase in retired or retiring residents who rely more on public services. Population decline, especially of the most productive segment, in turn means a declining tax assessment base for most municipalities. Meanwhile, transfer payments from the Ontario government are still not sufficient to enable municipalities to fund the programs that citizens in this region need.[6]

The challenges facing the northwest include how to enhance the remaining economy and provide work opportunities, not only for an idle and aging workforce, but also for the young people who continue to seek prosperity elsewhere. The region is thus at a crossroads: it can continue to rely on the provincial and federal governments to respond to legitimate requests, and hope that the answer is both timely and positive; or it can chart a course to making the structural changes in its economy to meet present and future challenges.

The traditional economy of northwestern Ontario has been dominated by the natural resources sector, but public policy has signalled an interest in diversifying the region's economy and addressing both longer-term resource depletion and changing markets. The results of policy interventions by the federal and provincial governments to address the north's economic challenges can be usefully juxtaposed with alternative institutional mechanisms of economic development policy intervention already under way in the northwestern region.

Development Attempts in Northwestern Ontario

All three orders of government have been involved in regional economic development in northwestern Ontario. Since the 1950s a number of institutional and organizational configurations, spearheaded by the federal government, have aimed to deliver economic development programs to Canada's disadvantaged regions, including northwestern Ontario. In 1987 the federal government effected several significant changes in regional development policy that led to the creation of regional development agencies for each of western Canada, Atlantic Canada, and northern Ontario; a fourth agency, for Quebec, followed in 1991. These new agencies were part of a trend towards larger regions for developmental programming in Canada. In all cases, the emphasis was on strengthening large-scale regional economies by concentrating on areas of potential comparative advantage.

The agency responsible for northern Ontario is the Federal Economic Development Initiative in Northern Ontario (FedNor), which plans and funds economic development.[7] Unlike other federal regional development entities, which are separate departments, FedNor is administered by Industry Canada.[8] FedNor is mandated to work as both a facilitator and a catalyst with a variety of partners to encourage an environment of regional economic development involving communities, businesses, and other levels of government. The agency has two main programs, the Northern Ontario Development Program (NODP) and the Community Futures Program. The goal of the NODP is to promote economic growth throughout a large and diverse geographic area that stretches from Muskoka Lakes to James Bay, and from the Manitoba border to western Quebec. It supports projects in six areas: community economic development, innovation, information and communications technology, trade and tourism, human capital, and business financing. The NODP is an all-embracing program covering almost every sector – its only limitation is spatial or geographic; it potentially could support any economic activity falling within FedNor's regional jurisdiction.

Through its Community Economic Development project, for instance, FedNor seeks to partner with community groups and not-for-profit organizations in helping to create employment and stimulate growth in socio-economically depressed communities. The agency's Innovation Project is an example of helping companies in northern Ontario to bring new products and services to market. FedNor does this by providing assistance to organizations that attend to the necessary infrastructure, environment, and conditions to facilitate applied research and development, and the development, application, and transfer of new technologies to the north.

The other component of FedNor is the Community Futures Program, which supports sixty-one Community Futures Development Corporations (CFDCs), twenty-four of which are located in the north; the rest serve rural eastern and southern Ontario. The CFDCs offer a wide variety of programs and services that support community economic development and small business growth. They also provide access to capital via loans, loan guarantees, or equity investments to create or maintain employment.

The provincial government also has its own development policy intervention in the north, delivered by the Ministry of Northern Development, Mines and Forestry. The Northern Development Division is responsible for economic and community development. Its key mandate is to promote economic growth and investment in northern Ontario and to ensure that provincial government policies and programs reflect a northern perspective. The division divides its economic and community development mandate into four somewhat overlapping thematic components – namely, business support, community support, support for youth, and transportation and roads.

The most important delivery agency of the Ministry of Northern Development, Mines and Forestry is the Northern Ontario Heritage Fund Corporation (NOHFC), which has two aims: to work with northern entrepreneurs and businesses to help them create jobs in the private sector; and second, to support critical infrastructure and community development projects that will help communities improve their economies and quality of life.

The NOHFC delivers a variety of government programs and services in the north, most of them are similar to FedNor's activities. For instance, it has programs in community and regional economic development, transportation, and community infrastructure. The NOHFC has northern development professionals in the north's six largest communities (Kenora, North Bay, Sault Ste Marie, Sudbury, Thunder Bay, and Timmins) and in a number of smaller communities across the north. Team members work with northern communities, institutions, and businesses to help them identify economic development opportunities in key economic sectors.

An Appraisal of Policy Governance in Northern Ontario

A key factor that fosters or hinders the interaction of a public agency and its local environment is the extent to which the agency's mission reflects the core values and interests of the local environment. The mandates of both FedNor and the NOHFC generally position them to provide some policy leadership in northern Ontario. Both are considered to be on a mission necessary for the region's economy. Their programs constitute well-intentioned interventions by the two levels of government in a socio-economically disadvantaged region, and, in fact, they have had some success. Their many programs have contributed to the development of new businesses and the retention of existing ones. They have also invested in the increased use of technology and in innovation in the region. One notable success has been to increase the number of rural and remote communities with access to high-speed Internet and cellular telephone service. The successful strides these agencies have made so far, however, should not blind one to their untapped further potential to transform the region's economy.

Deep institutional weaknesses at both FedNor and the NOHFC have undermined their legitimacy and effectiveness, reproducing in microcosm the broader tension in federal-provincial relations. The two orders of government have disagreed fundamentally about regional economic development policies since the 1960s, about both the right approach and each other's appropriate role. FedNor is the latest institutional expression of a long struggle over the legitimate role of Ottawa. For its part, Ontario, like other provincial governments, has shown little enthusiasm for federal strategies or plans in its own backyard. In general, provincial governments see regional economic development as their responsibility, on the grounds that they are closer to the problem than any national agency and have a better understanding of regional needs and priorities.[9] The NOHFC, then, appears to be Ontario's reaction to federal showmanship in its jurisdiction.

The degree of coordination among public agencies with similar mandates – their ability to broker power and resources and to negotiate conflicting interests among multiple players to further collaborative action – affects the strategic impact of their policy intervention.[10] Unfortunately, the heavy heritage of both FedNor and the NOHFC is one of intergovernmental tension over the conduct of regional economic development policy. The first thing that stands out in reviewing the mandates and programs of the two agencies is the incredible overlap: there is, simply, no coordination between the two. Their ability to make a strategic impact on the region's economy is weakened by fragmentation and duplication of program delivery. As early as 1995, Canada's auditor general advised the two agencies to streamline their programs and move away from disparate short-term projects towards more strategic investment in regionally designed and intersectoral programs.[11] Success at coordination would have transformed potentially conflicting, short-term, and fragmentary sets of development projects offered by similar agencies in silos into complementary and coherent programs with a more strategic, sectorally comprehensive, and longer-term orientation that led to structural transformation in the local economy. There is, however, no evidence that the auditor general's advice, given more than a decade ago, has been heeded: the agencies continue to offer a disparate set of multidimensional, fragmented, inconsistent projects mostly aimed at job creation, without any clear long-term plan.

Moreover, while each agency's mandate calls for partnership with communities and the private sector, in practice the agencies' claims to partnership are restricted to a tacit understanding about monitoring each other's funding initiatives that clients bring forward. The agencies' legitimacy and strategy, then, are affected by the perceptions of their key clientele. The more extensive the support and established feedback loops these agencies maintain with local organized actors (public and private), the better their chances of effecting enduring policy changes. A collaborative partnership implies mechanisms of joint action involving networks of actors in the private and community sectors engaged in strategic planning.[12] It also means jointly determining the strengths and weaknesses of the regional economy, and collaboratively seeking mechanisms for comprehensive policy and programs that promise to actualize its potential.

In short, economic development policy in northern Ontario requires a more coordinated and proactive approach; FedNor and the NOHFC are products of traditional bureaucratic departments with a bias towards passive approval of loan applications for silo projects. Instead, what is needed is strategic engagement in regionally comprehensive and long-term planning.

One solution to the agencies' duplication, rivalry, and waste would be to form a multilevel intergovernmental partnership that allows the actual delivery of economic development to be dispersed and devolved to the municipal level of government. Doing so could create the institutional mechanism for interagency coordination, and give the federal and provincial agencies a break from the intergovernmental rivalry that inhibits the sort of partnership their mandates profess to seek. Devolution to the lower level of government could also make it easier to implement programs in partnership with local actors to discover and tap local entrepreneurship and resources.[13] An example of such a framework can be found in New Brunswick, where the federal government's regional development agency, the Atlantic Canada Opportunities Agency (ACOA) has moved over time to partnership with a wide variety of governmental and non-governmental actors, an approach that has yet to occur in the northern Ontario context.[14]

A Collaborative Approach to Regional Economic Development

What are the chances of building the institutional infrastructure to support a regionally comprehensive and integrated approach to economic development in northern Ontario? How can existing mechanisms of regional economic development policy in the north be altered to improve partnerships among the various levels of governments and organized community interests? My goal here is not to be overly normative but, rather, to examine recent political developments in the region and then assess their potential for providing alternative mechanisms of policy intervention.

As the discussion that follows illustrates, these alternative institutional infrastructures will still be consistent with the centrality of the state in whatever form of state-society arrangement emerges. As Guy Peters notes,[15] the ideals of democracy necessitate some form of public authority, wielded by the state, to maintain the goals of accountability, coherence, steering, and a common set of priorities for the collective good of society. The significance of such a counterweight to society-centric perspectives is that the emergence of non-state actors and local municipalities in policy governance in northwestern Ontario does not necessarily presuppose the decline of senior levels of government. Rather, it presents an analytical context in which to assess the state's ability to adapt to changes in the external policy environment.

A key leading organization championing new institutional infrastructure for regional economic development is the Northwestern Ontario Municipal Association (NOMA). The organization, incorporated in

2001, consists of four components: the Kenora District Municipal Association, the Rainy River District Municipal Association, the Thunder Bay District Municipal League, and the City of Thunder Bay. NOMA's objectives are to consider matters of general interest to northwestern Ontario's municipalities and to procure policies that are advantageous to them. NOMA also seeks to engage in more strategic local governance by taking united action on matters that affect the economy and sustainability of the region. NOMA and the Federation of Northern Ontario Municipalities form the Northern Caucus of the Association of Municipalities of Ontario. Thus, NOMA also engages in extensive networking among municipalities that spread beyond northwestern Ontario to include the whole of the province's northern region.

Even more significant, NOMA is also forming increasingly strong strategic relationships with First Nations communities. Aboriginal communities represented through their treaty organizations in northwestern Ontario are increasingly being factored into the strategic vision of economic adjustment and transition. Indeed, Aboriginals are taking advantage of their much greater role in the economy of the region.[16] Significant numbers of Aboriginal individuals and families are relocating to the urban centres of Kenora, Sioux Lookout, and Thunder Bay to seek further education and employment. Their participation is thus crucial to any forward-thinking approach to the economy and health of the region.[17]

Aboriginal communities are not the only mobilized community groups, as other grassroots interests now include groups such as the Thunder Bay Economic Justice Committee and the Food Action Network, among others. As a 2007 report sponsored by the Ontario government concludes, there is a strong recognition within the region that all future efforts by municipalities, businesses, industries, and other stakeholders must be done in concert with the First Nations and other community groups.[18] One of the most encouraging signs of a change in attitude towards governance in northwestern Ontario is thus the cooperation and collaboration that is taking place between First Nations and non-Aboriginal communities across the region. Central to these changes is the leadership that municipalities are showing in dealing with the seismic shifts in their economy.

In the face of the worsening economic crisis in the region, NOMA has embarked upon building a policy infrastructure for more strategic economic intervention. The organization's economic development strategy has two key components: economic development investment incentives; and economic development population and business regeneration. The first incentive is aimed at attracting businesses to the region primarily through tax concessions and other subsidies that could be coordinated with upper levels of government. The second initiative has two dimensions: first, to reverse the tide of population decline by attracting and keeping industrious immigrants to the region; second, to engage in some form of intersectoral planning aimed at supporting existing businesses as well as stimulating new local entrepreneurship.

NOMA's intersectoral planning is an ambitious and innovative project for municipal governments – indeed, it goes beyond the traditional domain of municipal governments, as some of the areas identified as priorities for coordinated strategic action are energy, regional health and education, transportation, tourism, and destination marketing. A significant characteristic of NOMA's coordinated regional policy initiative is the recognition of the need to stop asking for more handouts from upper levels of government. Local governments do not have to deliver services passively, as has been their conventional role; rather, they can engage more proactively in the transitioning of their economies.

Even more important is NOMA's recognition that local municipalities will need to think beyond their immediate jurisdictions and adopt a more regional perspective if they are to overcome the structural disadvantages of a region of widely scattered rural enclaves and single-industry towns. Northwestern Ontario needs to be viewed as a single regional economy, and the establishment by municipalities of a suitable policy and institutional arena could pave the way to greater economic development.

Another feature of the NOMA initiative is the change in discourse with upper levels of government. Municipalities are constitutionally the creatures of the provinces, but a powerful shift is under way in political activism towards local and grassroots spaces. Citizens are often more directly involved with macro processes of governance in local communities, where the concept of collective or shared interest is most tangibly felt. Against this backdrop of increasing grassroots activism, local municipalities have the political legitimacy (even if not the constitutional authority) to engage other levels of government more strategically as partners. The goal of such engagement could be to move beyond merely requesting more funds for roads and sewage facilities towards collaborative formulation and implementation of regional economic development policies.

FedNor and the NOHFC have two options in responding to such initiatives. They can continue to give way to the impulse to intergovernmental rivalry and ignore or otherwise frustrate the municipalities' initiatives. Or they can see the opportunity to build a truly bottom-up institutional infrastructure that allows for intergovernmental partnership and state-society collaboration. Inasmuch as the most visible presence of government in the region is actually through FedNor and the NOHFC, these agencies are positioned to take a leadership role in overcoming the practical limitations to the strategic use of their funds. NOMA's initiative, however, should not be seen as replacing the involvement of higher levels of government. Rather, it should be a node of coordination among the key actors across the various levels of government and from within the community.

As the Ontario government noted in the 2007 report referred earlier, improved policy vision and governance in the region requires the two senior levels of government to encourage and support the NOMA-led initiative to bring the economic players in northwestern Ontario into a coalition to identify and take action on key economic issues and opportunities. A partnership involving the federal and provincial governments and an integrated body of municipalities in the region, the report suggests, could form a tripartite roundtable working group to form coordinated and collaborative economic adjustment and development policy and plans for the region. Participants should also include communities and non-governmental organizations in a truly strategic intervention to combat the forces of regional economic decline. FedNor and the NOHFC, as the key federal and provincial development agencies in the region, could facilitate the coordinated presence of those two levels of government.

The difficulty of coordinating federal and provincial policies, programs, and activities in northwestern Ontario relates also to coordination or joint action among non-state actors. For example, FedNor works with Community Futures Development Corporations in the region, while the provincial Ministry of Northern Development, Mines and Forestry has also created Development Councils to offer advice and feedback. Fostering joint action among these and other local or regional organizations, such as chambers of commerce, the Prospectors and Developers Association, the Forestry Association, unions, and others, remains a challenge.

Beyond sporadic consultations on timely issues among these local actors, the movement towards strategic economic development policy governance could consider leveraging the institutional potentials of joint municipal initiatives, such as NOMA, as a way of systematizing coordination at the local level. The multitude of local organizations thus could consolidate their links with FedNor and the provincial ministry. Indeed, the aforementioned political activities in the region point to the gradual emergence of municipalities as nodes or forums of spatial and sectoral coordination. Since I argue that municipalities should be included in the policy development and implementation processes in a much more meaningful way, then municipalities or, perhaps, more appropriately, regional municipal organizations (NOMA being one such) could be given the resources to become the heretofore missing link between the various local communities and the senior levels of government. The emphasis on local municipalities as nodes of coordinated joint action could be a way to deal with the frankly rather chaotic networks and policy discourse communities involved in economic development policy in the region.

If the institutional arrangement I have described were implemented, regional economic development policy could be undertaken on a truly regional and strategic scale, rather than preserving the current silos of community economic development initiatives, which often have little or no prospect of success. Such a move, however, would have certain consequences. First, it would involve less direct transfer of funds by government agencies to randomly selected private enterprises and a more strategic investment of funds following comprehensive planning and deliberation. Second, it would call for close collaboration among government agencies and local community organizations in which the latter play a greater role in identifying local economic and entrepreneurial potentials and investing in them. Third, if the primary mechanisms of delivery were community organizations, federal and provincial agencies would have less incentive for competition and would be compelled to channel their resources more through existing frameworks of policy collaboration. Fourth, separation of sectoral and spatial planning would be dissolved at the local level, since local policy stakeholders tend to have a more intersectoral view of their local economy.

Conclusion

In conclusion, FedNor and the NOHFC are performing roles that are highly relevant to the needs of northern Ontario. The current schematic basis of their policy delivery, however, faces considerable challenges that are partly rooted in the broader intergovernmental politics of Canada's federal system. Lack of effective coordination among agencies engaged in similar policy intervention, however, can be costly. The costs often include waste of resources in completely unrelated projects, vague or confused policy direction, unclear mechanisms of policy or program evaluation, and dubious legitimacy from economic and political standpoints.

In this chapter I have emphasized the need for more collaborative partnerships encompassing diverse expressions of cooperation between state agencies and organized societal interests. These kinds of interorganizational cooperation can be formal as well as informal strategic networks of complex relationships among agencies with similar mandates in the three orders of government, and state-society partnerships incorporating community development organizations and business groups. The proposed governance framework, therefore, emphasizes partnerships among governments, the private sector, communities, voluntary organizations, and others. It also values greater devolution to the regional and local levels. Moreover, it does not seek to do away with the role of the state in governing and steering policy; rather, it suggests a new vision of the state as enabler and convenor. Such a role would require the sharing of power and authority with the community itself. Given recent political developments in northwestern Ontario, including initiatives by NOMA, economic development policy governance in the region holds the potential for a more strategic and proactive orientation. Realizing this potential, however, would require better organizational and institutional capacities for policy planning and program implementation that involve collaborative partnerships with non-state actors and economic development agencies from all three levels of government.

NOTES

1 D.J. Savoie, *Federal-Provincial Collaboration: The Canada-New Brunswick General Development Agreement* (Montreal; Kingston, ON: McGill-Queen's University Press, 1981); idem, *Rethinking Canada's Regional Development Policy: An Atlantic Perspective* (Moncton, NB: Canadian Institute for Research on Regional Development, 1997); and R. Simeon, *Intergovernmental Relations*, study prepared for the Royal Commission on the Economic Union and Development Prospects for Canada (Toronto: University of Toronto Press, 1985).

2 P. Aucoin and H. Bakvis, "Organizational Differentiation and Integration: The Case of Regional Economic Development Policy in Canada," *Canadian Public Administration* 27 (3, 1984): 348–71; see also Savoie, *Rethinking Canada's Regional Development Policy.*

3 L. Di Matteo, "Strategies for Developing a Broadly Based Regional Knowledge Economy in Northwestern Ontario" (Thunder Bay, ON: North Superior Training Board, 2006).

4 R. Rosehart, *Northwestern Ontario: Preparing for Change*, Northwestern Ontario Economic Facilitator Report (n.p., 2008), available online at http://www.mndm.gov.on.ca/nordev/documents/noef/REPORT_FEB2008.

5 C. Southcott, *The North in Numbers: A Demographic Analysis of Social and Economic Change in Northern Ontario* (Thunder Bay, ON: Lakehead University, Centre for Northern Studies, 2006).

6 Northwestern Ontario Municipal Association, "Enhancing the Economy of Northwestern Ontario" (n.p., 2007), available online at http://www.northernontarioregion.ca/uploads/documents/NWORDA/EnhancingtheEconomyofNWO.pdf.

7 D. Webster, "Regional Development Planning," *The Canadian Encyclopedia* (1992), available online at http://www.thecanadianencyclopedia.com/index.cfm?PgNm=TCE&Params=A1ARTA0006746.

8 Canada, Auditor General of Canada, *Report of the Auditor General of Canada* (Ottawa, 1995), available online at http://www.oag-bvg.gc.ca/internet/English/parl_oag_199511_e_1155.html.

9 Webster, "Regional Development Planning."

10 L.J. O'Toole, "Research on Policy Implementation: Assessment and Prospects," *Journal of Public Administration Research and Theory* 10 (2, 2000): 263. See also R. Agranoff and M. McGuire, "Multinetwork Management: Collaboration and the Hollow State in Local Economic Policy," *Journal of Public Administration Research and Theory: J-PART* 8 (1, 1998): 67–91; J.V. Denhardt and R.B. Denhardt, *The New Public Service: Serving, Not Steering* (Armonk, NY: M.E. Sharpe, 2003); M. Hill and P. Hupe, "The Multi-layer Problem in Implementation Research," *Public Management Review* 5 (4, 2003): 471–90; E. Lindquist, "Organizing for Policy Implementation: The Emergence and Role of Implementation Units in Policy Design and Oversight," *Journal of Comparative Policy Analysis: Research and Practice* 8 (4, 2006): 311–24; L.J. O'Toole and K.J. Meier, "Desperately Seeking Selznick: Cooptation and the Dark Side of Public Management in Networks," *Public Administration Review* 64 (6, 2004): 681–93; and S. Winter, "Integrating Implementation Research," in *Implementation and the Policy Process: Opening Up the Black Box*, ed. D.J. Palumbo and D.J. Calista (New York: Greenwood Press, 1990).

11 Canada, Auditor General of Canada, *Report.*

12 J. Newman, "Joined-Up Government: The Politics of Partnership," in *Making Policy Happen*, ed. L. Budd, R. Paton, and J. Charlesworth

(New York: Routledge, 2006); J. Pierre and B.G. Peters, *Governing Complex Societies: Trajectories and Scenarios* (New York: Palgrave Macmillan, 2005); and O. Treib, H. Bahr, and G. Falkner, "Modes of Governance: Towards a Conceptual Clarification," *Journal of European Public Policy* 14 (1, 2007): 1–20.

13 R.P. Stoker, *Reluctant Partners: Implementing Federal Policy* (Pittsburgh: University of Pittsburgh Press, 1991); and G.L. Wamsley and M.N. Zald, *The Political Economy of Public Organizations: A Critique and Approach to the Study of Public Administration* (Lexington, MA: Lexington Books, 1973).

14 N.J. Bradford and D. Wolfe, "Regional Economic Development Agencies in Canada: Lessons for Southern Ontario" (Toronto: University of Toronto, School of Public Policy & Governance, Mowat Centre for Policy Innovation, 2010); and C. Conteh, "Public Management in an Age of Complexity: Regional Economic Development in Canada," *International Journal of Public Sector Management* 25 (6–7, 2012): 464–72.

15 B.G. Peters, *The Future of Governing: Four Emerging Models* (Lawrence: University Press of Kansas, 2001).

16 F. Abele, *The Art of the State: Northern Exposure, Peoples, Powers and Prospects in Canada's North* (Montreal; Kingston, ON: McGill-Queen's University Press, 2009).

17 F. Abele, "Policy Research in the North: A Discussion Paper" (Ottawa: Gordon Foundation, 2006).

18 Rosehart, *Northwestern Ontario*.

4 Results Measurement and Economic Development in Northern Ontario

BOB SEGSWORTH

Introduction

The Ontario government's 2009 *Places to Grow – Better Choices, Brighter Future: Proposed Growth Plan for Northern Ontario* assured that "a set of performance indicators will be developed to measure implementation of this Plan. Performance measures will be monitored and actions and strategies will be adjusted to ensure the Plan's successful realization."[1] By June 2010 work "to determine how the Growth Plan will be put in place, monitored and measured"[2] was in progress.

In this chapter I argue that the development and use of performance indicators is a part of contemporary public sector management commitments, and I demonstrate their implementation internationally, nationally, and provincially. I offer a results measurement report that illustrates, historically and comparatively, several dimensions of economic development in northern Ontario and argue that implementation indicators, although useful for some purposes, are insufficient to prove the outcomes (results) of government policy. Finally, I make some recommendations to improve the quality of results reporting and to develop and create access to better regionally relevant data to improve the quality of research and informed discussion and debate on the success of economic development policies and programs in northern Ontario.

"[P]erformance orientation in public management," as one researcher suggests, "is here to stay. It is essential for successful government."[3] Comparative studies of public management in Westminster systems have concluded that the enthusiasm for performance (or results) management has been greater in the United Kingdom, Australia, and New Zealand than in Canada.[4] Another argues that "considerable progress has been made," and points out that the focus of results-based management has changed from outputs to outcomes – that is, to "the benefits achieved as a result of those goods and services."[5] In an earlier work, I summarize the experience in Westminster systems as:

- the government's specifying its policy goals and setting targets;
- departments' specifying the policy goals to which they will contribute;
- departments' defining the means (activities and programs) by which they intend to contribute to attaining government policy goals, specifying the measures they will use for outputs and outcomes, and setting performance targets; and
- departments and agencies' reporting regularly on their performance against the targets.[6]

In the first decade of the twenty-first century, we have witnessed a commitment to results-based management by both the federal government and the provincial government of Ontario. In 2000 a Treasury Board report specified changes that would be required to establish results-based management in the federal government. One key point was the importance of performance information for the success of this new management framework: "The foundation of result-based management is accurate and timely performance information. Departments and agencies need to implement an information regime that measures, evaluates and reports on key aspects of programs and their performance in key areas; holds managers accountable for achieving results; and ensures unbiased analysis, showing both good and bad performance."[7]

Following the recommendations of the 1995 Ontario Financial Review Commission,[8] Ontario's then Progressive Conservative government introduced business planning. By 2000 it was clear that the notion of results included outcomes. The Draft Business Planning and Allocations Directive of the Ontario government's Management Board Secretariat required published business plans to "detail published core business performance measures, showing desired outcomes, targets, standards and commitments for the new year."[9]

The commitment to results measurement and reporting continued throughout the decade. In 2005 the federal government introduced its policy on Management, Resources and Results Structure (MRRS). Each government department's MRRS was expected to contain five basic sections, one each to deal with strategic outcomes, program activity architecture, actual and planned resource information, performance measures, and governance structure. Then, in 2007, the Treasury Board Secretariat produced a *Performance Reporting Good Practices Handbook* and, at about the same time, added a "Government of Canada Planning and Performance Gateway" to its Web site.[10] The Ontario Public Service (OPS) Modernization Initiative, initiated in 2006, also reflected a continuing commitment to results measurement. Its "Framework for Action" claimed that "to build a modern OPS, we must keep focused on common goals and we must continue to measure and report on results and continuously improve."[11] The 2009 "OPS Framework for Action" stated that "performance measurement is critical to demonstrate results and identify areas for improvement."[12] In terms of economic development, Figures 4.1 and 4.2 illustrate the similarity of the two perspectives.

Despite this commitment to results-based management and results reporting, a search of the Web sites of the Ontario Ministry of Northern Development and Mines, its Ministry of Natural Resources, the Federal

Figure 4.1. The Federal Government's Whole Government Framework, Economic Affairs

Government of Canada

Whole of Government Framework - Economic Affairs

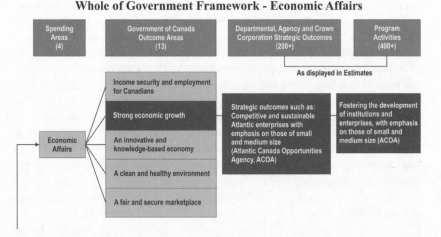

Source: Canada, Treasury Board Secretariat, *Canada's Performance, 2007–08* (Ottawa, 2008).

Figure 4.2. Ontario's Ministry of Northern Development and Mines and Government Priorities

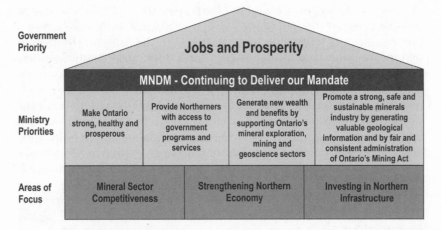

Source: Ontario, Ministry of Northern Development and Mines, *Results-based Plan Briefing Book, 2009–10* (Toronto, 2009), 4.

Economic Development Initiative in Northern Ontario (FedNor), and Industry Canada yields no public reports that measure the outcomes of government policy on economic development in northern Ontario, possibly evidencing the promise-versus-performance experience outlined in the context of federal evaluation policy and practice by Muller-Clemm and Barnes.[13] It might also give credence to Mayne's caveat that "lack of agreement on the usefulness of performance information has been a major stumbling block in the past – and no doubt still is in some quarters."[14] Accordingly, in this chapter, I provide a number of performance measures that capture dimensions of economic development for northern Ontario.

Methodology

A key problem in developing a results measurement report is knowing the number of indicators to provide. The World Bank statistical database contains information on two thousand indicators: the United Nations has forty-eight Millennium Indicators; the UK Audit Commission has recommended sixty regional development indicators;[13] the European Commission calls for fifty-six regional development policy measures;[16] while the government of Western Australia uses one hundred indicators of various aspects of regional development.[17]

Perhaps the most relevant for our purposes are the Regional Economic Indicators reports produced annually by the Alberta provincial government for each of fourteen economic regions.[18] The Alberta reports contain information on ten categories of indicators: major municipalities; demographics; immigration (permanent residents); labour force characteristics; employment by industry; income; investment; establishments with employees; small business establishments; and inventory of major projects. The reports also contain 154 quantitative indicators, of which seventeen demographic indicators, ten labour force indicators, and twelve employment by industry measures are derived from 2001 and 2006 census data provided by Statistics Canada, while twenty-three investment indicators are calculated from Statistics Canada data for 2005, 2006, and 2007. For the other categories, the data come from the Citizenship and Immigration Canada landing file for the period from 1997 to 2007 and from Alberta Finance and Enterprise databases. When I asked why these particular indicators had been selected, an Alberta public servant told me that they were based on the statistically reliable data the Alberta government could obtain.[19]

Two other noteworthy features of the Alberta reports are, first, that they provide longitudinal data – that is, measures over time that allow readers to see whether economic conditions are changing for each of the regions over time; and, second, they make a serious attempt to compare regional values with provincial values over time. For example, population indicators are expressed, in part, as a percentage of the provincial total over time, thus allowing readers to compare particular regions to the province as a whole.

For this analysis, I have borrowed both the longitudinal and the regional/provincial approach of the Alberta reports. For reasons of access and cost, the indicators I use are based on data provided by Statistics Canada for Ontario, northeastern Ontario, and northwestern Ontario from the 1981, 1986, 1991, 1996, 2001, and 2006 censuses.[20] Because industry classifications are adjusted at various intervals, I am unable to determine comparable measures of employment by industry over time, and have excluded them for the purposes of this study.

I chose the period of 1981 to 2006 for two reasons. First, it provides a base from which an observer might identify trends for each of the measures presented. Second, it was during the early part of this period that the Ontario government created the Ministry of Northern Affairs and Mines (1985, renamed Northern Development and Mines later the same year) and the federal government created FedNor (1987). Thus, the choice of the 1981–2006 period allows me to provide information about the state of the northern Ontario and Ontario economies both before and after these two important government initiatives. Unfortunately, this approach cannot be applied to the investment indicators, because data on building permit values were available only for the 1991–2006 period.

I provide fourteen performance results measures for both Ontario as a whole and northern Ontario in four main categories: demography; income; labour force characteristics; and investment. For each measure the ratio of the northern Ontario statistic divided by the Ontario value expressed as a percentage is included in the tables. Because Statistics Canada provides separate data for northern Ontario's two economic regions, I have had to calculate northern Ontario statistics from that base. For example, to calculate an unemployment rate for northern Ontario, I added the number of unemployed persons in northwestern and northeastern Ontario and divided that number by the labour forces of the two regions. I then multiplied that figure by 100 to arrive at an accurate unemployment rate for northern Ontario.

Results

As Table 4.1, shows, the province's population increased substantially over the twenty-five-year period, while that of northern Ontario declined in both absolute and relative terms (from 9.5 per cent of Ontario's population in 1981 to 6.5 per cent in 2006).

"Dependency Rate 1," shown in Table 4.2, is the number of the population below age fifteen and over age sixty-four divided by the number of adults ages fifteen to sixty-four – in other words, the population of children and the elderly who are dependent on the adult population to meet their economic needs. The table shows that the dependency rate by this measure for northern Ontario remains higher than for Ontario as a whole, but declined from 108.1 per cent in 1981 to 105.3 per cent in 2006. From a northern Ontario perspective, this would seem to be evidence of improvement over time.

Table 4.1. Population, Ontario and Northern Ontario, 1981–2006

Year	Ontario	Northern Ontario	Ratio of Northern Ontario to Ontario
1981	8,534,260	812,310	9.5
1986	9,001,165	790,530	8.8
1991	9,977,050	814,040	8.2
1996	10,642,790	818,495	7.7
2001	11,285,550	777,800	6.9
2006	12,028,895	776,975	6.5

Table 4.2. Dependency Rate 1, Ontario and Northern Ontario, 1981–2006

Year	Ontario	Northern Ontario	Ratio of Northern Ontario to Ontario
1981	0.459	0.496	108.1
1986	0.448	0.484	108.0
1991	0.462	0.487	105.4
1996	0.482	0.492	102.1
2001	0.472	0.494	104.7
2006	0.456	0.480	105.3

"Dependency Rate 2," the old age dependency rate, measures the population over age sixty-four divided by the number of adults ages fifteen to sixty-four. The result is the elderly population that is dependent on the adult population to meet its economic needs. As Table 4.3 shows, the old age dependency rate is increasing at a faster rate in northern Ontario than is the case for Ontario, and that it now exceeds the Ontario rate substantially. In 1981 the northern Ontario rate was 89.1 per cent of the Ontario rate, but by 2006 it had reached 119.1 per cent of the provincial rate.

Table 4.4 demonstrates that adults in northern Ontario have become poorer over time, as their average incomes declined from 92.5 per cent of the provincial average in 1981 to 86.7 per cent in 2006.

Table 4.5 illustrates that the situation for northern Ontario families has worsened, with average family income dropping from 92.5 per cent of the provincial average in 1981 to 82.3 per cent in 2006.

Table 4.3. Dependency Rate 2, Ontario and Northern Ontario, 1981–2006

Year	Ontario	Northern Ontario	Northern Ontario/Ontario
1981	0.138	0.123	89.1
1986	0.148	0.140	94.6
1991	0.161	0.159	98.8
1996	0.174	0.178	102.3
2001	0.181	0.205	113.3
2006	0.188	0.224	119.1

Table 4.4. Average Income, Adults, Ontario and Northern Ontario, 1981–2006

Year	Ontario	Northern Ontario	Ratio of Northern Ontario to Ontario
1981	$12,968	$11,998	92.5
1986	19,127	17,255	90.2
1991	25,993	22,897	88.1
1996	27,124	25,289	93.2
2001	32,767	27,463	83.8
2006	38,099	33,017	86.7

Table 4.5. Average Family Income, Ontario and Northern Ontario, 1981–2006

Year	Ontario	Northern Ontario	Ratio of Northern Ontario to Ontario
1981	$28,002	$25,879	92.5
1986	41,692	35,838	86.0
1991	57,227	49,627	86.7
1996	59,830	53,744	89.8
2001	73,849	60,268	81.6
2006	90,526	74,521	82.3

The labour force is defined as the number of persons who are fifteen years of age or older who were not institutional residents and were either employed or unemployed during the year in question. Table 4.6 indicates that the labour force of northern Ontario did not increase at the same rate as that of the province as a whole. In 1981, northern Ontario's labour force was 8.5 per cent of the province's, but by 2006 it had declined to 6 per cent.

Table 4.6. Labour Force Size, Ontario and Northern Ontario, 1981–2006

Year	Ontario	Northern Ontario	Ratio of Northern Ontario to Ontario
1981	4,464,050	377,355	8.5
1986	4,922,245	386,020	7.8
1991	5,511,235	409,020	7.4
1996	5,586,975	390,730	7.9
2001	6,086,815	384,795	6.3
2006	6,587,575	393,290	6.0

Table 4.7. Participation Rate Ontario and Northern Ontario

Year	Ontario	Northern Ontario	Ratio of Northern Ontario to Ontario
	(%)		
1981	67.1	61.8	92.1
1986	69.0	63.6	92.2
1991	69.9	64.5	92.1
1996	66.3	61.9	93.8
2001	67.3	61.3	91.5
2006	67.7	61.2	91.3

The participation rate is defined as the number of persons in the labour force expressed as a percentage of the population ages fifteen and over. Table 4.7 shows that the participation rate for northern Ontario relative to that for Ontario declined slightly from 92.1 per cent in 1986 to 91.3 per cent in 2006.

The employment rate is defined as the number of employed persons expressed as a percentage of the population fifteen years of age and over. Table 4.8 illustrates the decline in the employment rate for northern Ontario adults: in 1981 the rate was 98.1 per cent of the Ontario average; by 2006 it was 97.4 per cent of the Ontario average.

The unemployment rate is the number of unemployed persons expressed as a percentage of the labour force. Table 4.9 shows that the northern Ontario unemployment rate increased from 132 per cent to 140 per cent of the overall Ontario rate over the period 1981–2006. Unemployment remains a more serious problem in northern Ontario than in the province as a whole.

Table 4.8. Employment Rate, Ontario and Northern Ontario, 1981–2006

Year	Ontario	Northern Ontario	Ratio of Northern Ontario to Ontario
		(%)	
1981	94.4	92.6	98.1
1986	93.2	88.8	95.3
1991	91.5	90.1	98.5
1996	91.0	87.9	96.6
2001	94.0	90.2	96.0
2006	94.0	91.6	97.4

Table 4.9. Unemployment Rate, Ontario and Northern Ontario, 1981–2006

Year	Ontario	Northern Ontario	Ratio of Northern Ontario to Ontario
		(%)	
1981	5.6	7.4	132
1986	6.8	11.2	165
1991	8.5	9.9	116
1996	9.0	12.1	134
2001	6.0	9.8	163
2006	6.0	8.4	140

Table 4.10 shows that the value of residential building permits issued in northern Ontario declined over the period from 1991 to 2006, even as the value of such permits for the province as a whole more than doubled. The value of residential building in northern Ontario accordingly declined from 6.3 per cent to 2.7 per cent of the Ontario total over the period. Ontario's housing boom did not extend as far as the north.

As Table 4.11 shows, the value of commercial building permits issued in northern Ontario increased only slightly from 1991 to 2006, while the value of permits in the province as a whole more than doubled. Over the period, the value of commercial building in northern Ontario declined from 5.2 per cent to 3.4 per cent of the Ontario total.

A similar pattern exists for industrial building permit values; as Table 4.12 shows, northern Ontario's declined from 5.9 per cent to 3.4 per cent of the province's over the 1991–2006 period.

Table 4.10. Value of Residential Building Permits, Ontario and Northern Ontario, 1991–2006

Year	Ontario	Northern Ontario	Ratio of Northern Ontario to Ontario
1991	$7,019,481	$442,458	6.3
1996	5,939,335	221,549	3.7
2001	11,166,741	231,951	2.1
2006	14,293,993	380,639	2.7

Table 4.11. Value of Commercial Building Permits, Ontario and Northern Ontario, 1991–2006

Year	Ontario	Northern Ontario	Ratio of Northern Ontario to Ontario
1991	$2,271,650	$119,219	5.2
1996	1,828,240	95,888	5.2
2001	3,648,195	110,045	3.0
2006	4,814,978	165,667	3.4

Table 4.12. Industrial Building Permit Value Ontario and Northern Ontario

Year	Ontario	Northern Ontario	Ratio Northern Ontario to Ontario
1991	$1,140,421	$67,655	5.9
1996	1,080,471	55,733	5.2
2001	1,552,721	41,242	2.7
2006	1,843,893	61,842	3.4

Table 4.13 illustrates a somewhat different pattern in terms of the value of institutional building permits. In 1991 the value of such per-mits in northern Ontario was 12.3 per cent of the value for the province as a whole. Northern Ontario's values then declined significantly, but had recovered somewhat by 2006.

In terms of the value of all building permits, northern Ontario's slipped from 7.4 per cent to 3.6 per cent of Ontario's over the period (Table 4.14).

These results do not encourage optimism about the economic future of northern Ontario. On thirteen of the fourteen indicators, the region

Table 4.13. Value of Institutional Building Permits, Ontario and Northern Ontario, 1991–2006

Year	Ontario	Northern Ontario	Ratio of Northern Ontario to Ontario
1991	$1,567,139	$193,532	12.3
1996	749,506	34,499	4.6
2001	2,701,654	175,980	6.5
2006	2,339,312	218,803	9.4

Table 4.14. Value of All Building Permits, Ontario and Northern Ontario, 1991–2006

Year	Ontario	Northern Ontario	Ratio of Northern Ontario to Ontario
1991	$11,998,691	$882,864	7.4
1996	9,597,552	407,669	4.3
2001	19,069,311	559,218	2.9
2006	23,292,176	826,951	3.6

fared worse than the province as a whole from 1981 (or 1991) to 2006. Northern Ontario is more disadvantaged now than it was in the latter part of the twentieth century.

Even with respect to the one indicator of improvement in northern Ontario – dependency rate 1, the population of children and the elderly who are dependent on the adult population to meet their economic needs (Table 4.2) – the data are not as positive as they appear. In fact, the proportion of northern Ontario's population that is under age fifteen has been declining relative to that of the province, from 24.9 per cent in 1981 to 17.3 per cent in 2006 in the case of the north, and from 22.1 per cent to 18.4 per cent for the province as a whole, which explains the relative improvement in northern Ontario's total dependency rate over time.

This trend raises some concern about the population forecasts in the Ontario government's 2009 *Places to Grow*, which projects a northern Ontario population in excess of 808,000 by 2036. If the population of northern Ontario is getting older and the percentage of children in the region is declining – indeed, *Places to Grow*[21] acknowledges that the youth population of northern Ontario has declined at every interval from 1986 to 2008 – it is difficult to understand the projection of a population increase. Indeed, it is more likely that the region's population will continue to decline for the foreseeable future.[22]

Conclusion

The economy of northern Ontario has performed far less well than that of the province as a whole since the early 1980s, despite the creation of federal and provincial agencies intended to assist the region. Yet, results measures, as Hendricks has noted, do not allow for attribution.[23] They cannot tell us, for example, if the decline of the northern Ontario economy relative to that of the province is the result of government action. In the context of the research presented in other chapters of this book, however, the results measures might indicate that:

1. the federal and Ontario governments are pursuing the wrong policies;
2. the federal and Ontario governments are not committing sufficient resources to achieve the desired results;[24]
3. the policies of the two governments are being implemented poorly; or
4. some combination of these three possibilities.

Several years ago a senior official in the Management Board of the government of Ontario argued that performance measures should be seen as "red flags."[25] The argument was a simple one. If performance measures do not indicate the desired results, then more intensive evaluation of the relevant policies and programs should take place. Thus far, despite numerous studies in recent years,[26] there has been no adequate explanation of the deterioration of the northern Ontario economy compared with the provincial economy. For such a meaningful process to occur, some small initiatives would be most helpful.

Stiglitz, Sten, and Fatoussi note that "gross domestic product (GDP) is the most widely used measure of economic activity."[27] Some governments monitor the economic health of their regions closely – Western Australia, for example, provides gross regional product statistics for each of its nine economic regions, and compares their values with that of the chosen comparator, the urban centre of Perth. In Canada, unfortunately, despite the rhetoric about the value of the northern Ontario economy and the investments the federal and provincial governments have made in it,[28] GDP statistics are not produced for Ontario's economic regions. Yet, it is difficult to engage in intelligent dialogue about economic development in Ontario without such data.

Stiglitz, Sten, and Fatoussi also suggest that we need better measures of economic performance, that we look at income and consumption jointly with wealth, and that we provide more indicators of well-being. The Organisation for Economic Co-operation and Development notes that "indicator systems promote learning," and that "partnership between central and sub-central levels of government is crucial."[29] In Western Australia, the indicators cover economic, social, and environmental aspects of regional development. *Places to Grow*, too, includes a commitment to develop performance indicators "to measure implementation of this Plan."[30] Yet, two elements of this commitment are noteworthy: nine months after the commitment was made public, no publicly available set of performance indicators existed; and, perhaps of greater concern, the commitment goes only so far as to develop implementation indicators – there is no commitment to measure the outcomes or results of the implementation of the plan.

One element of *Places to Grow* is its vision that "[n]orthern Ontario has a skilled, educated and healthy population"[31] in the future. What indicators will be provided regularly to assess the extent to which that vision is being realized? The "Results-based Plan Briefing Book 2009–2010" issued by the Ministry of Northern Development and Mines states that the ministry "strives to make Northern Ontario and the provincial mineral sector strong, healthy and prosperous."[32] If the Northern Economic Development Activity performance measures the briefing book provides – the percentage of northern highways in good condition, percentage of northern bridges in good condition, investment dollars leveraged from other partners and number of full-time jobs created or sustained – are an example of current thinking in the ministry on the subject, then there is little reason to be optimistic. As Bill Jenkins and Andrew Gray expressed it so aptly in 1993, "the good delivery of bad policy is hardly the measure of a healthy state."[33]

There is an indication of some serious thought on this subject on the part of FedNor. Given its mandate as "a regional development organization in Northern Ontario that promotes economic development, diversification, and job creation and encourages sustainable, self-reliant communities in Northern Ontario,"[34] Industry Canada's 2008 finding that "there is a continuing debate about whether longer term measures should be included" is a positive sign. "At issue is the appropriate balance between immediate outcomes and later evidence related to intermediate or ultimate outcomes."[35]

If we are to measure the results of regional development policy in northern Ontario, we need better information. In the 1980s then-premier David Peterson promised the development of a northern Ontario database. Although discussions between Laurentian and Lakehead universities and the Ministry of Northern Development and Mines on the subject were quite extensive, the promise never was fulfilled. Researchers need access to such a database to be able to respond to recommendations about the information needed to measure development more appropriately. The failure to develop such information resources and to provide easy access to them tends to confirm the remarks of a colleague in the Economics Department at Laurentian University: "Either they do not want to know, or they know, but do not want us to know."[36] In either case the lack of a genuine commitment to transparency and accountability for results is obvious.

NOTES

The support and advice of Alyson Hazlett of Statistics Canada has been invaluable, and she deserves recognition for her superb service in the form of the efficiency with which she responded to my every request and question. The constructively critical comments of my colleague, Dr Mary Powell, and of Dr Charles Conteh provided a basis for reflection and significant improvements to the original version of the manuscript. I accept full responsibility for any errors in the chapter.

1 Ontario, Ministry of Energy and Infrastructure and Ministry of Northern Development, Mines and Forestry, *Places to Grow – Better Choices, Brighter Future: Proposed Growth Plan for Northern Ontario* ([Toronto]: Queen's Printer for Ontario, 2009), 58.
2 "Message from the Ministers: Building the Growth Plan for Northern Ontario," *Ontario Bulletin* 1 (4, 2010): 1; available online at http://www.placestogrow.ca/images/pdfs/North_bulletin_4_ENG.pdf.
3 C. Curristine, "Government Performance: Lessons and Challenges," *OECD Bulletin* 5 (1, 2005): 150.
4 See P. Aucoin, *The New Public Management: Canada in Comparative Perspective* (Montreal: Institute for Research on Public Policy, 1995); and B. Segsworth, "Accountability, Evaluation and Performance Monitoring: A Comparative Perspective," Research Report 15 (Toronto: Panel on the Role

of Government in Ontario, 2003); available online at http://www.law-lib.
utoronoto.ca/investing/reports/rp15.pdf.

5 J. Mayne, "Challenges and Lessons in Implementing Results-Based
Management," *Evaluation* 13 (1, 2007): 88.

6 Segsworth, "Accountability, Evaluation and Performance Monitoring," 50.

7 Canada, Treasury Board Secretariat, *Results for Canadians: A Management
Framework for the Government of Canada* (Ottawa: Treasury Board
Secretariat, 2000), 6–7.

8 Ontario Financial Review Commission, *Beyond the Numbers: A New
Financial Management and Accountability Framework for Ontario* (Toronto:
Ministry of Finance, 1995).

9 Ontario, Management Board Secretariat, Program Management and
Estimates Division, "Business Planning and Allocations Directive"
(Toronto: Management Board Secretariat, 2000), 6.

10 Canada, Treasury Board Secretariat, *Performance Reporting Good
Practices Handbook* (Ottawa: Treasury Board Secretariat, 2007). See
also idem, "The Government of Canada Planning and Performance
Gateway"; available online at http://www.tbs-sct.gc.ca/ppg-cpr/home-
accueil-eng.aspx.

11 Ontario, Ministry of Government Services, "Framework for Action 2007"
(Toronto: Queen's Printer for Ontario, 2007), 25.

12 Ontario, Ministry of Government Services, "2009 OPS Framework for
Action: Driving Changes, Delivering Results" (Toronto: Ministry of
Government Services, 2009), 10.

13 W. Muller-Clemm and M. Barnes, "A Historical Perspective on Federal
Program Evaluation," *Canadian Journal of Program Evaluation* 12 (1, 1997):
47–70.

14 Mayne, "Challenges and Lessons," 88.

15 Organisation for Economic Co-operation and Development (OECD),
Governing Regional Development Policy: The Use of Performance Indicators
(Paris: OECD, 2009), 190–1.

16 Ibid., 192–3.

17 See Western Australia, Department of Local Government and Regional
Development, "Indicators of Regional Development in Western Australia"
(East Perth, WA: URS Australia, 2003); and idem, "Indicators of Regional
Development in Western Australia: Supplementary Report 2007" (Perth:
Government of Western Australia, 2007).

18 Alberta, "Regional Economic Indicators" (Edmonton); available online at
http://www.alberta-canada.com/about-alberta/regional-economic-indicators.
html, accessed January 2009.

19 Interview with a senior official with the Alberta Ministry of Finance and Enterprise, 9 February 2010.

20 Specifically, Statistics Canada's "Basic Profile for Ontario and Northeast and Northwest Economic Regions" for 1981, 1986, 1991, 1996, and 2001; and "Semi-custom Profile for Ontario and Northeast and Northwest Economic Regions and Statistics Canada: Value of the Total Buildings, Residential, Non-residential 'ICI' Buildings for the Selected ERs in Ontario from 1989–2006."

21 Ontario, Ministry of Energy and Infrastructure and Ministry of Northern Development, Mines and Forestry, *Places to Grow*, 3.

22 As suggested in an interview with a senior official at Statistics Canada, 30 October 2009.

23 M. Hendricks, "Attribution: Can We Soothe the Achilles Heel of Performance Measurement," in *Using Evaluation to Support Performance Management: A Guide for Federal Executives*, ed. K. Newcomer and M. Scheirer (Arlington, VA: Pricewaterhousecooper Endowment for the Business of Government, 2001).

24 For a statement to this effect regarding FedNor funding, see Performance Management Network, Inc,. *Evaluation of FedNor Final Report* (Ottawa: Industry Canada, May 2002).

25 R. Segsworth, "Evaluation Policy and Practice in Ontario," *Canadian Journal of Program Evaluation*, Special Issue (2001).

26 See, for example, Urban Metrics, "Pan-Northern Ontario Investment Attraction Strategy: Final Report" (Toronto: Urban Metrics, 2006); R. Rosehart, *Northwestern Ontario: Preparing for Change*, Northwestern Ontario Economic Facilitator Report (n.p., 2008), available online at http://www.mndm.gov.on.ca/nordev/documents/noef/REPORT_FEB2008.; and H. Hall and B. Donald, *Innovation and Creativity on the Periphery: Challenges and Opportunities in Northern Ontario* (Toronto: Martin Prosperity Institute, 2009).

27 J. Stiglitz, A. Sen, and J.-P. Fitoussi, *Report by the Commission on the Measurement of Economic Performance and Social Progress* (n.p., 2010), available online at http://www.stiglitz-sen-fitoussi.fr.

28 See, for example, C. Peet, "Representing the Great White North: The Northern Ontario M.P.P. Experience" (paper presented to the annual meeting of the Canadian Political Science Association, Ottawa, 2009); and City of Greater Sudbury, Advisory Panel on Municipal Mining Revenues, *A Refined Argument* (Sudbury, ON, 27 February 2008), available online at http://www.greatersudbury.ca/content/div_councilagendas/documents/MMR%20_Report_final_Feb_27_2008.pdf, accessed 12 March 2008.

29 OECD, *Governing Regional Development Policy*, 12, 13.

30 Ontario, Ministry of Energy and Infrastructure and Ministry of Northern Development, Mines and Forestry, *Places to Grow*, 58.

31 Ibid., 6.

32 Ontario, Ministry of Northern Development and Mines, "Results-based Plan Briefing Book 2009–10" (Toronto), available online at http://www. mndm.gov.on.ca/en/about-ministry/results-based-planning/results-based-plan-2009-2010.

33 B. Jenkins and A. Gray, "Reshaping the Management of Government: The Next Steps Initiative in the UK," in *Rethinking Government: Reform or Reinvention*, ed. L. Seidle (Montreal: Institute for Research on Public Policy, 1993), 92.

34 Canada, Industry Canada, "Highlights of the 2009–2010 FedNor Business Plan, 1" (Ottawa, 2010).

35 Canada, Industry Canada, Audit and Evaluation Branch, "Mid-Term Evaluation of the Northern Ontario Development Program (NODP)" (Ottawa: Industry Canada, 2008), iii.

36 Interview, October 2009.

5 First Nations Inclusion: A Key Requirement to Building the Northern Ontario Economy

DAWN MADAHBEE

The Context

Society in general does not really understand the perspective of First Nations people. In fact, the First Nations are often referred to as the "Indian problem" and as a burden to society. There is a sense – a mistaken sense – that First Nations are completely satisfied to live in the vicious cycle of dependence and social handouts. Mainstream society does not realize that an innate pride and sense of honour beats in the hearts of this land's original people. And this comes from knowing that we have strong principles, values, and traditions. We also have legal contracts – treaties – in place. Moreover, we have a strong sense of survival, and tons of resolve.

The textbooks from which we learn the history of North America, Canada, and Ontario teach very little about the First Nations peoples' perspective. In this chapter, I attempt to shed some light on that perspective, with a particular focus on economic autonomy and sustainability for First Nations. We need to start with the treaties. Some might perceive treaties as agreements of an irrelevant past, or simply as broken promises; but treaties are being upheld as binding, lawful agreements in Canada's highest courts. I then provide some demographic statistics on First Nations in northern Ontario. In the rest of the discussion, I highlight and analyse the new economic factors influencing the climate for northern Ontario First Nations' economic success – namely, economic autonomy and sustainability.

For the purposes of this chapter, northern Ontario is defined by the major treaty areas of Robinson-Huron, the Robinson-Superior, Treaty

#9, Treaty #3, the Williams Treaty, and the Manitoulin Treaty – that is to say, the geographic area north of Barrie around the Georgian Bay, Parry Sound, and Muskoka to the shores of James Bay and Hudson Bay, from the Manitoba border in the west to the Quebec border in the east. In identifying the treaty areas, it is important to note that it is the treaties that specifically set out the relationship between First Nations people and the federal Crown (Canada). These treaties are generally interpreted as stating that the original peoples of these lands entered into agreements to share the lands with the newcomers – not to give up the lands to them – in exchange for certain concessions.[1] Careful review of these treaties by researchers and lawyers has upheld the sharing notion. And although it has been said over the years that these treaties are "of the past," it is fairly certain that no one whose family had owned land for several generations would be happy to be told the original land deeds were no longer valid simply because they were agreements of the past.

Canada has delegated some of its authority under the treaties in areas such as resource management to the provinces[2] – although it should be noted that this delegation of authority has not received the formal approval of First Nations people. Recent court decisions throughout Canada and in international forums have upheld the legally binding nature of treaty agreements, and have recognized the unique status, governance authority, and land ownership that First Nations legally hold as a result of them.[3] So, although successive non-Aboriginal governments in Canada have disregarded these trea-ties, recent legal decisions in favour of the First Nations require non-Aboriginal governments to work with them. It is thus increasingly urgent that Canadians learn the significance and the implications of these treaties with respect to the development of Canada and regions such as northern Ontario – in particular, the need to consult and accom-modate First Nations on all development on or near their traditional territories.

The First Nations population, the number of First Nations post-sec-ondary graduates, and recognition of Aboriginal rights and titles all continue to grow, as do First Nations land bases through the resolution of land claims. Conditions have improved tremendously, to the point where First Nations are full participants in the Canadian economy. The number of Aboriginal entrepreneurs is also growing at a rate faster than the Canadian average, producing significantly improved business success rates.[4] This positive economic climate is further enhanced by several recent factors,[5] such as:

- recent Supreme Court of Canada rulings that mandate the Crown (federal and provincial governments) with a "duty to consult and accommodate the interests of Aboriginal people" on resource development; by osmosis, industry is beginning to adopt and integrate the practice of consulting with Aboriginal people;
- the ideal situation of First Nations to take advantage of the growing global emphasis on alternative energy sources;
- the expanded resource bases of First Nations communities through the settlement of land claims and reclamation of traditional territories;
- the increase in the number of international travellers interested in indigenous culture and tourism;
- improved access to capital by First Nations people; and
- the growing sophistication of educated Aboriginal leadership.

In addition, many First Nations are building on the success of other First Nations who are actively focused on strategizing ways to eliminate poverty, create community wellness, generate revenues, and reduce their reliance on external governments whose key focus has been social, rather than economic, solutions. All of these factors are especially characteristic of a growing number of First Nations in northern Ontario.

The People

Ontario has the largest population of First Nations people in Canada (158,400, or 22.6 per cent of Canada's total First Nations population). Next to British Columbia, Ontario has the largest number of First Nations communities of all the provinces and territories: 130, of which 105 are located in northern Ontario, or the region north of Parry Sound/Muskoka. First Nations people represent a minority in the overall provincial population, at 1.4 per cent of the total,[6] but approximately two-thirds reside in northern Ontario, where they make up just over 13 per cent of the population – a significant force. In addition, the First Nations population is growing at four times the Canadian average even as population growth in northern Ontario as a whole is declining.[7] Projected growth suggests that Aboriginal people will make up 25 per cent of northern Ontario's population over the next generation.[8]

There are two distinct First Nations cultures in northern Ontario: the Northern Cree, who are primarily located in the far north, in the resource-rich regions of the province; and the Anishinabek, who reside in the near north around the Great Lakes, in northern Ontario's five main urban centres, and alongside main transportation corridors such as the Trans-Canada Highway.

Combining all of these factors, it stands to reason that any regional economic development in northern Ontario would benefit from the direct involvement of First Nations people. Not content with their status quo on the periphery of development or with the views of those who regard them as an impediment, many First Nations are prepared to be a valuable resource and interested partners in the well-planned development of the region.[9]

First Nations are strongly attached to the land and to the region overall. First Nations people are protective of the lands and of the legacy of generations of ancestors who have lived on them. That is why First Nations people regard this area as their ancestral homelands, and they believe they are entrusted with keeping these homelands in an honourable state for future generations. Reference to homelands is not limited to the boundaries of Indian reservations, but is tied to all those surrounding lands on which current community members and their ancestors have held ceremonies, hunted, picked berries, collected herbs and medicines, made trails, camped, and buried their dead. They consider all of that land their home and their traditional territories to which they have title. Therefore, in the view of First Nations people, any development has to be mindful of their ongoing traditional activities on these lands, as well as well-managed and controlled with a strong consideration of environmental concerns and regeneration.

The New Economic Factors Influencing the Climate for First Nations Economic Success

Natural Resource Development Opportunities

In Canada over $315 billion in major resource developments have been identified in or near Aboriginal communities.[10] During the past five years, one significant change to the rules of the game with respect to resource development has been rulings by the Supreme Court of Canada[11] requiring all levels of government to have meaningful consultations and discussions with First Nations communities present or nearby on all developments on lands in traditional territories, Crown lands, and areas on or near those communities. Therefore, no permits for developments can be issued by the federal or provincial governments without consulting and accommodating the interests of First Nations. These rulings, known as the "duty to consult and accommodate Aboriginal peoples," specify that "the Crown, acting honourably, cannot cavalierly run roughshod over Aboriginal interests where claims affecting these interests are being seriously pursued in the process of treaty negotiation and proof." The rulings go further to state that "[t]he government's duty to consult with Aboriginal peoples and accommodate their interests is grounded in the honour of the Crown."[12] There is also acknowledgment in these rulings of the "pre-existence of aboriginal societies," which basically acknowledges the right to a say on traditional territories and any agreed-upon resource revenue sharing. There is, in effect, no place in Canada where development can take place without the meaningful involvement of First Nations. With this legal requirement, the First Nations now have the opportunity to be full partners in all developments. This is particularly true of northern Ontario, where the economy relies primarily on the resource development sector.

Corporate interests are also recognizing the significance of this requirement to consult and accommodate as a smart business strategy. Industry is now avoiding confrontations and long project delays by taking the initiative to engage directly with First Nations during the project development stage, addressing their issues, and, in several cases, involving them as business partners in their projects or in revenue sharing.[13] The private sector sees the benefit of working cooperatively with the First Nations in these developments. Although, unlike government, the private sector does not have a formal duty to consult and accommodate Aboriginal peoples, it does owe Aboriginal peoples a duty of care, and may be held legally liable should they breach contracts with Aboriginal peoples or deal with them dishonestly. Accordingly, many resource development companies, such as De Beers, Weyerhaeuser, and Tembec, have taken the initiative to work in partnership with the First Nations in northern Ontario to develop the mineral and timber resources. They have in place corporate policies that create a positive working relationship with First Nations through Impact and Benefit Agreements, employment policies, and purchasing arrangements for the procurement of supplies and services. Across Canada, especially in resource-rich Alberta and British Columbia, corporations are recognizing and reaping the benefits of working cooperatively with First Nations.

Of course, to ensure this duty is discharged, First Nations need to have consultation protocols in place to communicate to government and industry how they wish to be consulted – one that clearly outlines a process that is acceptable to the community and that can be understood by both government and industry. Many of these protocols are now in place, but every First Nation needs to have such a document that is meaningful to its community.[14] It is thus important that First Nations receive support to develop these consultation protocols, and that any regional economic development policy for northern Ontario include a policy for consultation with First Nations that provides clear direction in terms of operational guidelines for government departments, ministries, and agencies. Such a policy, developed with the full cooperation, involvement, and agreement of First Nations, would guard against unstructured discretion and constitute a guide for all parties involved.

The Global Emphasis on Alternative Energy

First Nations in northern Ontario are ideally situated to be involved directly in the growing number of alternative energy projects. Because many First Nations are located on or near ideal water, solar, or wind resources, or some combination of these, and because they have lands isolated from large populations, they can partner with environmentally conscious companies to harness these resources for connection to the provincial electricity grid or to provide a local power source. According to the Ontario Power Authority, "Ontario's 250,000 lakes and countless rivers and streams hold nine per cent of the world's fresh water. This vital resource currently provides 25 per cent of the province's electricity via more than 200 generating stations."[15] Of course, northern Ontario, with its natural geography and large number of First Nations is a vital partner in the production of alternative energy. Ontario's 2009 Green Energy Act also recognizes, in section 1 (2), titled *Interpretation*, that "[t]his Act shall be interpreted in a manner that is consistent with section 35 of the *Constitution Act, 1982* and with the duty to consult aboriginal peoples," once again demonstrating that First Nations involvement in power site developments is crucial and a legal requirement.

The Ontario Water Association, for instance, which has mapped Ontario's potential water power sites in relation to First Nations lands, as well as parklands, finds that almost every potential site is on or near

First Nations land and traditional territories. Maps of potential power (water and wind) sites across Canada by Natural Resources Canada confirm this finding. Many First Nations in northern Ontario, such as Long Lac #58 First Nation and Dokis First Nation, are already involved in water power projects that are generating revenues for their communities. Several wind power companies are also working with First Nations, particularly those near the northern shores of Lake Superior, Lake Huron, and James Bay.

Two issues First Nations experience in the development of energy projects are the lack of technical expertise to develop such projects effectively, and the need for capital to assess, structure, and invest in them properly.[16] In short, First Nations need to build capacity in this sector, which appeals to Aboriginal peoples because green energy is consistent with their philosophy of protecting the land and the environment. Many First Nations people thus regard harnessing energy through well-planned and well-controlled green energy concepts as a more viable option than other current energy sources.

A Growing Land Base

The development of resources and energy presupposes the availability of an appropriate land base. In addition to the many lands they already possess in northern Ontario, First Nations have launched many land claims with respect to their traditional territories/homelands and requests for "Additions to Reserve" to add to their land base.[17] Through extensive land research, many First Nations have successfully proven that their lands were misappropriated, expropriated, or inappropriately surrendered for sale, or that their boundaries were incorrectly described. As a result, hundreds of land claims have been filed across the country.

In the land claims process, there are *specific claims* and *comprehensive claims*.[18] Specific claims generally relate to obligations under historic treaties or the way in which the Crown managed a First Nation's funds or assets. Comprehensive claims refer to those where Aboriginal rights and title have not been addressed through a treaty. In Ontario, there are 111 specific land claims in progress with the federal government and 60 land claims in progress with the provincial government – some claims are filed with both, others with only one, depending on the nature of the claim.[19] In addition, there are three comprehensive claims, two of which, the Algonquin and Anishinaabeg claims, include sections of land that might be considered on the fringe of northern Ontario. A number of First Nations have also filed for "Additions to Reserve Lands" to address the need for community growth or in finalization of legal claims. For example, the Manitoulin Land Claim of 1990 left a twenty-five-year window for First Nations to purchase lands to add to their reserve land base.

Through all of these processes, First Nations land and resource bases are growing, along with the economic opportunities.

Aboriginal Tourism

Another economic sector that has much potential and upon which First Nations people can build is tourism. Worldwide there is growing interest on the part of and in the number of international travellers who wish to learn about indigenous people. Cultural tourism generally refers interest in the lifestyle of the people in a particular country or region, and the Canadian Tourism Commission (CTC) has identified Aboriginal tourism as one of six strategic issues on which to focus. In a comprehensive study conducted in the United Kingdom, Germany, and France in 2007, just over 1,500 travellers were surveyed who had not yet visited Canada but had expressed an interest in doing so.[20] When asked about their ideal trip to Canada, the number interested in Aboriginals proved significant, as shown in Table 5.1.

The table also shows that a total of 136,257 visitors annually from three European countries alone were interested in Aboriginal tourism.

Table 5.1. Interest in Aboriginal Tourism, Selected European Countries

Country	% Interested in Aboriginal Tourism	Total Visitors to Canada, 2008	Total Visitors to Canada, 2009	Average Number of Visitors Interested in Aboriginal Tourism per Year
France	85	66,759	63,283	55,268
Germany	72	44,949	44,388	32,161
United Kingdom	46	117,745	94,549	48,828

Sources: Derived from Insignia Group, *Aboriginal Tourism Opportunities for Canada: U.K., Germany, France* (Ottawa: Canadian Tourism Commission, 2007), 5; and Canadian Tourism Commission, *Tourism Snapshot 2009 Year-in-Review* (Ottawa, 2010), 5.

Table 5.2. Four Northern Ontario Aboriginal Tourism Products

Company	Location	Product Offering
Great Spirit Circle Trail	Manitoulin Island	Small group tours involving a selection of daily cultural experiences; powwows; bus tours; Great Lakes cruise ship land excursions
Canadian Cultural Tours	Kenora	M.S. *Kenora* cruise ship tour; powwows; fishing packages
Temagami Anishnabai Tipi Camp	Temagami	Camping; storytelling; traditional foods
Cree Village Eco Lodge	Moose Factory	Fully serviced rooms in a modern ecologically designed hotel with a full-service restaurant on the shores of James Bay

If just half of those visitors came to Ontario and spent a thousand dollars each on food, lodging, and transportation, that would translate into more than $68 million. Diverting them for a time to enjoy their stated interest in Aboriginal tourism thus implies a significant potential infusion of tourist dollars into the region. Recognizing this potential, the CTC has established a list of "Significant 28 Aboriginal Tourism Products in Canada," which includes only those Aboriginal products regarded as ready to receive international markets. Of the twenty-eight, four are in Ontario, including the Great Spirit Circle Trail (GSCT), a company owned by seven First Nations communities in and around Manitoulin Island, Canadian Cultural Tours in Kenora, the Temagami Anishnabai Tipi Camp in Temagami, and Cree Village Eco Lodge in Moose Factory (see Table 5.2).

It is noteworthy that much of the global interest in Aboriginal tourism is based on the human need for self-discovery through holistic experiences offered by other cultures in tune with nature, such as natural remedies and their spiritual beliefs. These types of visitors seek unique, authentic, experiential products.[21] According to the CTC report on Aboriginal tourism, these visitors are looking for "the opportunity to feel something different and do something different in a unique environment through a unique culture." GSCT, in particular, has developed expertise and capacity in the industry, with contracts and partnerships with several European-based companies, and hosts several Great Lakes cruise ships that bring visitors to Manitoulin on day trips to enjoy Aboriginal culture. The company's success has spilled over to all mainstream tourism and service sector businesses in the region.

In the early 1990s a number of tourist-filled motor coaches regularly drove through the First Nations land on Manitoulin. They would not stop in the communities to purchase food or crafts, and their commentary-providing guides were non-Aboriginal. Even though the First Nations people regarded "tourism" as exploitive of their culture, they got together with Waubetek, an Aboriginal-owned and controlled organization that delivers business financing and economic development services to First Nations and Aboriginal entrepreneurs in northeastern Ontario, and resolved that: First Nations people needed to tell their own story; First Nations could no longer be on the outside of this industry; First Nations needed to have some control over this industry, otherwise it could adversely affect them; and, most important, First Nations needed to ensure their cultural integrity and the protection of the sacred aspects of their traditional practices. In 1997 they created the Great Spirit Circle Trail to coordinate and market Aboriginal tourism in the Manitoulin region. Their first step, in consultation with the Elders, was to develop cultural integrity guidelines. Since then, the Aboriginal tourism industry has enhanced and helped to grow tourism in the region in a controlled way. The Great Spirit Circle Trail is also recognized internationally as the partner of choice for several major global tourism companies that promote cultural and nature-based tourism in Ontario.

Even though Australia is generally perceived as the world leader in the provision of indigenous tourism products, in Canada much of the product is owned and operated by Aboriginal people themselves.[22] This ensures authenticity and allows Aboriginal people to share only those aspects of their culture that are endorsed by the community – for example, sweat lodge ceremonies are not allowed to be commercialized as part of any tourism package. It is also important to educate people about the many differences among the cultures and histories of the various Aboriginal groups in Canada – many have a stereotyped image of the prairie native riding horseback across the horizon. International visitors to northern Ontario might be surprised to find that our geography of lakes and woodlands differs from landscapes elsewhere in the country, and that the cultures of the Anishinabek and Cree – their styles of dress, languages, songs, and traditional practices – differ greatly from one other and from those of other Aboriginal groups. Overall, northern Ontario would benefit by investing in, and helping to grow, the Aboriginal tourism industry to continue to draw international visitors to the region. The industry in the region is in need of more resources generally, but it particularly needs a source of both product development funds to enhance or expand existing market-ready products and marketing dollars to produce quality promotional campaigns to reach these global markets.

Access to Capital

Economic and business development requires capital, access to which has been significantly limited for Aboriginal people. A 2009 study found a gap of more than $43.3 billion between the business capital that First Nations and Inuit people have access to and that available to mainstream Canadians. The authors of the study also point out that, of mainstream sources of market capital, 95 per cent is derived from financing instruments that operate *without* incentives from government to support the Canadian economy, but "First Nations/Inuit business financing access levels, trends and gaps all point to historical over-reliance on insufficient levels of government contribution capital and growth stalled at the early expansion phases for both the small and the mid-sized ventures for lack of an organic connection to market capital."[23]

In fact, up to 97 per cent of funds in First Nations budgets are provided through government transfer payments that are non-discretionary and specifically for social programming. Since that leaves as little as 3 per cent for economic development, it is not surprising that First Nations economies are only marginally developed. The cycle of dependence and social challenges naturally continues when there is no investment in the economy. To escape this cycle of dependence, many First Nations have taken steps to generate revenues for economic development through other means, such as community-owned businesses, equipment rentals, commercial land leases, taxation, and service charges.[24] A growing number, including, for instance, Membertou in Nova Scotia, are now generating revenues in excess of $30 million per year, mainly through strategic business partnerships and investments that are a result of concerted plans and efforts to rebuild First Nations economies.

Conventional lenders have also shied away from granting commercial loans to businesses on First Nation lands because the Indian Act prevents those lending in First Nation communities from accessing loan security or collateral,[25] since all fixed property located on First Nation property is communally owned, and cannot be pledged or seized as security.

The need for commercial financing is being partly met by a network of fifty-eight Aboriginal financial institutions (AFIs) across the country. The Waubetek Business Development Corporation in northeast Ontario is one such institution. These organizations are not-for-profit entities owned by Aboriginal people from the areas they serve. Established twenty years ago, they struggled greatly during their formative years, but their capacity has grown along with their capital base. The AFIs have had to be creative in growing their capital, and extremely careful with their investments, as the majority rely on their earnings from investments to cover operating costs. Some have established their own, creative, mutual fund share offerings, while others have partnered through loan pools with similar organizations or established businesses: one organization in Winnipeg, for example, established a call centre. Through this cross-country AFI network, more than $1.1 billion in loans has been granted to Aboriginal businesses in Canada for amounts as high as $250,000, although the average investment is around $20,000.

Six AFIs serve northern Ontario: the Nishnawbi-Aski Development Fund, based in Thunder Bay, serves the Cree communities in the far north; Wakenagun Development Corporation, based in Timmins, serves the Cree communities in the James Bay region; Waubetek Business Development Corporation, based near Manitoulin Island on the Whitefish River First Nation in Birch Island, serves the Anishinabek communities, the Wahta Mohawks in northeast Ontario, and Aboriginal people outside the First Nations communities throughout the region; Rainy Lake Tribal Area Business and Financial Services Corporation, based in Fort Frances, serves the Anishinabek communities in the Kenora and Fort Frances area of northwest Ontario; the Indian Agriculture Program of Ontario, based on Tyendinaga First Nation land in southern Ontario, provides commercial financing for agriculture businesses to First Nations people throughout the province; and the Métis Voyageur Development Fund, based in Ottawa, finances Métis businesses throughout Ontario.

These AFIs are able to help meet the demand for commercial financing that conventional lenders cannot. Known as "developmental lenders," AFIs work closely with their clientele from the concept phase to the actual start-up and, in some cases, through ongoing advisory support during the initial years of operation, thus contributing to better business success rates. With their knowledge of Aboriginal markets and of the business challenges First Nations people face, AFIs are in the best position to deliver financing to Aboriginal entrepreneurs. The main limitations of AFI financing, however, are the growing need for financing beyond their $250,000 cap and the lack of investment funds to service the larger projects. This is particularly true of the AFIs serving northern Ontario.

With the commercial capital available for small and medium-sized businesses, opportunities for the development of Aboriginal businesses have grown significantly. In fact, according to Statistics Canada's 2002 "Aboriginal Entrepreneurs Survey," the number of Aboriginal businesses was growing faster than the Canadian average at that time. The survey also notes that there are "over 250 Aboriginal start-ups/acquisitions annually, with 92.3 per cent of businesses surviving to the critical one-year mark," and that "between 1996 and 2001, the increase in Aboriginal self-employment (31 per cent) was nine times that of the overall Canadian population."[26] The continuing growth of small and medium-sized Aboriginal businesses is expected to meet the need for services in First Nations, and thus stem the economic leakage from First Nations communities and enhance regional opportunities for procurement as a supplier to resource development initiatives. .

To prepare for this growth, a source of infrastructure capital has been developed. Through an instrument known as the First Nations Finance Authority,[27] First Nations now have an opportunity to access affordable financing in the same way all other orders of governments in Canada do: directly from capital markets. In the past, First Nations had to go to conventional lenders who charged high interest rates for financing improvements to infrastructure, public works, and local services needed to build and maintain safe communities. To access funds under the First Nations Finance Authority, repayment risk is to be assessed independently in a review of the First Nation's sources of revenue, although the membership of the review board is still being finalized, so no First Nation in northern Ontario has yet availed itself of this new tool. In the meantime, First Nations need to seek ways to increase their own sources of revenue to repay infrastructure debt and to determine whether future government transfers for infrastructure capital can be used to leverage this financing.

Building Capacity

Today's First Nations leadership is poised to take advantage of this new economic climate and seize the opportunities it offers. A growing number of leaders have university degrees, particularly in the legal field. Large gaps still exist, however, between Aboriginal and non-Aboriginal high school and post-secondary graduation rates. As a report by the C.D. Howe Institute says, "[w]hile younger Aboriginals are indeed seeking more education than previous generations, they have not kept pace with the increase in education among other Canadians."[28] According to Statistics Canada's 2006 *Aboriginal Peoples Survey*,[29] 42 per cent of First Nations adults ages twenty-five to sixty-four had post-secondary education, compared with 61 per cent of non-Aboriginals in that age group. One area where education levels are comparable is trades training. In 2006, 12 per cent of First Nations and 13 per cent of non-Aboriginal people had a trades certificate, which might indicate the success of government training programs (primary First Nation certification is in carpentry). With a focus on trades training and boosting education levels, First Nations could address the labour force issues of an aging workforce and industry's ability to compete in global markets. In northern Ontario, it might be best to focus on targeted trades training in the resource development fields to help fill the need for qualified technical expertise.

The Road Ahead

Many First Nations recognize that the only way to address the wide range of social issues they face is to focus on economic development and to take the reins of control from external governments. This is not to say that external governments do not have a role to play: they have both a fiduciary obligation and a responsibility to provide the economic tools that will allow First Nations to harness their resources to be full participants in the Canadian economy. In 2008, the Anishinabek Nation in Ontario released its Economic Blueprint,[30] intended to function as a step-by-step practical guide for First Nations to use in rebuilding and strengthening their local economies. Many of its recommendations are actions that First Nations themselves can take to make changes in their communities and to begin to change the mindset of reliance. Collectively, as First Nations people, we owe it to future generations to remove the shackles of dependence and to raise our own standards. First Nations such as Membertou in Atlantic Canada, the Osoyoos Indian Band in British Columbia, Fort McKay in Alberta, the Meadowlake Tribal Council area in Saskatchewan, and the Tribal Council Investment Group of Manitoba have advanced economically through implementing long-term strategies. Many of these efforts grew out of desperation to address the needs of their communities, as other, externally originating efforts were not succeeding.

Rather than reinventing the wheel, First Nations in Ontario are taking advantage of the lessons learned. Whether it be the Sagamok Anishinabek in the Lake Huron North Shore region, who have achieved ISO certification to work in partnership with corporate Ontario, or Attawapiskat First Nation in the James Bay region, who have developed a partnership with De Beers in the mining industry, or the Rainy Lake First Nation near Fort Frances, who export timber to US markets, First Nations in northern Ontario are beginning to take their rightful place as partners in the development of the region. First Nations want to play a role in the future development of the Canadian economy and society.

Ottawa's "Federal Framework for Aboriginal Economic Development"[31] is intended to help provide some of the legislative and financial support First Nations need to achieve a level of economic well-being that equals that of other Canadians. The Ontario government is also looking at recommendations put forward in the Anishinabek Nation Economic Blueprint[32] and in roundtable discussions on First Nations economic development to support the province's *Proposed Growth Plan for Northern Ontario.*[33]

Now is the time to change the thinking that has been an obstacle to understanding the needs and perspective of First Nations and Aboriginal people. Is there a meaningful role Aboriginal people can play in the development of the northern Ontario economy? I say a resounding "Yes!" Aboriginal people have a role in ensuring development of lands and resources takes place responsibly and that specific areas stay untouched as a legacy for our future. I believe Aboriginal people have a responsibility to share their traditional values and principles with respect to the lands and the wildlife on those lands. I believe Aboriginals must be key partners in all aspects of planning for the region. I believe that Aboriginal people have, and want, an integral role as contributors to society, in creating wellness and getting rid of poverty. There is a new economic climate, and Aboriginal people are poised to be part of it.

NOTES

1 K.L. Ladner, "Indigenous Governance Questioning the Status and the Possibilities for Reconciliation with Canada's Commitment to Aboriginal and Treaty Rights" (West Vancouver, BC: National Centre for First Nations Governance, 2006). See also F. Abele, "Policy Research in the North: A Discussion Paper" (Toronto: Walter and Duncan Gordon Foundation, 2006).

2 R. Rosehart, *Northwestern Ontario: Preparing for Change*, Northwestern Ontario Economic Facilitator Report (n.p., 2008), available online at http://www.mndm.gov.on.ca/nordev/documents/noef/REPORT_FEB2008.

3 Ladner, "Indigenous Governance."

4 Many Aboriginal financial institutions are experiencing business success: between 72 per cent and 94 per cent are still operating after five years, as tracked by the National Aboriginal Capital Corporation Association.

5 Rosehart, *Northwestern Ontario*.

6 Statistics Canada, *2006 Aboriginal Population Profile*, Cat. no. 92-594-XWE (Ottawa, 2010). The population statistics in this chapter refer only to the First Nations population and do not include the Métis population.

7 Canada, Minister of Indian Affairs and Federal Interlocutor for Métis and Non-Status Indians, "Federal Framework for Aboriginal Economic Development" (Ottawa: Public Works and Government Services Canada, 2009), confirmed by Statistics Canada, *2006 Aboriginal Population Profile*.

8 Ontario, Ministry of Energy and Infrastructure and Ministry of Northern Development, Mines and Forestry, *Places to Grow – Better Choices, Brighter Future: Proposed Growth Plan for Northern Ontario* ([Toronto]: Queen's Printer for Ontario, 2009).

9 See, for example, the Web site of the Nishnawbe Aski Nation, http://www.nan.on.ca/.

10 Canada, Minister of Indian Affairs and Federal Interlocutor for Métis and Non-Status Indians, "Federal Framework."

11 Specifically, the cases of *Haida Nation v British Columbia*, 2004; *Taku River Tlingit First Nation v British Columbia*, 2004; and *Mikisew Cree v Canada*, 2005.

12 See, for example, Canada, Transport Canada, "Aboriginal Consultation: A Review of the Taku, Haida and Mikisew Cree Decisions" (presentation to

the National Executive Forum on Public Property, Victoria, BC, 11–12 May 2006), 2–9.

13 Rosehart, *Northwestern Ontario*.

14 L.A. Knafla and H.J. Westra, *Aboriginal Title and Indigenous Peoples: Canada, Australia, and New Zealand* (Vancouver: UBC Press, 2010).

15 See the Ontario Power Authority Web site at http://www.powerauthority. on.ca.

16 Rosehart, *Northwestern Ontario*.

17 Ladner, "Indigenous Governance."

18 L. Miljan, *Public Policy in Canada: An Introduction*, 5th ed. (Don Mills, ON: Oxford University Press, 2008).

19 See the land claims sections of the Web sites of the federal Department of Indian and Northern Affairs at http://www.ainc-inac.gc.ca and the Ontario Ministry of Aboriginal Affairs http://www.aboriginalaffairs.gov.on.ca.

20 Insignia Group, *Aboriginal Tourism Opportunities for Canada: U.K., Germany, France* (Ottawa: Canadian Tourism Commission, 2007).

21 Canada, Minister of Indian Affairs and Federal Interlocutor for Métis and Non-Status Indians, "Gathering Strength: Canada's Aboriginal Action Plan" (Ottawa: Minister of Indian Affairs and Northern Development, 1997).

22 Knafla and Westra, *Aboriginal Title and Indigenous Peoples*.

23 D. Collin and M.L. Rice, "Access to Capital for Business: Scoping Out the First Nation and Inuit Challenge" (presentation to the Statistics Canada Socio-Economic Conference, Gatineau, QC, 4 May, 2009).

24 See the Web site of the Nishnawbe Aski Nation, http://www.nan.on.ca/.

25 Canada, Royal Commission on Aboriginal Peoples, *Report*, vol. 5, *Renewal: A Twenty-Year Commitment* (Ottawa: Parliamentary Research Branch, 1996).

26 Statistics Canada, "Aboriginal Entrepreneurs Survey, 2002," *Daily*, 27 September 2004, 1.

27 See the Web site of the First Nations Finance Authority at http://www. fnfa.ca/.

28 J. Richards, "Closing the Aboriginal/non-Aboriginal Education Gaps," *Backgrounder* 116 (Toronto: C.D. Howe Institute, October 2008), i.

29 Statistics Canada, *Aboriginal Peoples Survey* (Ottawa, 2006), available online at http://www.statcan.gc.ca/cgi-bin/imdb/p2SV.pl?Function=getSurvey&SD DS=3250&lang=en&db=imdb&adm=8&dis=2.

30 H. Tarbell, C. Manual, R. Martin, and D. Madahbee, *The Anishinabek Nation Economy: Our Economic Blueprint* (Nipissing First Nation, ON: Union of Ontario Indians, 2008), available online at http://www.anishinabek.ca/ download/FINALpercent20Consolidatedpercent20ANEB_PDF-sm.pdf.

31 Canada, Minister of Indian Affairs and Federal Interlocutor for Métis and Non-Status Indians, "Federal Framework."

32 Tarbell et al., *Anishinabek Nation Economy.*

33 Ontario, Ministry of Energy and Infrastructure and Ministry of Northern Development, Mines and Forestry, *Places to Grow.*

6 A Historic Overview of Policies Affecting Non-Aboriginal Development in Northwestern Ontario, 1900–1990

MICHEL S. BEAULIEU

In the mid-1970s, in one of the foundation works exploring the history of political economy in Ontario, H.V. Nelles provided the first in-depth examination of the impact that resource development played in shaping the politics in Ontario.[1] Building upon the work of Harold Innis and Donald Creighton, Nelles turned his attention to the "new" staple economy of the twentieth century – mines and forests.[2] And yet while Nelles's work remains the most detailed examination of the government of Ontario's role in the exploitation of natural resources and the resource politics at the heart of central Canadian economic development, the adversarial nature and sense of alienation by northerners due to government actions and decisions, while touched upon in places, remained largely ignored.[3]

Building upon the work of Geoffrey Weller and Chris Southcott, this chapter provides a historical overview of development policies in northwestern Ontario.[4] Central to the argument I lay out is that the development of "policy" in the post-Second World War era cannot be understood without a grasp of historical antecedents. In fact, it is often the case that, on those rare occasions when politicians and economic planners do look to the past to learn lessons for current policy development, they focus on the early twentieth century and the literature on the development of "New Ontario," or works that frame the discussion in terms of the Ontario government's exercising what it perceived was in the "public's interest."[5] State policies towards the northwest have not only reinforced a hinterland-metropolis relationship (as Weller argues) and a sense of alienation (as Southcott establishes); they have also been adversarial, and steeped in attitudes of colonialism that regional concerns are secondary.[6]

Defining the Northwest

The relationship between the various "norths" of Ontario and the provincial government seated in Toronto has been defined in numerous ways by those living in the "north" and the south.[7] The definition of what constitutes northern Ontario has changed a number of times in the past one hundred years, often for political reasons having little to do with the north itself. For much of its history, however, northern Ontario has consisted of five distinct regions: the northwest, the northeast, "north of the larger towns," "smaller communities," and "north of the fiftieth parallel."[8]

The northwest, the largest and most sparsely populated region of the province, is geographically defined as lying north and west of Lake Superior, and west of Hudson Bay and James Bay. It includes most of subarctic Ontario. Its western boundary is the province of Manitoba, which once disputed Ontario's claim to the western part of the region. The area consists largely of rural municipalities and Aboriginal communities. Aside from the city of Thunder Bay, Kenora is the only municipality in the entire region with a population of greater than ten thousand.

The political, economic, and, some could argue, cultural epicentre of the region for the past four hundred years has been the head of Lake Superior, where present-day Thunder Bay now sits. To create Thunder Bay, the province forced the amalgamation of Port Arthur and Fort William, two communities that had long been rivals for regional dominance.[9] In fact, much of the existing literature on northwestern Ontario and its two primary cities attempts to highlight the similarities, differences, and tensions that have existed between them since the late nineteenth century. In particular, recent work has highlighted municipal political culture during the first term of the city council of Thunder Bay between 1969 and 1972. Anecdotally, many in the region have a pessimistic view of local politics. A real belief exists that successive city councils are unaware of the larger issues, ill equipped individually and as a group to deal with the region's ongoing problems, or simply corrupt. No doubt, as Peter Raffo establishes, some of these beliefs are resonant of the problems and issues, both real and imaginary, that dominated the first city council.[10]

Non-Aboriginal Development Policy to 1939

There can be no denying that the early development of northwestern Ontario was determined largely by outside forces. The decision to locate and build Fort William, the first permanent non-Aboriginal centre, was reached in response to Jay's Treaty between the United States and Britain. Its policies, procedures, and governance, however, were determined not in consultation with the local population but by the North West Company and those in Montreal who controlled it and acted as a kind of government in the interior.[11] Fort William became the inland headquarters of an economic empire, but the merger in 1822 of the North West Company with its chief rival, the Hudson's Bay Company, relegated Fort William to a small supply post. The community's importance continued to wane for nearly thirty years, until exploratory expeditions began to discover minerals throughout the region. Treaty negotiators were dispatched, and the region was carved up largely without input from or care for those who inhabited it. The earliest infrastructure, in the form of roads and later railways, came from the desire of the newly formed Dominion of Canada to assert its control of the Red River colony and the rest of the region.[12]

The establishment of Fort William and Port Arthur as competing communities came about as a result of government railway policies concerning the establishment of the Canadian Pacific and Canadian Northern railways.[13] By 1890 railways connected both towns to the populous eastern part of the country and to the vast western expanse, and they had become, both figuratively and literally, the "gateway to the west." Sir Oliver Mowat, the premier of Ontario, who visited the northwest in 1893, was one of a number of politicians who shared a belief in the importance of the region; he claimed he would not rest "until this part of the province was equal in point of development to any other portion."

As the twentieth century unfolded, the southern part of Ontario increasingly began to see itself as "Empire Ontario," as evidenced by the branding of its northern reaches as "New Ontario."[14] Provincial policy for "New Ontario" was colonial in nature, concerned only with the exploitation of the region's natural resources to ensure the continued expansion of southern industrial manufacturing.[15] When policy did move beyond resource extraction, as advocated by John Dryden, agriculture minister in the Mowat government, systems were imposed and agricultural communities laid out in a fashion that might have worked for southern Ontario but was wholly unsuited for the north.

Considering such colonial treatment, it is not surprising that Ontario owed much of its success in the late nineteenth and early twentieth centuries to revenues derived from northern resources. As the work of Livio Di Matteo reveals, between 1871 and 1911, "Northern Ontario contributed disproportionately to Ontario government revenues" as profits procured from natural resources from the north were used to subsidize Ontario government expenditures in the south. Once the population of northern Ontario increased, however, the provincial government did direct more revenues to the region, but these were used primarily to build and improve transportation routes, which only bound the north more closely to the south.[16]

By the end of the nineteenth century, Toronto had established itself as the metropolis of prosperous agricultural and industrial southern Ontario, and was eyeing control of the immense mineral deposits of the north.[17] The transportation network needed to exploit these resources determined the development of many northern Ontario communities. The construction of the Canadian Pacific Railway and Canadian Northern Railway led to the establishment of depots to provide supplies for trains moving east and west. Many of these depots became villages and then towns in those areas where mining and logging took hold. The major employers in the immediate area, with the blessing of the province, dictated the development of villages and towns such as Red Lake, Nipigon, and Fort Frances.[18] Such a reality, in turn, dictated provincial development policy and often placed attempts by residents of these communities to shape their municipal development through local action and lobbying at odds with provincial desires.

The First World War and the resources needed for the war effort led to a period of unprecedented growth in northern communities that provided labour and services for resource-extraction industries. Growth continued during the 1920s, and northwestern Ontario's population experienced its largest percentage increase in the modern era.[19] By this time, there was some hope of improvement in provincial policy towards northern communities. The death of Premier James Pliny Whitney shortly after being elected in 1914 had led to the appointment of William Hearst of Sault Ste Marie as premier. The former minister of lands, forests and mines, it was felt, would not treat the north as his predecessors had. However, although he attempted to reduce the amount of US ownership of industry in the north, he also favoured southern investors and the use of the north to continue building the industrial south.[20]

During the 1920s successive provincial governments actively promoted northern Ontario, while also favouring a form of imperialism that believed in the prominence of British culture and ideals.[21] Appointing the province's first legislative secretary for northern Ontario, Premier Howard Ferguson also created a new agency to promote settlement in the north by immigrant farmers. Northwestern Ontario's lack of arable land made this a pointless endeavour except in isolated areas such as the Slate River Valley south of Fort William and the region surrounding Fort Frances, but it did result in some much needed infrastructure development and the opening up of remote regions through the construction of colonization roads and airstrips.

It was also during this period that a policy of limited government involvement in resource industries was instituted. Throughout the 1920s governments encouraged investors from Canada and the United States to treat northwestern Ontario's entire wilderness and towns in terms of its productive capacity and revenue potential, and how it could be maximized to assist in further southern growth. The provincial government of William Henry further reduced restrictions on mining and forestry development and cut much of the funds for conservation programs and infrastructure development in northwestern Ontario – in many respects handcuffing regional municipal development goals to create an industrial base. Although the Henry government is notable as having established the province's first Ministry of Northern Development, its goal was to promote northern Ontario to potential settlers for colonization, not industrial development.[22] Political awareness of the north ended dramatically with the election of Mitch Hepburn's Liberals in 1934. Hepburn abolished the Ministry of Northern Development and ended all economic and colonization assistance.

The 1940s and 1950s

The Second World War had a profound influence on the development of northwestern Ontario. The role of Port Arthur Member of Parliament Clarence Decatur Howe in Prime Minister William Lyon Mackenzie King's cabinet ensured that the region's wartime development would be considered. Nicknamed the "Minister of Everything," C.D. Howe and his Department of Munitions and Supply essentially controlled every aspect of the country's home war effort.[23] Howe looked to the northwest and its vast natural resources communities to provide the materials needed for that effort. One result was the expansion of industrial manufacturing in in the twin cities of Fort William and Port Arthur, but this came at the expense of many rural communities in the region, depopulated by the demand for labour in the twin cities.

Following the war, northwestern Ontario entered what historians have described as the third phase of the forest industry in the region, one that continues to this day, in which mechanization has dramatically altered the nature and characteristics of the industry.[24] Small changes such as the introduction of gasoline-powered chainsaws and larger ones such as snowmobiles and wheeled skidders have combined to alter the nature of the workforce and skills required. The spread of all-weather roads, seen as a boon for economic activity for communities throughout the region, has opened up new areas and allowed the industry to harvest year-round.[25]

During the late 1940s and the early 1950s, the provincial government under Leslie frost focused on three main priorities: expansion, development, and finance. These priorities were shared by the federal Liberal government of Louis St Laurent, who became prime minister following the retirement of Mackenzie King in 1948. St Laurent used C.D. Howe as much as his predecessor had. The resource industries boomed, so few were concerned about the relative lack of industrial and municipal growth outside the Lakehead. Year-round operations combined with the construction of pulp and paper mills throughout the region led to the development of larger communities, and in the 1950s and early 1960s northwestern Ontario experienced its single largest population increase, much of it in communities designed and laid out by professional planners to meet the needs of the resource industry before settlement began.

Using the federal government's Trans-Canada Highway program, the Drew and Frost governments undertook a massive expansion of highways and roads in Ontario. As Peter Baskerville writes, however, the province continued a tradition whereby "the north received less attention than the south ... [and] interminable discussion of cost-sharing with the federal government delayed significant highway construction until the mid-1950s."[26] Some communities were not linked by a reliable all-weather road until the 1980s, thus stunting new areas of growth such as tourism. Successive provincial and federal government concerned themselves only with ensuring that the arteries that facilitated and promoted natural resource movement to the south remained open. Lumber and mining communities were at the whim of companies as technological changes. And although the construction of thousands of miles of roads led to increased tourism and some economic diversification, it also ensured that communities remained at the mercy of private interests.[27]

The opening of the St Lawrence Seaway in 1959 was seen as the solution to many of the region's economic problems. It was a belief supported by the construction of the giant Keefer Terminal in Port Arthur in 1962 and it was accompanied by hopes of regional diversification. Between 1958 and 1965 northwestern Ontario experienced an economic, social, and cultural boom as the twin cities established themselves once again as major transshipment points. The Seaway provided the means for manufactured goods to move west and grain to flow east at levels unseen since the gold age of shipping in the early twentieth century. The Seaway also allowed, for the first time in over a century, ocean-going vessels – previously unable to navigate the St Lawrence due to their size – to pick up cargo at the Lakehead and ship it directly to any port of call in the world. With the development of the oil fields of Alberta, the port of Thunder Bay was seen as vital to the continued success of industrial Canada.[28]

Fort William and Port Arthur continued in the post-war period to be the largest urban centre in the northwest, benefiting from the demand for resources and acting as a transportation hub for exporting resources and importing commercial goods and supplies for regional communities. The combined population of the twin cities climbed dramatically from 65,000 in 1951 to 90,000 in 1961 to 121,000 by 1981.[29] Both communities increasingly worked together and often were treated by the provincial and federal governments as single entities. However, the development associated with the Seaway and Keefer Terminal was never truly fulfilled. While the twin cities flourished, other towns did not: the goods flowing west flowed right past them.

Regional Development Plans of the 1960s and 1970s

In 1965 representatives from towns and cities across northwestern Ontario attended a conference on "Regional Development and Economic Change" in Toronto. Organized by the Ministry of Economic Development and chaired by its minister, Stanley J. Randall, the keynote speaker was Paul G. Hoffman, director of the United Nations Special Fund. Hoffman spoke on how advances in science and technology had "made the world a single neighbourhood." He went on to state that "Canada's problem is somewhat similar to that which exists in underdeveloped countries – slow diversification of industry and slow integration of agriculture ... Also, where exploitation of natural resources and water has taken place, this should be now directed [towards] logical development."[30]

For many, one of the legacies of the John Robarts government of the 1960s was its dedication to "make local government strong and meaningful as possible."[31] Dedicated, like premiers Drew and Frost before him, to making Ontario appealing to private investors, Robarts used the conference and its subsequent "Design for Development" document to "forecast regional plans, the selection and stimulation of growth centres, and particular regional economic specializations, using the program as an 'umbrella' for guiding the 'smoothing-out' of conspicuous regional differences."[32] A cabinet committee was established to examine and submit regional development plans and to have the Regional Development Branch of the Ministry of Treasury and Economics liaise with federal programs. An intensive process of research and coordination led by Richard S. Thoman, Director of Regional Development, began in 1967. A series of "independent" local government reviews was undertaken, including the Lakehead Government Review that led to the amalgamation of Fort William and Port Arthur as Thunder Bay. Although new grant structures were initiated and existing ones modified to assist the new municipalities that emerged, the policy of provincial development under the Robarts government was not beneficial to the region.

The political reorganization that occurred during this time on a massive scale at the Lakehead and the smaller but pronounced changes at the district level across northwestern Ontario profoundly influenced the shape and form of regional government, but it did little to solve the systemic economic and development issues facing the region. In part, this was due to contradictory views of municipal development. Although the Robarts government sought more efficient and "meaningful government," its economic policies, as instituted by Stanley Randall, ensured communities would benefit from infrastructure improvements designed to assist only traditional economic activities.[33] Randall is perhaps best known for his infamous 1963 statement, "show me a resource, and I'll sell it,"[34] words that encapsulate the provincial government's movement back to an early twentieth century view of the northwest's role in the province.

Meanwhile, the federal government introduced such initiatives such as the Agriculture Rehabilitation and Development Act (1961) and the Fund for Rural Economic Development (1966), which were intended to promote non-agricultural development in rural areas to deal with issues such as high unemployment, out-migration of labour, and declining populations. The northern hinterlands of the wealthiest province in the federation, however, were largely excluded from such assistance.

As Chris Southcott has demonstrated, during this period, of the "types of strategies issue[d] from the metropolis,"[35] one kind merely supported the existing type of development that had occurred in the region since the end of the Second World War, and was characterized by seeing no "need to change the hinterland status of the region." It fostered policies centred on forestry, mining, and a desire for smaller municipalities, implemented through existing mechanisms such as the Ministry of Northern Affairs, Ontario Hydro, and agencies of the Ontario government.

These strategies also worked through new federal agencies established under the government of Pierre Elliott Trudeau in the late 1960s. In 1969, Trudeau charged Jean Marchand with the regional development portfolio, and the result was the Department of Regional Economic Expansion (DREE). Two programs were established within DREE: one intended to fund the construction of highways, water systems, industrial parks, and schools; the other to provide incentives, through loan guarantees and grants, to companies in designated regions for job creation.[36] Both programs were roundly criticized, however, for Marchand's focus on eastern Canada (the Maritimes and Quebec), and the department itself was reorganized following the Trudeau government's electoral losses in western Canada in 1972.

To the extent that Thunder Bay benefited from the programs, it was in the area of infrastructure to accommodate the growth taking place there due to the in-migration of people from smaller communities in the northwest due to the lack of jobs and provincial and federal development assistance that addressed the unique circumstances of the region.[37] At the same time, the need for municipal government to keep taxes low to encourage development led to lack of money for industrial development, which in turn led to the need for provincial and federal programs such as DREE. Such funding was also outcome based, requiring a demonstration of the immediate benefits, and, as a result, money tended to flow into established industries such as forestry and mining, rather than diversifying the economy.

The circumstances of the 1950s through to the 1970s thus led to Thunder Bay's future being tied to the health of the forest industry.[38] As a "Design for Development Study" commissioned by the Ontario government in 1971 concluded, for example, northern Ontario "has a narrow and relatively slow growing economic base ... If ... the dominant industry declines substantial hardships follow because few, if any, alternative forms of employment are available."[39] Southcott writes that, "[i]n response to this lack of direction from the provincial and federal governments," many town and cities in the region took upon themselves to their "own strategy of development based on the diversification of local economy through the creation of secondary industry."[40] To address these concerns, Thunder Bay and many other towns created "development bureaus" – predecessors of such present-day entities as Development Thunder Bay – to bring business to the region and, in particular, to increase the region's manufacturing base.

Thunder Bay initially attempted to implement such a strategy by returning to policies that had already been detrimental to the former Port Arthur and Fort William: tax breaks and cash bonuses. Thunder Bay badly needed such a strategy as the region was being affected by the profound restructuring of the Canadian forestry industry in the face of its need to become more efficient, get out from under its debt load, and rid itself of excess capacity. By the mid-1970s restructuring and recession caused unemployment in the region to skyrocket as mills and mines closed and populations declined – many people headed for the oil fields of Alberta and the factories of southern Ontario. Youth out-migration, in particular, became a serious problem, with many leaving for post-secondary educational opportunities elsewhere and not returning.

Thunder Bay: A Case Examination

Thunder Bay's Development Bureau was largely unsuccessful in bringing new industry to the city, given the economic realities of the day. It noted, however, that, although the city's dependency on natural resource exports meant that its economy could by affected by foreign situations beyond its control, the bureau's director reported that the city and area had "an excellent buffer against these potential conditions. History indicated resource areas are, in many cases, the last to feel the pinch of a recession. This area could continue momentum of activity, by contracts long after areas such as Toronto, were into a hard recession – then we could be affected while they recover their momentum, building up their activities." The director argued, in fact, that Thunder Bay needed to prepare for a predicted "surge" in the primary industries by planning for support or services industries. For example, the need for chemicals by the region's small and medium pulp and paper mills warranted the construction of a production facility in northwestern Ontario, rather than having chemicals transported from southern sources.[41]

Thunder Bay was unable to capitalize on such suggestions, however, due to a perceived shortage of land zoned for industrial use. Development officers and city officials disagreed about the supply, but much of it was in the hands of the railway companies, which wanted to hold on to their land for future needs in relation to the port. In fact, the city had erred in October 1973 when it determined the supply of industrial land that would be required to meet immediate and foreseeable needs.[42]

The Development Bureau, in part, was merely responding to the funds that were being made available through the Ontario Land Corporation (OLC), one of whose goals was to "steer new development away from the fertile fields of southwestern Ontario into growth-starved eastern and northern regions." The question for the Treasurer of Ontario was not whether the OLC would be in competition with the private sector, but what the government had "to do to get you to build your next plant on the rock in Eastern Ontario." Key among the ideas floating around were freeing up funds to develop serviced industrial parks in the north and "filling them with plant attracted by serviced land sold below cost."[43]

The Thunder Bay City Council, however, expressed some concerns. For example, the ability to assemble land for housing purposes would be restricted to regional municipalities, which excluded the city. The council was also concerned about committing to a large capital debt only to "find that serviced land was no longer needed" – although it admitted that, "under today's conditions it would appear that this is unlikely." City officials argued that Thunder Bay needed to be dealt with in a unique way. The provincial treasurer had informed the mayor that OLC planning would be restricted to delegations from the "upper tier of regional government systems," which again excluded Thunder Bay. In response the city council called for "regional" legislation for Thunder Bay, and said that the Ontario government knew well the argument that the city was a regional municipality and that such an "experimental" program should also be tried there.[44] It even suggested that limitations on spending and other criteria could be imposed in greater degree. These calls also came with the city's initial exclusion from the DREE program.

Regional Examples

With provincial infrastructure programs tending to favour the south,[45] municipalities in the northwest attempted to address the issue from a regional perspective. For example, a 1977 presentation by the Municipal Advisory Committee on Provincial Planning for Northwestern Ontario focused on four "Priorities for Action": a more effective management of forest resources; an improved transportation policy; greater support for local initiatives; and life in small communities.[46] Indeed, by 1979, many of the recommendations had been acted upon, including a more sustainable management policy.[47]

Protests from municipal governments in northwestern Ontario, however, were usually dismissed rather than being taken seriously. At a 1977 conference, for example, in a panel discussion of "A View of Northwestern Ontario as Others See It," Jim Carnegie, General Manager of the Ontario Chamber of Commerce, contended that residents of northwestern Ontario have a reputation of complaining, although that was now diminishing. Tom Campbell, Deputy Minister of Northern Affairs, presented the politicians' perspective, focusing on the government's view that the region was "a major asset to the Province and that it should be assisted to exploit natural resources." Doug Fisher, former MP for Port Arthur-Rainy River, suggested there was as much "brain-power in northwestern Ontario as in Toronto or Ottawa," and that the thick levels of bureaucracy could be handled if residents didn't go hat in hand to them when requesting change to improve life in the north. He further suggested the government experts making decisions affecting the north should be brought into the area for discussions, rather than residents going to Ottawa or Toronto seeking improvements to progress.[48]

In an attempt to address these types of concerns, during the summer of 1978 Thunder Bay, with support from other municipalities in the northwest, explored the establishment of a Research Development Centre in an attempt to access a federal grant designed to increase support for centres of research innovation and technology transfer to improve the competiveness of Canadian industry.[49] The idea of some form of development research centre located at Lakehead University was not new – a study in the early 1970s had already revealed its feasibility – and, as Mayor Dusty Miller noted in 1978, "it would fill the technological gap between the research establishments in Toronto-Ottawa in the East and Saskatoon in the West."[50] Thunder Bay, however, had competition: a paper presented to the Municipal Advisory Committee in Northeastern Ontario reached similar conclusions,[51] a more aggressive approach was advocated as Laurentian University in Sudbury had already received increased grants for these types of activities.[52] Neither the provincial nor the federal government was interested in the Lakehead proposal, however, and the centre was never established. Indeed, according to provincial officials, Thunder Bay enjoyed a "diversified economy which has given it strength to weather the storms of economic downturn better than some."[53] Such was the response by Leo Bernier, Minister of Northern Affairs, in April 1974 to Thunder Bay Mayor Dusty Miller's request for funds for an Economic Development Strategy for her city.[54] Miller had pointed to the numerous studies whose recommendations had been ignored by the province,[55] and Bernier's support of yet another in a long list of studies calling for greater government investment in regional economic diversification seemed pointless. It did not help that such economic base studies were "met with outright hostility by the Ministry of Industry and Tourism."[56]

The 1980s and 1990s

At the beginning of the 1980s, it appeared to some as if the north would no longer be ignored. The Ontario government initiated a Royal Commission on the Northern Environment to investigate the effects of development on northern environments and communities. Much to the chagrin of municipalities in much of the northwest, its initial mandate included only communities "north or generally north of the 50th parallel."[57] After protests from towns and cities across the northwest and a number of First Nations, the Royal Commission's scope was expanded. However, as Thunder Bay's chief administrative officer reported to other municipal leaders in 1977, "the reports coming out of the ... Northern Environment hearings run the gamut of personal feeling from elation to frustration and discouragement, to the question of the usefulness of the hearings, and finally to a possible return to Southern Ontario to obtain the feelings there of its citizens."[58]

The Royal Commission eventually conceded what northerners had long complained of: that the north "serves and is dominated by Ontario's more populated industrial south. This reality underlines the environmental degradation and social malaise that has characterized the exploitation of Northern natural resources ... [T]he bulk of development benefits have flowed south ... The North has not shared equitably in the profits that have flowed from the exploitation of its natural resources."[59] The Royal Commission concluded: "Many northerners still consider that the north has become an economic colony of the south, receiving an insufficient share of the benefits of development while bearing most of the adverse impacts. They feel that they have little control over shaping their own destinies and lack of power to significantly influence decisions about development made in corporate and government boardrooms elsewhere."[60]

The result was the creation of the Northern Ontario Heritage Fund to facilitate tourism and infrastructural improvements. In the intervening decade, however, little actual change occurred, as resources still went predominately to traditional industry.

Federal and provincial policy decisions determined the course of the softwood lumber industry,[61] and the Western Grain Transportation Act provided a subsidy to railway companies to lower the cost of transporting grain, a policy instituted not for the benefit of northwestern Ontario communities, but for that of the railways and western farmers; that it helped to promote transportation at Thunder Bay was incidental. By the early 1980s, northwestern Ontario accounted for 5.3 per cent of the country's wood pulp production. 9.5 per cent of its paper board production, and 2.6 per cent of lumber and marginal panel board, veneer, and plywood production; within Ontario, these numbers were 26.7 per cent, 38.1 per cent, 27 per cent, and 28.5 per cent, respectively.[62] Although a certain level of diversification of the economy had occurred, as witnessed by the success of Bombardier's streetcar production in Thunder Bay, manufacturing depended increasingly on the forestry industry, particularly with respect to logging equipment, chemical production, pulp, newsprint, kraft paper, and fine paper manufacturing. Thunder Bay's port also experienced a surge in Prairie grain, which represented almost three-quarters of the total volume of the port, as well as increases in coal, potash, and sulphur – so much so that the District Economist's Office thought they were joining newsprint and lumber as important products.[63]

Contemporary predictions were that grain handling would increase, but that the port would find it difficult to maintain efficiency without implementing such strategies as revised labour agreements, rail reconfiguration, and expanded storage and workhouse capabilities. Although coal was seen as growing only modestly, optimistic long-range forecasts of increased demand and capacity promised to improve Thunder Bay's economic situation. Transshipments of potash – the port handled 1.6 million tonnes in 1982[64] – and sulphur were also expected to increase substantially. In contrast, shipments of iron ore through the port had declined significantly with the phased closure of the Atikokan mines in 1978, although the discovery of deposits at Lake St Joseph and Bending Lake promised a recovery with the improvement of market conditions.[65]

By the 1990s, northwestern Ontario's labour force had undergone a significant shift, with jobs in the services industry having increased substantially – more than 4,500 additional jobs between 1986 and 1991[66] – while traditional manufacturing jobs continued to decrease, from 11,779 in 1970 to 10,000 in 1990,[67] with most of the losses coming between 1986 and 1990. The transportation industry also shed more than 900 full-time jobs between 1986 and 1991. The natural resources industries experienced a comparable decline, with jobs lost during a bust cycle not replaced during a boom. Many of these jobs were relatively high paying, unionized jobs, with good benefits, and although the total number of jobs lost was offset by increases in services sector employment, there was a substantial decrease in real family income across the region.[68]

Conclusion

One historian of Thunder Bay has commented that, "in terms of development, not much has really changed since the 1970s."[69] The 1980s and 1990s brought the city even more problems as the boom and bust cycles that had defined the region since the Second World War were compounded by technological and other changes, so that booms produced fewer new jobs while busts produced large-scale job losses. Job losses in the grain industry, the railways, and the pulp and paper industry have been countered by gains in retail and other services sector jobs. With the growth of employment in the health and post-secondary sectors, the region is transition from its old economic base to a new knowledge economy.

The snapshot this chapter has provided should encourage us to rethink our conceptions of economic development in northwestern Ontario, much of which to date has been dictated largely by outside forces rather than by regional decision making. Recent Ontario government initiatives, however, perpetuate a century of adversarial relationships between those who live in the north and southern politicians. Once again regional planners are arguing that "[n]orthwestern

Ontario is at a cross-road! It can continue to rely on the Provincial and Federal Governments to respond to legitimate requests from the region and hope that the answer is both timely and appropriate to the expressed needs. Or, it can chart its own course by taking on those challenges and developing its own solution."[70] Yet provincial and federal governments historically have undermined regional attempts to diversify and industrialize the economy, and it is clear that change will come only when the two levels of government abandon the nineteenth-century idea of northwestern Ontario as a colony.

NOTES

1 See H.V. Nelles, *The Politics of Development: Forests, Mines & Hydro-electric Power in Ontario, 1849–1941* (Toronto: Macmillan of Canada, 1974).
2 D. Creighton, *The Commercial Empire of the St. Lawrence* (1937, repr., as *The Empire of the St. Lawrence,* Toronto: Macmillan and Company, 1956); and H. Innis, *The Fur Trade in Canada: An Introduction to Canadian Economic History* (1930; repr., Toronto: University of Toronto Press, 1999).
3 For more on regional development issues, see F.J. Anderson, *Regional Economic Analysis: A Canadian Perspective* (Toronto: Harcourt Brace Jovanovich Canada, 1988); M. Bradfield, *Regional Economic Analysis and Policies in Canada* (Toronto: McGraw-Hill Ryerson, 1988); A. Careless, *Initiative and Response: The Adaptation of Canadian Federalism to Regional Economic Development* (Montreal; Kingston, ON: McGill-Queen's University Press, 1977); Economic Council of Canada, *Living Together: Regional Disparities in Canada* (Ottawa: Minister of Supply and Services, 1977); N. Hansen, "Regional Development Policies: Past Problems and Future Possibilities," *Canadian Journal of Regional Science* 19 (1, 1996): 107–18; J.R. Melvin, "Regional Inequalities in Canada: Underlying Causes and Policy Implications," *Canadian Public Policy* 13 (3, 1987): 304–17; Organisation for Economic Co-operation and Development, *Regional Problems and Policies in Canada* (Paris: OECD, 1994); and D.J. Savoie, *Regional Economic Development: Canada's Search for Solutions* (Toronto: University of Toronto Press, 1986).
4 This chapter is a preliminary attempt to articulate the historic state-regional policy relationship. The author recognizes that no complete understanding of the complexities of the topic is possible without further, much needed work on the Aboriginal-state relationship in regional development policy. During the period before the 1970s, however, it is safe to say that governments at all levels ignored dialogue with Aboriginal

people in their development plans. For a general historical overview of the region, see M.S. Beaulieu and C. Southcott, *North of Superior: An Illustrated History of Northwestern Ontario* (Toronto: James Lorimer, 2010); T.J. Tronrud and A.E. Epp, eds., *Thunder Bay: From Rivalry to Unity* (1995, repr., Thunder Bay, ON: Thunder Bay Historical Museum Society, 2008); and W.R. Wightman and N.M. Wightman, *The Land Between: Northwestern Ontario Resource Development 1800 to the 1990s* (Toronto: University of Toronto Press, 1997).

5 For the classic discussion, see Nelles, *Politics of Development*, chaps. 3 and 4.

6 See C. Southcott, "Alternative Development Strategies for Resource Hinterlands: Thunder Bay as a Case Study," in *Social Relations in Resource Hinterlands*, ed. T.W. Dunk (Thunder Bay, ON: Lakehead University, Centre for Northern Studies, 1991); and G.R. Weller, "Hinterland Politics: The Case of Northwestern Ontario," in *Provincial Hinterland: Social Inequality in Northwestern Ontario*, ed. C. Southcott (Halifax: Fernwood Publishing, 1993). See also Tom Miller, "Cabin-Fever: The Province of Ontario and Its Norths," and D. Scott, "Northern Alienation," both in *Government and Politics in Ontario*, 2nd ed., ed. D.C. MacDonald (Toronto: Van Nostrand Reinhold, 1980).

7 For more on the history of northern Ontario, see K. Abel, "History and the Provincial Norths: An Ontario Example," in *Northern Visions: New Perspectives on the North in Canadian History* (Peterborough, ON: Broadview, 2001). For an extensive historiographical look, see A.E. Epp, "Northern Ontario: History and Historiography," in *The Historiography of the Provincial Norths*, ed. K. Coates and W. Morrison (Thunder Bay, ON: Lakehead University, Centre for Northern Studies, 1996).

8 The definition used is one put forward by the late Tom Miller in "Cabin Fever."

9 It is important to note that, although the 1969 amalgamation was a top-down decision, previous discussions on amalgamation in 1910, 1920, and 1958 had fluctuated between being driven regionally or by Queen's Park. See "Amalgamation of Fort William and Port Arthur, 1910–69," City of Thunder Bay Archives (hereafter cited as TBA), 2401. For more on this intercity rivalry, see E. Arthur, "The Landing and the Plot," *Lakehead University Review* 1 (1, 1968): 1–17E; idem, ed., *Thunder Bay District, 1821–1892* (Toronto: University of Toronto Press, 1973); T. J. Tronrud, *Guardians of Progress: Boosters and Boosterism in Thunder Bay, 1870–1914* (Thunder Bay, ON: Thunder Bay Historical Museum Society, 1993); and Tronrud and Epp, *Thunder Bay*.

10 See P. Raffo, "Municipal Political Culture and Conflict of Interest at the Lakehead, 1969–72," Thunder Bay Historical Museum Society, *Papers and Records* 26 (1998): 26–45.

11 Material on the fur trade is extensive. For more on the fur trade in northwestern Ontario, see, for example, J. Morrison, *Superior Rendezvous Place: Fort William in the Canadian Fur Trade* (Toronto: Natural Heritage Books, 2001); and idem, *Lake Superior to Rainy Lake: Three Centuries of Fur Trade History* (Thunder Bay, ON: Thunder Bay Historical Museum Society, 2003).

12 Weller, "Hinterland Politics," 7.

13 See B. Muirhead, "The Evolution of the Lakehead's Commercial and Transportation Infrastructure," in Tronrud and Epp, *Thunder Bay*.

14 For more on the concept of "Empire Ontario," see J. Schull, *Ontario since 1867* (Toronto: McClelland & Stewart, 1978); and P.A. Baskerville, *Sites of Power: A Concise History of Ontario* (Don Mills, ON: Oxford University Press, 2005).

15 Nelles, *The Politics of Development*, 51; and H.A. Innis, "An Introduction to the Economic History of Ontario from Outpost to Empire," in *Profiles of a Province: Studies in the History of Ontario*, ed. E.G. Firth (Toronto: Ontario Historical Society, 1967), 153–5.

16 L. Di Matteo, "The Government of Ontario and Its North, 1871–1911," Research Report 33 (Thunder Bay, ON: Lakehead University, Centre for Northern Studies, 1992), 8.

17 See J.M.S. Careless, "Limited Identities in Canada," *Canadian Historical Review* 1 (1, 1969): 6.

18 For more on this development, see T.J. Tronrud, "Building the Industrial City," in Tronrud and Epp., *Thunder Bay*, 101.

19 M. Bray, "The Place and the People," in *A Vast and Magnificent Land: An Illustrated History of Northern Ontario*, ed. M. Bray and E. Epp (Toronto: Ministry of Northern Affairs, 1984), 14.

20 Baskerville, *Sites of Power*, 173–7.

21 For more on the Ferguson government, see P.G. Oliver, *Public & Private Persons: The Ontario Political Culture, 1914–1934* (Toronto: Clarke Irwin, 1975); and idem, *Howard Ferguson: Ontario Tory* (Toronto: University of Toronto Press, 1977).

22 Baskerville, *Sites of Power*, 193–4.

23 For more on C.D. Howe, see L. Roberts, *C.D.: The Life and Times of Clarence Decatur Howe* (Toronto: Clarke Irwin, 1957); and R. Bothwell and W. Kilbourn, *C.D. Howe: A Biography* (Toronto: McClelland & Stewart, 1979).

24 See I. Radforth, *Bushworkers and Bosses: Logging in Northern Ontario, 1900–1980* (Toronto: University of Toronto Press, 1987).

25 O. Saarinen, "Cities and Towns," in Bray and Epp, *Vast and Magnificent Land*, 159.
26 Baskerville, *Sites of Power*, 213.
27 G. Wheeler, "Politics and Policy in the North," in MacDonald, *Government and Politics in Ontario*, 288; and N. Wightman and R. Wightman, "Road and Highway Development in Northwestern Ontario," *Geographica* 36 (4, 1992): 366–80.
28 For more on the development and impact of the Seaway, see B. Muirhead, "The Evolution of the Lakehead's Commercial Transportation Infrastructure," in Tronrud and Epp, *Thunder Bay*.
29 For a detailed analysis of population trends, see C. Southcott, *The North in Numbers: A Demographic Analysis of Social and Economic Change in Northern Ontario* (Thunder Bay, ON: Lakehead University, Centre for Northern Studies, 2006), 24–7.
30 Paul G. Hoffman, Remarks to the Conference on Regional Development and Economic Change, Thunder Bay, ON, 15–17 February 1965, TBA 5225–80.
31 N. Peterson, "Regional Government and Development," in MacDonald, *Government and Politics in Ontario*, 186.
32 Ibid., 183.
33 See Ontario, Ministry of Treasury and Economics, *Design for Development: Northwestern Ontario Region – Phase Two, Policy Recommendations* (Toronto, 1970); and idem, *Design for Development: A Policy Statement on the Northwestern Region* (Toronto: Queen's Printer, 1971).
34 Quoted in R. White, *Ontario, 1610–1985: A Political and Economy History* (Toronto: Dundurn Press, 1985), 282.
35 Southcott, "Alternative Development Strategies for Resource Hinterlands," 36.
36 For more on DREE, see Geoffrey J.D. Hewings, *Regional Industrial Analysis and Development* (Oxford: Methuen, 1977), 134–42. For a regional analysis, see British Columbia, Legislative Assembly, Select Standing Committee on Agriculture, *The Impact of the Department of Regional Economic Expansion on the Food Industry in Western Canada* (Victoria, 1978).
37 Weller, "Hinterland Politics," 19–20.
38 Tronrud, "Building the Industrial City," 119.
39 For this quotation, see J. Struthers, *The Limits of Affluence: Welfare in Ontario* (Toronto: University of Toronto Press, 1994), 123; and C. Martin, "The Politics of Northern Ontario: An Analysis of the Political Divergencies at the Provincial Periphery" (MA thesis, McGill University, 1999), 49.
40 Southcott, *Provincial Hinterland*, 36.

41 G.W. McFadden, Director, Development Bureau of the City of Thunder
  Bay, to W.E. Mokemela, Assistant Co-ordinator, Operations, City of
  Thunder Bay, "Economic Review," 23 August 1974, 1, TBA, Series 117,
  4703–23.
42 G.W. McFadden, Director, Development Bureau of the City of Thunder
  Bay, to E.C. Reid, City Co-ordinator, City of Thunder Bay, 1 April 1974,
  TBA, Series 117, 4703–23.
43 *Globe and Mail*, 27 July 1974. TBA, Series 17, 4701–23.
44 John White, Minister of Treasury Economics and Intergovernmental Affairs,
  to Walter Assef, Mayor, City of Thunder Bay, 7 March 1974, TBA, Series 17,
  4703–23; City Co-ordinator to John White, Minister of Treasury Economics
  and Intergovernmental Affairs, 1 April 1974, TBA, Series 17, 4703–23.
45 Weller, "Hinterland Politics," 8–9.
46 Municipal Advisory Committee on Provincial Planning for Northwestern
  Ontario, "Priorities for Action" (Thunder Bay, ON, 1977).
47 See Other Government – Ontario, Ministry of Treasury, Economics
  and Intergovernmental Affairs, Municipal Advisory Committee for
  Northwestern Ontario, "Proceedings of Forest Management Seminar,"
  Thunder Bay, ON, 10 February 1979, 1, TBA, Series 117, 5102–9.
48 City of Thunder Bay, *Industrial – Commercial News Report* 11 (1, 1977): 2.
49 Planning, Economic Development Bureau, General, telegram from Michael
  Gravelle, Special Assistant to the President of the Board of Economic
  Ministers, to Mayor Dusty Miller, City of Thunder Bay, 22 December 1978,
  TBA, Series 117, 5029–27.
50 Planning, Economic Development Bureau, General, Mayor Dusty Miller,
  Dr Norman Grace, and Jerry McFadden to Hon. R.K. Andreas, MP,
  President, Board of Economic Development Ministers, ca. December 1978,
  TBA, Series 117, 5029–27.
51 N.S. Grace, "The Role of Innovative Research in Regional Economic
  Development," in *Proceedings of Second Annual Conference on Regional
  Development in Northeastern Ontario, North Bay, ON, 5–6 May, 1977* (North
  Bay, ON: Municipal Advisory Committee on Provincial Planning in
  Northeastern Ontario, 1977).
52 Planning, Economic Development Bureau, Enterprise Development Study
  Group, "A Report of the Enterprise Development Group: Support Material
  and Appendix," May 1978, 31–4, TBA, Series 117, 5029–28. See also
  "Resource Centre: need here but no money," *Chronicle Journal* (Thunder
  Bay), 31 August 1977 and 1 September 1977.
53 Planning, Economic Development Bureau, Enterprise Development Study
  Group, "A Report of the Enterprise Development Group: Support Material
  and Appendix," May 1978, 1, TBA, Series 117, 5029–28.

54 See Planning, Economic Development Bureau, Dusty Miller to Hon. Leo Bernier, Minister of Northern Affairs, 28 February 1979, and Bernier to Miller, 4 April 1979, TBA, 5107.

55 Those mentioned include Ontario, Ministry of Treasury and Economics, *Design for Development*; Ontario, Ministry of Treasury, Economics and Intergovernmental Affairs, *Northwestern Ontario: A Strategy for Development* (Toronto, 1978); and Enterprise Development Group, "A Competitive Enterprise for Growth" (Thunder Bay, ON, 1978).

56 Planning, Economic Development Bureau, "Economic Market Development of Thunder Bay's Market Area," J.R. Picherack to Mayor D. Miller, 21 August 1979, TBA, Series 117, 5107–47.

57 Planning, Economic Development Bureau, General, G.W. McFadden, Director, Development Bureau, to Mayor Walter Assef, 23 August 1977, TBA, Series 117, 4988–6.

58 City of Thunder Bay, *Industrial – Commercial News Report* 11 (3, 1977): 7.

59 Martin, "The Politics of Northern Ontario," 49–51.

60 Ontario, Royal Commission on the Northern Environment, *Final Report and Recommendations* (Toronto: Ministry of the Attorney General, 1985), 10–11.

61 Tronrud, "Building the Industrial City," 106.

62 Thunder Bay Economic Development Corporation, "Come Grow with Us" (Thunder Bay, ON: City of Thunder Bay, 1983), E1/1.

63 Canada, Department of Employment and Immigration, Economic Planning & Analysis Directorate, Ontario Region, "Thunder Bay CEC Area Profile" (Ottawa, 1986), 12.

64 Thunder Bay Economic Development Corporation, "Come Grow with Us," G1/4.

65 Ibid., G1/5.

66 See Thunder Bay Economic Development Corporation, "Review of the Local Economy" (Thunder Bay, ON: City of Thunder Bay, 1992).

67 B. Dagostar, W.B. Janowski, and M. Moazzami, "The Economy of Northwestern Ontario: Structure, Performance, and Future," Research Report 31 (Thunder Bay, ON: Lakehead University, Centre for Northern Studies, 1992), 40.

68 Thunder Bay Economic Development Corporation, "Trends and Forecasts" (Thunder Bay, ON: City of Thunder Bay, 1993), 16, 17.

69 M.E. Kosny, "Thunder Bay after a Quarter Century," in Tronrud and Epp, *Thunder Bay*, 234.

70 Northwestern Ontario Municipal Association, "Enhancing the Economy of Northwestern Ontario" (n.p., 2007), 5, available online at http:// www.northernontarioregion.ca/uploads/documents/NWORDA/ EnhancingtheEconomyofNWO.pdf.

7 Destiny Delayed? Turning Mineral Wealth into Sustainable Development

DAVID ROBINSON

Introduction

Metal mining has been and will continue to be a distinctive feature of the economy of northern Ontario. All of Ontario's twenty-eight metal mines are in the north of the province, and they produced $7.4 billion worth of metals in 2008,[1] most of which was exported (mineral production in southern Ontario is predominantly of construction materials, such as gravel). A region commonly is considered to be specialized if it has an industry whose share of the regional economy is 1.4 or more times its share of the general economy. By that criterion, northern Ontario is both specialized in and dependent upon the mining sector – with forestry, mining accounts for more than 6 per cent of the goods-producing sector in northern Ontario, ten times the share of these industries in southern Ontario. Furthermore, almost all of the $660 million spent on mineral exploration in Ontario in 2008 occurred in the north. Indeed, the degree of specialization in mining in Northern Ontario is actually increasing.

Mining, however, is not a sustainable industry, so that a regional economy based on it eventually must make a transition to other sources of income or it will decline. Thus, mineral wealth can be either extracted or used to build a sustainable economy. The Ontario government, however, in its 2009 *Places to Grow: Proposed Growth Plan for Northern Ontario*, which is described as "a long-term economic blueprint that sets out a framework to guide decision-making over the next 25 years,"[2] reveals that it remains committed to extraction rather than development.

I begin the chapter by defining "mineral wealth," and then proceed to the concepts of development based on mineral wealth and sustainable development based on mineral wealth. I follow these definitions by briefly describing the main features of the economic policies governing northern Ontario to the present, with an emphasis on mineral and mining policies; I argue that the results of these policies have been unsatisfactory with respect to several natural criteria, although they have had some limited success. I move on to consider whether, based on historical policies, northern Ontario should be understood as an internal colony, and I examine the implications of that status.

I then identify necessary features of a sustainable development strategy for northern Ontario, with an emphasis on mineral and mining policies, and consider whether a sustainable mineral development policy has begun to emerge as the region becomes less important as a source of revenue for the province. Finally, I draw several conclusions about the prospects for sustainable development based on the mineral wealth of northern Ontario.

Key Concepts

The title of this chapter contains several words that are ill defined or even undefined. "Wealth," "sustainable," and "development" are contested terms in a set of linked and often confused conversations. "Wealth," for example, takes 3,900 words in the *Oxford English Dictionary* (OED).[3] The meaning of "sustainable" is disputed, and "development" is a mystery in the economics literature. Add that northern Ontario has disputed boundaries and a contested political identity. What, then, are defensible and useful interpretations of these terms?

Wealth

Mineral wealth is a subtler and far more complex notion than it seems. Elliot Lake, once the Uranium Capital of the World, is now a retirement town. The uranium is still there, but it exists in a curious state of being potentially valuable. Is it wealth? Mining it today would make one poorer. Nonetheless, the option to mine it at some future time has a positive price in a well-defined market.

Only economically recoverable ore counts as mineral wealth. The value and even the size of a mineral reserve depend on the price of the minerals extracted. Figure 7.1 is a conventional marginal-cost-marginal-revenue figure for a given mine. Assume that the capital cost of getting the mine into production has been spent, and is now a sunk cost. If one were to consider buying the mine, one would be willing to pay no

Figure 7.1. The Value of a Mine

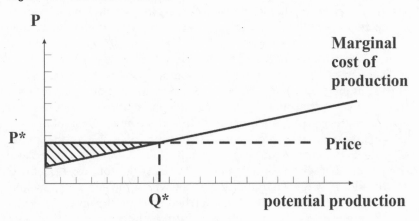

Figure 7.2. Windfall Gain Due to Rising Prices

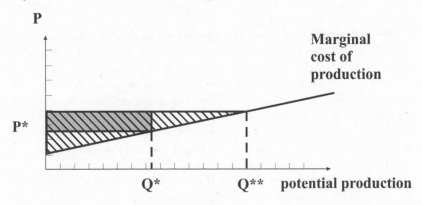

more than the value of the ore that can be extracted economically minus the cost of extraction. The cost of extraction is shown as a rising marginal cost curve. The hatched area represents the net value of known reserves. Beyond Q*, production costs more than it brings in. Indeed, the mine would never have been built if the investors had not believed that the hatched area would be larger than the cost of development.

Clearly, if the price rises, Q* moves to the right, and the hatched area increases. Part of the increase is "windfall profit" (the shaded rectangle in Figure 7.2), part is the net value of the expansion of the economic reserve. A potential buyer who believes prices will rise will value the reserves more than an owner who expects them to fall. Even if the international price stays the same, a decline in the value of the domestic currency would make the cost lower in international currencies. Reserves also become more valuable if the costs fall. A mine is like a lottery ticket: initial costs are known, but the return is uncertain.

There are additional complications. Some of the reserves can be extracted immediately; the current price applies to this part of the reserve. For the part that cannot be extracted immediately, some future price applies. Future prices are unknown, but futures markets might make it possible to commit to production for a future date at a known price. Of course, the cost of future production is also unknown, and reducing price risk might mean taking on cost risk. The story can be refined to consider new and marginal mines for which the entire production is near the right-hand side of the hatched triangle in Figure 7.1. Such mines might come into and go out of production as prices fluctuate; others might never make money. There are also discoveries – such as the Hemlo find – that come in near the left-hand side of the figure and produce very large profits.

Figure 7.1, however, lacks an explicit treatment of the development costs of mines, ignores distinctions between national and international markets, and takes no account of discounting, resource depletion, or exploration. It does make clear the fact that mineral wealth is the net value of production at various prices and costs, and that the value is speculative in a fundamental sense. The conventional economic term for the hatched areas in Figures 7.1 and 7.2 is "economic rent" or "resource rent." It arises because price is determined at the margin while costs apply across the entire range.[4]

Another important feature of the mining sector is illustrated by Figure 7.3: mining offers the highest average weekly wage in the economy. It does this partly as "compensating variation," or extra payment for risk, remoteness, and employment variability. At least a part of the wage, however, is rent. Figure 7.3 illustrates how higher wages take a slice out of the rent triangle that would otherwise go to owners. One result is that the level of output is lower, perhaps Q^U, because owners experience this form of rent sharing as higher costs. Reducing the rate of extraction might have a positive effect, since it could prolong the life of the mine, stabilizing the community. The "nickel bonus" negotiated by INCO workers is an additional form of rent sharing that comes into play only when the price rises above a specified level.[5]

Figure 7.3. Dividing the Rents

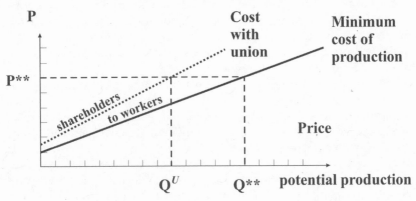

Sustainable

The OED is more helpful in defining "sustainable development" than in defining "wealth," despite the common assertion that sustainability is a recent and vague notion. Two senses apply: "sustainable development n. (a) Econ. economic development which can be sustained in the long term; (rare, and perh. not a fixed collocation in this sense); (b) Ecol. utilization and development of natural resources in ways which are compatible with the maintenance of these resources, and with the conservation of the environment, for future generations."

Surprisingly, the first sense, focused on the economy, is described as "rare, and perh. not a fixed collocation in this sense." The OED's editors are uncertain about the use of "sustainable development" to refer to "economic development which can be sustained in the long term." When we speak of sustainable economic development, it is very likely to be understood first, and possibly last, in terms of environmental sustainability.

The second sense is the part of the notion of sustainability popularized by the Brundtland Commission, convened by the United Nations in 1983.[6] It is the dominant sense of the phrase "sustainable development," and is obviously a necessary condition for the sustainability in the first sense. In the time since the Brundtland report, researchers from many disciplines have attempted to operationalize the concept of sustainable development.[7] Economists generally prefer the "capital approach" to sustainable development, in which the economic concept of capital is broadened to incorporate both social and environmental assets. In this framework sustainable regional development is "development that ensures non-declining per capita *regional*[8] wealth by replacing or conserving the sources of that wealth; that is, stocks of produced, human, social and natural capital."[9]

Mineral stocks are not replaced in the process of development, so sustainable mining begins to look like an oxymoron. Two responses are possible. Focusing on the notion of economically exploitable stocks leads to the view that the stock of exploitable reserves might be "renewed" through exploration. Sustainability in a mining region then simply requires a sufficiently energetic program of exploration.

A focus on the depletion of mineral stocks leads to the concept of "weak sustainability,"[10] which allows stocks of one form of wealth to decline as long as other stocks are built up at the same time, so that the total stock is sustained (population growth requires that the total stock actually grow).

Development

The concept of development provides a way to choose between the two conceptions of sustainable mining. Referring again to the OED, "economic development" is: "e. The economic advancement of a region or people, esp. one currently underdeveloped." "Advancement" is somewhat vague. The definition provided by Wikipedia clarifies the notion: "Economic development refers to social and technological progress. It implies a change in the way goods and services are produced, not merely an increase in production achieved using the old methods of production on a wider scale. Economic growth implies only an increase in quantitative output; it may or may not involve development."

Other sources confirm that "development" is change tending towards a more complex state. The *Online Business Dictionary* defines economic development as the "[q]ualitative measure of progress in an economy. It refers to development and adoption of new technologies, transition from agriculture based to industry based economy, and general improvement in living standards." The *Penguin Dictionary of Economics* calls it "[t]he growth in total and per capita income of developing countries, accompanied by fundamental change in the structure of their economies," and the *HarperCollins Dictionary of Economics* refers to the "structural transformation of an economy through industrialization."

A policy based on sustainability through exploration is not a development policy because it is not transformative. The "weak sustainability" approach, on the other hand, is consistent with development, since it requires that the mineral wealth of a region be transformed into a different form of productive capital – into human and social capital. For northern Ontario development can only mean a shift from exporting natural resources for use as raw materials towards the export of products that include larger amounts of value added.

Resource-based economies do not automatically make the transition to sustainable growth. Many suffer from the "resource trap," the "resource curse," or, for developed countries, the "Dutch disease." The "resource curse" refers to the "paradox," described by Sachs and Warner, "that economies abundant in natural resources have tended to grow slower than economies without substantial natural resources."[11] Hussain, Chaudhry, and Malik conclude that "[t]here is [an] adverse nexus between export[-]related natural resources as [a] ratio of [gross domestic product] and economic growth."[12] Collier argues that "the surplus from natural resource exports significantly reduces growth ... [and] over time, countries with large resource discoveries can end up poorer ... the resource trap is a binding problem for countries with governance capacities below a certain level."[13] Both Norman[14] and Brunnschweiler and Bulte[15] find that the direct effect of resource wealth (particularly the subset of mineral resource wealth) on income growth is positive and significant, although small. The authors argue that resource dependency, rather than resource wealth, is the problem, and that dependency is a result of government failure: countries with bad institutions attract little investment, and as a result they grow more slowly and remain dependent on exports of commodities.

Economic Development Based on Mineral Wealth for Northern Ontario

Figure 7.4 illustrates the typical life cycle of a mining town. While the resource is being extracted, the mine supports a growing community. When the resource is exhausted, people leave to find other work. The mine becomes a hole in the ground. Where is the wealth at the end of the process? Part goes to the owners of the company. Some of it is collected as tax revenue. Much of what is collected is used to provide services for the extraction – meaning that much of the government revenue from mining is actually just an indirect cost of extraction.

Figure 7.4. Mining-based Growth without Development Produces a Ghost Town

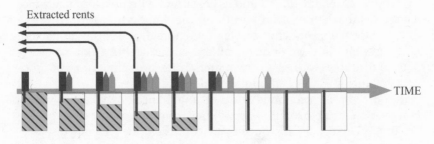

The houses built and the wages paid are not, in general, wealth. They are simply part of the cost of operating the mine. They are expenditures. Houses are not wealth when a town becomes a ghost town, because they have almost no market value. Houses in Elliot Lake were an exception because they were successfully sold to retirees. In that case mineral production produced a capital asset that could be applied to another economic activity.

Wages are a cost to the owner, but in the mining sector wages are often supported above the opportunity cost of labour by unions. This union wage premium transfers a share of the net wealth produced from owners to workers, and hence to the local community. Unionized workers capture some of the resource rents. These rents might be dissipated on toys and quality of life, or invested to educate a new generation or to start businesses.

Look again at Figure 7.4. Resource rents build wealth in other places. Much of the wealth is captured by speculators, some perhaps by the public sector, some by the workers. There is an inflow of wages and other income, but it is spent on producing a large hole and homes in a location where they are not needed. Wages and infrastructure investment are simply costs of extraction.

The process might be quite efficient, in the sense that resource rents are generated. The process might produce economic development as well. Montreal and Toronto, in fact, developed by capturing wealth extracted from northern Ontario as well as from other parts of the country. The feature that is most significant for the people of northern Ontario is that the process minimizes development in their region. The process begins and ends with empty territory.[16]

The Economic Policies Governing Northern Ontario

Figure 7.5 shows a mining community at B in some indefinite future sustainable state. Industrial or services facilities earn revenue from outside the community, perhaps from outside the country, to sustain the community. As it stands, Figure 7.5 is a reasonably accurate representation of Ontario's strategy for mining-based northern development. There is a clear appreciation of the fact that mining towns are not sustainable under the current policy regime; there is reference to an undefined sustainable state; and the steps from A to B are completely lacking.

Active policy generally has been confined to the period just before or after a mine closes. At that point the resource rents have been extracted and distributed, but the community has not been planned with a transition strategy in mind. The resources remaining in the community, including the housing stock and utilities, have been built for a style of life that might not be affordable once the very high mining wage is no longer available. There is no transition fund, there are no plans in place, and community leaders have no experience in promoting development.

The *Proposed Growth Plan for Northern Ontario* provides a loose sketch of the Ontario government's current ambitions for the north. The summary for the very short section on mining states that "there will be a greater emphasis on new technologies, value added products and services, and sustainable resource management practices."[17] "Sustainable resource management" is not defined. The seven-part "plan" can be paraphrased as follows (the official version is given in the appendix to this chapter):

1. Grow the northern mining cluster.
2. Continue to invest some money in the mineral sector.

Figure 7.5. Development as an Ideal Combined with Crisis Management

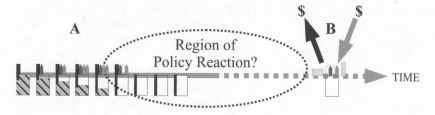

3. Improve regional infrastructure planning.
4. Continue to provide incentives for exploration.
5. Identify mining supply and service firms, and come up with an export strategy for the sector.
6. Hope the revisions to the Mining Act work out.
7. Work on the public image of the mining industry.

Items 1 and 5 represent an important shift in emphasis. To speak of a "Northern Ontario mineral industry cluster"[18] or of "the northern mining cluster," as in item 1 above, contradicts the view taken by the Ministry of Northern Development and Mines (MNDM) in 2003, when the provincial government announced its intent to form an Ontario Mining Industry Cluster Council (OMICC).[19] OMICC was explicitly created on the premise that there was only an Ontario-wide mineral sector cluster. As recently as 2004 MNDM analysts questioned the view that there were even 150 mining supply and services firms in Sudbury, and argued that the sector was actually concentrated in southern Ontario. Indeed, a ministry map shows only a "Sudbury Micro-Cluster."[20]

Items 1 and 5 represent the beginning of a coherent development strategy. Diversification around an existing specialization is generally recognized as the most promising route to successful regional diversification.[21] The remaining five items can be seen as a list of vaguely stated intentions to continue doing what the province was doing before the Growth Plan consultation began. The plan is strikingly short of specifics, and contains almost nothing new.[22] The role of the Ontario government in the proposal is explicitly limited to "[w]orking collaboratively with other partners to coordinate, facilitate and monitor implementation of the growth plan."[23]

The process of creating the document might have served to align the views of analysts in the fourteen ministries that are said to have participated in developing the plan. Achieving a common vision across ministries is inherently difficult; each agency has its own set of programs, in which its staff members are embedded. A shift in general policy can occur only when staff members actually change the language they use, and begin adjusting their activities to a new understanding of objectives.[24]

Questions that are not dealt with in the Growth Plan include how to capture a larger share of the rents from mining and how to channel rents to produce more sustainable communities. As Walls remarked, in a discussion of underdevelopment in Appalachia, "[t]he most important decisions are the 'non-decisions': the questions that are never raised and the subjects that never make the public agenda. Examples include public ownership of the region's natural resources and worker or community-owned and controlled industry."[25]

To summarize the policies presented in the Growth Plan, the government of Ontario proposes to continue the approach that has been in place for the past one hundred years, to continue to increase regulation of environmental impact, and to develop an active program to involve persons of Aboriginal descent. In addition the government has recently recognized that a cluster of mining supply and services enterprises is already having a positive effect on northern employment and the provincial balance of trade.

A Sustainable Development Strategy

Any reasonable economic development strategy for northern Ontario as a distinct geographical entity has to include a plan for getting at least some mining-dependent communities from A to B. Conceptually the problem is not difficult: 1) identify the features of a sustainable community; 2) decide if the features identified in step one are present or can be induced at reasonable cost for a given community; and 3) for communities that pass the test in step 2, create or reinforce features identified in step 1.

This is a proactive approach, in contrast to the reactive approach that has characterized northern policy. A proactive approach should be in place before a community goes into decline. During the life of the community, government and community members should be identifying steps to make the community more viable in the long run or to ensure that its members are prepared for the eventual decline.

Step 1: Identify the Features of a Sustainable Community

A good deal of work has been done to identify the general features of a sustainable community. Some of the most interesting appears in the literature on "resilient communities,"[26] which has two features: a focus on grassroots involvement, and a focus on building the human capital needed. Strikingly, the assumption in most of this literature is that senior government will not have promoted planning for sustainability.

Among the features of a sustainable community are:

1. Low-cost infrastructure. During boom times the focus is on add-ing infrastructure. Few communities have planned settlement patterns and infrastructure to minimize operating and mainte-nance costs. When a mine or mill closes and population declines, however, communities mighty be forced to spread the burden of substantial fixed costs over a smaller population. The prospect of rising taxes and declining services makes an economic transition very difficult.[27]
2. Facilities that can be converted to new uses cheaply.
3. A pool of leaders with an understanding of economic and social development.
4. A network of contacts and partnerships.
5. A pool of entrepreneurs and small businesses engaged in pro-ducing for sale elsewhere. Without a pool of revenue-generating businesses, a community has to start from scratch at a time when incomes have declined, and is forced to compete to attract large outside players.
6. A highly skilled workforce. Businesses increasingly go where the workers are. A community that does not have a surplus of talent is at a disadvantage. A community that is losing its young people is at a disadvantage.
7. Design capacity. The market demands high-quality goods. High-quality products are high in design content: they are beautiful, well made, safe, and interesting. Design and quality fabrication are value added, and adding value is what provides an economic base for any community.[28]
8. Quality of life. People are the main resource for any community. Providing amenities through community action is as effective as increasing wages. Quality schools, security, recreational facilities, and community support are all part of family income defined broadly.[29]
9. Revenue sources that can be used for development projects. Slack, Bourne, and Gertler identify some of the financial challenges for small and remote communities, and propose several possible solutions.[30]
10. Access to resources needed for producing an export. The resource might be tourism amenities, although tourism is generally the industry of last recourse for northern communities. A high-quality wood supply is one of the most obvious resources for northern communities.

11. Locally produced and controlled power. Power is a major cost of living and a crucial input for most industries. All small hydro and almost all local biomass energy resources should be transferred to communities. It makes little sense to subsidize the export of whole-sale power in the face of significant efficiency losses when it is possible to build the local economy using the same power valued at retail rates.

Step 2: Decide If the Requirements for Sustainability Are Present or Can be Induced

The first eight items are forms of physical, social, or human capital. The province necessarily plays a major role in putting many of these elements in place. Yet even a casual examination of the requirements suggests that there are major gaps for northern Ontario as a whole, and that smaller communities often lack most of the conditions for sustainability. Local infrastructure has not been designed for sustainability and reuse. As a result many communities will struggle if the primary source of employment declines.

Leadership capacity is a crucial element. Since local leadership has a significant role, we might expect provincial agencies to promote the development of strong and independent local leadership. On the other hand, it might be difficult for agencies to encourage competition for their political masters and their clients. Whether provincial agencies do promote local leadership, how, and in what contexts are empirical questions. It is not apparent that they do.

The education system is failing to produce the trades people the region requires, and appears to prepare young people to leave the region.

The final three items in the list above represent control of local resources. In general it has been the policy of the government not to allow local control. The result has been to limit diversification and inhibit the development of local leadership.

Step 3: Put the Preconditions for Sustainable Development in Place

It is significant that the *Proposed Growth Plan for Northern Ontario* mentions several items in the list. It is also significant that the plan lacks details and explicit targets. The lack of a coherent and workable development strategy for northern Ontario within a highly developed province and country presents a puzzle. The research mentioned earlier suggests that institutional factors explain underdevelopment in resource-based regions. It is therefore natural to look to the historical and political setting of the region to explain underdevelopment in the north.

Northern Ontario as a Colony: The Internal Colony Hypothesis

Northern Ontario presents a strange case within Canada. It is a historical accident that it is not a province like the comparable areas that became Manitoba, Saskatchewan, and Alberta. Had it become a province, resource revenues would have flowed to the provincial capital, which probably would have been Sault Ste Marie. As the capital city the Sault would have been larger and richer than it is today. That difference would have made northern Ontario at least as populous as Manitoba, Saskatchewan, or Alberta by the mid-twentieth century.

The province would have become part of Canada at Confederation, or would have joined Canada soon after, as several western provinces did. The region would have had its own university system, based on institutions founded in, perhaps, 1877 (University of Manitoba), 1906 (University of Alberta), 1907 (University of Saskatchewan), 1911 (University of Regina), or 1915 (University of British Columbia). The northern universities would have had professional and research programs in mining and forestry comparable to those of Quebec and British Columbia.

There are other intriguing implications of this *Gedankenexperiment*. Toronto would never have become the world centre for financing exploration and mining. Montreal might have. The counterfactual story is most useful when we attempt to evaluate the level of mineral-based development in northern Ontario. It is virtually inconceivable that the region would still be so heavily dependent on resource extraction if it had been a province. Northern Ontario is less developed economically and socially as a result of its status as a region of the province of Ontario, and southern Ontario is more developed as a result of the relationship.

John Roemer's formal definition of exploitation in *A General Theory of Class and Exploitation*[31] offers a clear basis for interpreting this thought experiment:

S exploits N in the coalition if
1. S is better off with N in the coalition than without N in the coalition;
2. N is worse off in the coalition than outside of the coalition.

By this criterion, southern Ontario has clearly exploited the north.

Efforts of mainstream social scientists to explain persistent under-development in regions like northern Ontario fall into two categories, according to Walls:[32] the subculture of poverty model and the regional development model. In response to the inadequacy of these models, and the social policy that followed from them, radical intellectuals developed a third model: internal colonialism, a situation in which one region within a political unit is exploited by another politically dominant region.[33]

A difficulty with applying internal colonialism to northern Ontario is that the concept is generally applied to cases in which one culture or race dominates another. Gonzalez-Casanova[34] explicitly defines internal colonialism as domination and exploitation among culturally heterogeneous, distinct groups. Van den Berghe[35] proposes to treat internal colonialism as an ideal type with the following characteristics:

1. Rule of one ethnic group (or coalition of such groups) over other such groups living within the continuous boundaries of a single state.
2. Territorial separation of the subordinate ethnic groups into "homelands," "native reserves," and the like, with land tenure rights from those applicable to members of the dominant group.
3. Presence of an internal government within a government, especially created to rule the subject peoples, with a special legal status ascribed to the subordinate groups.
4. Relations of economic inequality, in which subject peoples are relegated to positions of dependency and inferiority in the division of labour and the relations of production.

The concept of an internal colony might provide a useful metaphor for understanding northern Ontario, but the region does not completely satisfy van den Berghe's conditions. It is clear the population of northern Ontario differed ethnically from that of Upper Canada when the region was annexed, but it does so less today. The system of reserves and municipalities in vast tracts of Crown land has some of the features of homelands, but clearly lacks others. The Ministry of Northern Development and Mines was created within the Ontario government to consolidate government functions for northern Ontario, but it is far too feeble to be described as "an internal government."

There are alternative explanations. Walls proposes that, for Appalachia, which shares features with northern Ontario, a core-periphery model is more appropriate than the internal colony model. In his model,

[c]ommerce and trade among members of the periphery tend to be monopolized by members of the core. Credit is similarly monopolized. When commercial prospects emerge, bankers, managers, and entrepreneurs tend to be recruited from the core. The peripheral economy is forced into complementary development to the core, and thus becomes dependent on external markets. Generally, this economy rests on a single primary export, either agricultural or mineral ... Where the core is characterized by a diversified industrial structure the pattern of development in the periphery is dependent, and complementary to that in the core. Peripheral industrialization, if it occurs at all, is highly specialized and geared for export. The peripheral economy is, therefore, relatively sensitive to price fluctuations in the international market. Decisions about investment, credit, and wages all tend to be made in the core. As a consequence of economic dependence, wealth in the periphery lags behind the core.[36]

The core-periphery model does appear to fit northern Ontario. Other models provide useful insights as well. One approach focuses on patterns of dependent industrialization and the formation of clientele social classes. Characteristics of dependent industrialization that seem to be present in northern Ontario include foreign domination of the most dynamic sectors of industry, increasing competitive advantage for foreign monopolistic enterprises over local firms, and the introduction of advanced, capital-intensive technology without regard to resulting unemployment. Clientele classes have a "dual position as partners of metropolitan interests, yet dominant elites within their own societies."[37] They might include not only the industrial bourgeoisie, but also the state bureaucracy and other sectors of the middle class when their positions are tied to foreign interests.

Rent-seeking models are built on the assumption that resource rents can be appropriated by local elites.[38] Resources are then spent capturing rents rather than in productive activities. Torvik[39] presets a model in which increased resource abundance increases the payoffs from rent-seeking behaviour, leading to more rent seeking and lower growth. Auty[40] argues that resource-rich countries characterized by "point resources" such as mines are particularly vulnerable to exploitation by narrow sectional interests. A rent-based explanation emphasizes the collaboration among corporate interests, large unions, and the government to maintain control of the resource rents.[41] The three groups might struggle over the division of the rents, but they are united in defending the system that provides them.

Like the internal colony model, each of the alternatives emphasizes social formations and power, issues that the *Proposed Growth Plan for Northern Ontario* entirely ignores.

A Summary

The most striking feature of northern Ontario's development is that the region retains little of the wealth generated from its mineral resources. Provincial policies cannot be said to have failed, in the sense that they were never intended to create wealth *in* northern Ontario. It is only when evaluated from within the region, and by a population that was not present when the policies were adopted, that the provincial strategy can be said to have failed. The province simply has not attempted to achieve sustainable regional development in the North. Furthermore, the *Proposed Growth Plan for Northern Ontario* suggests that the province has no intention of making structural changes for at least twenty-five years.[42] There is no significant political pressure to change the situation. As a result, the prospects for sustainable northern growth based on northern mineral wealth continue to be very limited.

Recent research has identified governmental and institutional failure as the underlying cause of the so-called resource curse.[43] The literature that examines the possibility of resource-based development or underdevelopment concentrates on national economies. Northern Ontario is a subnational economy that appears to suffer a version of the "resource curse," and its case might offer additional support for the thesis, with a small modification: national economies might fail to develop because of corruption and other forms of government failure, but northern Ontario has failed to develop because of government success. The economic retardation of the region is a result of long-established policies intended to extract resources for the benefit of the metropolitan regions.

Appendix

The "Plan of Action" for the mineral industry in the Ontario government's 2009 *Places to Grow: Proposed Growth Plan for Northern Ontario* consists of the following seven elements.

1. Through the Ontario Mineral Industry Cluster Council and other opportunities, strengthen Ontario's positions as a leading global mining jurisdiction, maintain the competitive edge in Ontario Operations, and grow the northern mining cluster.
2. Invest in research and innovation (for example, deep-mining techniques, exploration and environmental technologies, mine closure and rehabilitation processes) to improve the efficiency of Ontario Operations. Implement "green" mining initiatives to improve energy efficiency and tailings management.
3. Link potential mine development with regional infrastructure planning.
4. Continue incentives to stimulate exploration investment in Ontario.
5. Undertake and maintain an inventory of mining supply and service companies in the north, and implement an export strategy to expand into new domestic and international markets.
6. Amend the Ontario Mining Act to ensure environmentally sustainable development stewardship, support Aboriginal participation in the mineral sector, and increase timeliness and clarity in the regulatory processes, supported by a "one-window" approach for approvals.
7. Develop initiatives that increase public understanding of current exploration and mining practices, environmental impacts, and the importance of minerals and metals to daily lives.

Section 8.4 states that the Minister of Infrastructure and the Minister of Northern Development, Mines and Forestry will "develop a set of performance indicators ... monitor overall implementation ... [and] report on what progress provincial ministries and municipalities have made to implement the policies in this Plan."[44]

NOTES

This chapter is for my friend Dr Derek Wilkinson, who was committed to both scholarship and public education in the service of all the people of northern Ontario.

1 Ontario, Ministry of Energy and Infrastructure and Ministry of Northern Development, Mines and Forestry, *Places to Grow – Better Choices, Brighter Future: Proposed Growth Plan for Northern Ontario* ([Toronto]: Queen's Printer for Ontario, 2009), 10.

2 Ibid., 57.
3 The main groups of meanings are summarized below. The first two are
   archaic but revealing.

   1. The condition of being happy and prosperous; well-being.
   2. Spiritual well-being.
   3. a. Prosperity consisting in abundance of possessions ... the collective
      riches of a people or country.
   4. Economics. A collective term for those things the abundant possession
      of which (by a person or a community) constitutes riches, or wealth in
      the popular sense. There has been much controversy among economists
      as to the precise extent of meaning in which the term should be used.
   5. Plenty, abundance, profusion.

4 In other markets the rents are called producer surplus, and might give
   rise to "supernormal profits" or "quasi-rents." These tend to be competed
   away through entry and technological innovation. Resource rents are
   reduced by competition as well, and especially by new finds, but mineral
   resources are subject to depletion, which tends to increase their scarcity
   value even while exploration decreases it.
5 It is interesting that, in Sudbury, when nickel prices reached record highs
   and the bonus exceeded the annual income of many families, the executive
   director of the Social Planning Council suggested publicly that the workers
   should share some of the bonus with the less well off in the community.
   The suggestion angered Steelworker leaders. It is likely that the union
   would have enjoyed much greater public support during the 2009–10
   strike had it voted to share even 10 per cent of the bonus with community
   agencies.
6 World Commission on Environment and Development (Brundtland
   Commission), *Our Common Future* (New York: Oxford University Press,
   1987). The report offers the following definition: "Sustainable development
   is development that meets the needs of the present without compromis-
   ing the ability of future generations to meet their own needs. It contains
   within it two key concepts: ... the concept of needs, in particular the
   essential needs of the world's poor, to which overriding priority should be
   given; and ... the idea of limitations imposed by the state of technology
   and social organization on the environment's ability to meet present and
   future needs" (15, 37).
7 For a detailed discussion of the effort to put sustainability into a system
   of national accounts, see United Nations, *Handbook of National Accounting:
   Integrated Environmental and Economic Accounting* (New York, 2003).

8 The word "regional" used here replaces "national" in ibid.
9 United Nations et al., "Handbook of National Accounting: Integrated Environmental and Economic Accounting," Final draft submitted for information prior to official editing (New York, 2003), 4.
10 According to the Organisation for Economic Co-operation and Development, "[a]ll forms of capital are more or less substitutes for one another; no regard has to be given to the composition of the stock of capital," *OECD Glossary of Statistical Terms*, available online at http://stats.oecd.org/glossary/detail.asp?ID=6611.
11 J.S. Sachs and A.M. Warner, "Natural Resource Abundance and Economic Growth," NBER Working Paper W5398 (Cambridge, MA: National Bureau of Economic Research, 1995), 2.
12 S. Hussain, I.S. Chaudhry, and S. Malik, "Natural Resource Abundance and Economic Growth in Pakistan," *European Journal of Economics, Finance and Administrative Sciences* 15 (2009): 189.
13 P. Collier, *The Bottom Billion: Why the Poorest Countries Are Failing and What Can Be Done about It* (New York: Oxford University Press, 2007), 38.
14 C.S. Norman, "Rule of Law and the Resource Curse: Abundance versus Intensity," *Environmental and Resource Economics* 43 (2, 2009): 198–207.
15 See C.N. Brunnschweiler and E.H. Bulte, "Linking Natural Resources to Slow Growth and More Conflict," *Science* 320 (5876, 2008): 616–17; and idem, "The Resource Curse Revisited and Revised: A Tale of Paradoxes and Red Herrings," *Journal of Environmental Economics and Management* 55 (3, 2008): 248–64.
16 While we were studying the effect of layoffs in Elliot Lake, we were told by federal and provincial administrators that the suffering of mining communities would be avoided in the future by relying on fly-in miners. The new approach moves a step closer to pure, efficient extraction mining that leaves nothing behind: no people, no buildings, no infrastructure, no development.
17 Ontario, Ministry of Energy and Infrastructure and Ministry of Northern Development, Mines and Forestry, *Places to Grow*, 9.
18 Ibid., 11.
19 The government of Ontario announced the formation of OMICC on 13 November 2003, and appointed the members of OMICC on 26 February 2004.
20 The map is reproduced in D. Robinson, "Ontario's Strategy for the Mineral Industry: Will It Be Right for the North?" INORD Commentary (Sudbury: Laurentian University, Institute of Northern Ontario Research and Development, 2 December 2004); available online at http://inord.laurentian.ca/1_05/OIMICC2.htm.

21 Slack, Bourne, and Gertler argue: "While it is fashionable to pursue economic development strategies for smaller and remote communities that
promote diversification, it should be acknowledged that regionally appropriate activities must form the basis for a sound economic development
effort. For many such communities, these opportunities will continue to
be found in the resource development sector or in tourism"; see E. Slack,
L.S. Bourne, and M.S. Gertler, "Small, Rural and Remote Communities:
The Anatomy of Risk" (paper prepared for the Panel on the Role of
Government in Ontario, Toronto, 2003), 21; available online at http://www.
law-lib.utoronto.ca/investing/reports/rp18.pdf.

22 To be fair, the Growth Plan was presented as a document for further
discussion.

23 Ontario, Ministry of Energy and Infrastructure and Ministry of Northern
Development, Mines and Forestry, *Places to Grow*, 61.

24 As an example, consider the long process of adopting a cluster approach
to industrial development in Canada. The theoretical underpinnings were
in place by 1990. The concepts were part of opposition policy in the early
'90s, and part of government policy by the mid-1990s. Conferences and
workshops were held across the country in the early 2000s, and
by about 2005 the approach had become conventional wisdom. More
than a decade was spent propagating the new understanding within
federal departments.

25 D. Walls, "Internal Colony or Internal Periphery," in *Colonialism in Modern
America: The Appalachian Case*, ed. H. Lewis, L. Johnson, and D. Askins
(Boone, NC: Appalachian Consortium Press, 1978). This is one of several similar papers by Walls that examine the nature of Appalachian
underdevelopment.

26 See, for example, the Resilient Communities Project at the University of
British Columbia, http://www2.arts.ubc.ca/rcp/; the Canadian Centre for
Community Renewal, http://www.cedworks.com/; the Ontario Healthy
Communities Coalition, http://www.ohcc-ccso.ca/; and the J.W. McConnell
Family Foundation, http://www.fondationmcconnell.ca.

27 See D. Robinson and M. Bishop, "The Impact of Layoffs on Municipal
Finances: An Overview," in *Boom Town Blues: Collapse and Revival in
a Single-Industry Town*, ed. A.M. Mawhiney and J. Pitblado (Toronto:
Dundurn Press, 1999).

28 INORD identified this gap in 2004, and has been promoting northern
design capacity by initiating the campaign for a school of architecture in
northern Ontario.

29 Richard Florida is the best-known proponent of amenity and quality of life
as essential elements in development.

30 Slack, Bourne, and Gertler, "Small, Rural and Remote Communities."
31 J.E. Roemer, *A General Theory of Class and Exploitation* (Cambridge, MA: Harvard University Press, 1982).
32 Walls, "Internal Colony or Internal Periphery."
33 See A. Gorz, "Colonialism at Home and Abroad," *Liberation* 16 (6, 1971): 22–9; M. Hechter, *Internal Colonialism and the Celtic Fringe in British National Developments, 1536–1966* (Berkeley: University of California Press, 1975); J. Persky, "The South: A Colony at Home," *Southern Exposure* 1 (summer/fall 1973): 14–22; and L. Webb, "Colonialism and Underdevelopment in Vermont," *Liberation* 16 (6, 1971): 29–33.
34 P. Gonzalez-Casanova, "Internal Colonialism and National Development," in *Studies in Comparative International Development* 1 (4, 1965): 27–37.
35 P. van den Berghe, "Education, Class, and Ethnicity in Southern Peru: Revolutionary Colonialism," in *Education and Colonialism*, ed. P.G. Altbach and G.P. Kelly (New York: Longman, 1978).
36 Walls, "Internal Colony or Internal Periphery."
37 Ibid.
38 E.H. Bulte, R. Damania, and R.T. Deacon, "Resource Abundance, Poverty and Development," ESA Working Paper 04-03 (Rome: United Nations, Food and Agriculture Organization, Agricultural and Development Economics Division, January 2004), 3.
39 R. Torvik, "Natural Resources, Rent Seeking and Welfare," *Journal of Development Economics* 67 (2, 2001): 455–70.
40 R.M. Auty, "The Political Economy of Resource-driven Growth," *European Economic Review* 45 (4, 2001): 839–46. The argument is developed more broadly in Auty, ed., *Resource Abundance and Economic Development* (Oxford: Oxford University Press, 2001).
41 P. Marchak, *Falldown: Forest Policy in British Columbia* (Vancouver: David Suzuki Foundation, 1999).
42 Ontario, Ministry of Energy and Infrastructure and Ministry of Northern Development, Mines and Forestry, *Places to Grow.*
43 See Brunnschweiler and Bulte, "Linking Natural Resources"; idem, "Resource Curse Revisited and Revised"; Collier, *Bottom Billion*; Norman, "Rule of Law and the Resource Curse"; and S.M. Murshed, "When Does Natural Resource Abundance Lead to a Resource Curse?" Environmental Economics Programme Discussion Paper 0401.2004 (London: International Institute for Environment and Development, 2004), available online at http://www.iied.org/pubs/pdfs/9250IIED.pdf.
44 Ontario, Ministry of Energy and Infrastructure and Ministry of Northern Development, Mines and Forestry, *Places to Grow*, 49.

8 Agri-Food Policy in Northern Ontario: Is It Possible to Steward a Local or Regional Agri-Food Economy?

DOUG WEST

Introduction

In geopolitical terms, northern Ontario is at least half as big as Europe; its scattered settler and indigenous populations and its economic history have created issues and concerns quite different from those of other areas of the province. Northern Ontario is really four Norths: the North of cities, the North of small towns, the North of resource extraction, and the North of indigenous peoples. We could add a fifth North, the fictitious one that animates the imagination of southern Ontario: the frozen, inhospitable, wild, and untamed frontier North. Each of these Norths has developed specific policy needs and articulates a relationship with the rest of Ontario, and indeed the rest of Canada, that is minimally heard and largely unnoticed in larger, provincial and national, policy communities. More important in the North, however, is the policy map that brings them all together to be called northern Ontario. Each northern subregion has its own set of voices and advocates, and each has its strengths and weaknesses. There is also a strong tradition of cooperation and conflict among First Nations communities and their non-native allies. This means that, when any resource policy is made, including agri-food policy, indigenous peoples should be at the table so that their interests are heard. Furthermore, rising energy costs and less accessible natural resources have resulted in the development of a crisis economy for many communities in the region. Thus, many communities have banded together to approach Toronto and Ottawa with a single voice. The same is true for the sectors of the northern economy that drive the policy debates that give the North its policy character. The needs of the North are different, isolated from the rest of Ontario, and under different sorts of pressures. Also, while immigration is causing populations in larger metropolitan areas to grow, northern cities and towns are further weakened by out-migration and by negative economic and demographic trends.

In this chapter, I address issues of policy debate, design, and implementation in the agri-food sector in northern Ontario. I attempt an outline of the roles of the provincial and federal governments in developing policy alternatives and the relationships among the federal, provincial, and local governments and interested non-state actors; I focus on both formal organizations and looser structures of policy networks of public sector and community actors. In the process, I reveal the key players and the degree of conflict or congruence over government relations with the agri-food sector in northern Ontario. It becomes clear that a united northern Ontario voice in the agri-food policy sector does not exist; rather, there are subregional studies and movements that have similar aims but are not coordinated. A number of questions help to guide the discussion on the viability of the agri-food sector as a potential economic driver.

- What have been the policy responses to the decline of agricultural activity in northern Ontario? What steps have the Ontario and federal governments taken to encourage the creation and nurturing of new farms and opportunities for new and traditional new farmers?
- What policy options have emerged to encourage and stimulate localized farming activities? Can northern Ontario achieve a degree of sustainable production, processing, and distribution of food following these alternatives?
- What is the "place" or use of agri-food policy among First Nations communities in northern Ontario? Is farming another form of cultural colonialism, and can First Nations communities return to a habitus of "country food"?
- How have the province and northern communities responded to food insecurity? Are there alternatives to food redistribution policies beyond the logic and practice of food banks that will provide a sustainable agri-food structure in the North?

In the agri-food sector many communities are actively pursuing new opportunities that have arisen as a result of their transitioning economies. Ventures such as community-shared agriculture, urban and community gardens, farmers' markets, and food charters that include respect for a reinvigorated farming culture are some of the options that northern agri-food policy makers have chosen. Given the challenges of climate in northern Ontario, which may or may not be changing, hydroponic greenhouses powered by surplus waste heat, biomass peat fuel production, and straw bale construction are now becoming more viable elements of the agri-food sector. There is also a growing movement towards the development of non-timber forest products (blueberries, mushrooms, Canada yew), and eco- and agri-tourism are small glimmers of hope on the northern horizon.[1] It is noteworthy, however, that in 2005 the Northern Ontario Large Urban Mayors Group, the Northwestern Ontario Municipal Association, and the Federation of Northern Ontario Municipalities released a document entitled "Creating Our Future: A New Vision for Northern Ontario" that did not include a single word about the viability of an agri-food sector in the North.[2]

In recent years there has been a concerted effort to measure the capacity of the agri-food sector in the various subregions of northern Ontario. These sponsored studies are a testament to the growing local food movement and concern for the development of an Ontario-wide agri-food context in the face of climbing fuel prices, climate change, and global markets for agri-food products. In the end, northern Ontario can never hope to compete with the southern part of the province in the global market, but steps can be taken to ensure that northern Ontarians have access to sustainable agri-food resources if the goal is to relieve the demand for food that has to travel an enormous distance to reach its consumer destination. At the same time there is pressure on the land and farmers to produce more for the cities, towns, and First Nations communities of the North, to feed the growing numbers of people who are becoming frustrated and worried about the integrity of the system that brings them their daily bread.

In terms of the development of a comprehensive agri-food policy in northern Ontario that actually drives a portion of a new northern economy, a number of points must be made. The recent rapid decline of resource-based industry has resulted in a severe economic downturn in the region – the unemployment rate is already double that of other areas of the province and rising. The North's economy is really many economies tied together through fiscal and regulatory policies that emanate from well-wishing and well-intentioned government officials. The North's economy is also tied to the development of capital flows that emanate from money markets controlled by banking, investment, and insurance institutions around the world. Finally, the North's economy is made by individual and corporate consumers purchasing and selling goods and services in a market atmosphere. Any shift in any of the variables in any economy affects the other variables. Therefore, to speculate about the viability of a local or regional economy, one must determine the interest and willingness of those who maintain and sustain the economy's variables to change their economic and social habits. The findings of the Rosehart Report, an in-depth analysis of the prospects for the development of the economy of northwestern Ontario – commissioned and published by the Ontario government in 2007, well before the current economic malaise that surrounds all policy planners – pays little notice of the agri-food sector, focusing primarily on the traditional drivers: natural resource exploration and retrieval.[3]

Northern Ontario has a history of cooperative ventures between its settler and indigenous populations, beginning with the traditional sharing economies of the First Nations peoples prior to contact, through the political economy of the fur trade, to today's declining resource-based industries. The central component in all cases has been the decided comparative advantage in economic cooperation in the North. Cooperation can take many forms and have many indices: formal economic cooperation that is regulated through shared rules of operation; informal information-sharing cooperation that considers the contextual specificities of individual communities of interest; and cultural and spiritual cooperation that begins with an ethic of respect and that permeates every aspect of economic operations.[4] The idea is to become a participant in one's economy instead of a consumer. Research is needed to describe and analyse this cultural-economic shift at the local and regional levels of the economy. Building a new economy literally from the ground up, based on the principles of sustainability and cooperation, also requires a degree of public re-education.

Northern Ontario: Rural by Nature

Early settlers of northern Ontario were entirely occupied with the taming of the wilderness, and acted as what some call ecological revolutionaries: "transforming woodland into farmland." This idea permeated the psychology of settler populations, who insisted on their "rights to deal roughly with the natural environment."[5] The policies of settler expansion into "unused" lands meant that Ontario became a province of agricultural opportunists, and government policy became focused on expansion and profit through land settlement and export development. Ontario remained a primarily rural province until the early part of the twentieth century; as industrialism and urbanization increased, the agricultural sector was pressed to keep pace with the demands of an increasing population. Since the 1920s Ontario has been the centre · point of immigration to Canada, and most settlers have gone to urban environments. At the same time agricultural policy in Ontario has been largely eclipsed by industrial and social policy, clear evidence of changing patterns of urban colonization.

In the past thirty years the diminishment of rural landscapes has increased as urban centres have sprawled to meet the needs of growing immigrant populations and economic prosperity. In 1981 critics of northern Ontario's lack of a plan to preserve the heritage of its rural consciousness began to put pressure on Queen's Park to identify rural landscapes as a crucial heritage of Ontario's history.[6] Because the province allowed individual municipalities to supervise their own land-use planning, urban cityscapes were beginning to encroach on valuable rural and agricultural landscapes. In the Greater Toronto Area (GTA), farmland was disappearing at an alarming rate – leading to a very public debate over contested green and agricultural spaces that food activists deem crucial to the food sovereignty of the GTA and Ontario in general. The Ontario agricultural heartland is increasingly industrialized and urbanized.

As small farms still comprise the majority of Ontario farm operations, governments have attempted to shore up the farm way of life by continually offering subsidies for training that supplement dwindling farm incomes. Governments are also encouraged to coordinate production techniques and facilitate knowledge transfer within the agricultural sector. The real challenge is to facilitate without directing; those who choose a life in agriculture understand what they need and what they want to share. In 2006 Agriculture and Agri-Food Canada announced the Canadian Farm Families Options Program, giving farm families the opportunity to receive business planning skills training to help them develop their off-farm income potential. The program, which expired in 2008, was one of many that focused on keeping people on the farm while helping them to make ends meet by increasing off-farm skills. The Options Program underscored the situation of most small farms in rural Ontario: to remain on the land, farmers – especially those with limited access to large markets – and their families rely on off-farm income to survive. The challenge in the past thirty years has been to integrate small farms into a food system that is technologically driven and highly differentiated in terms of production methods and

Table 8.1. The Two Faces of Farming – Financial Performance by Revenue Class, Ontario, 2004

Class	Number of Farms	Total Revenue	Total Net Income	Total Government Payments	Total Off-farm Income
		($ millions)			
$10,000–99,999	19,145	737	–52	54	861
$100,000–250,000	7645	1261	171	63	244
$250,000–500,000	5745	1981	334	69	145
$500,000–999,999	2720	1814	276	57	55
$1,000,000–2,499,999	1045	1518	227	31	24
Over $2,500,000	365	1820	213	27	7
Total	36,457	8971.1	1142.3	299.1	1646.6

Source: Statistics Canada, Farm Financial Survey, 2004.

yields, and that focuses on the development of food for export – a policy strategy that essentially distances people from the source of their food and farmers from their markets, and causes agriculture to be more concerned with expansion than sustainability.[7]

The policy environment for agriculture and food production in Ontario is complex, and involves many perspectives and positions. As David Sparling and Pamela Laughland suggest:

No single, all-encompassing policy can address all of the opportunities and challenges facing Ontario farmers today. One important factor to consider in policy development is the difference between small farms and large scale farms. To accelerate growth and competitiveness in Ontario agriculture we must develop policy streams tailored to the different objectives, needs and capabilities of the members of the industry. Some will be policies related to enhancing investment and growth aimed mainly at larger businesses while others will target increasing farm family incomes from all sources and sustaining and promoting rural communities.[8]

There are really two faces of farming in Ontario: as Table 8.1 shows, in 2004 large-scale farms had significantly higher profit margins and were less dependent on off-farm income sources. The difference in activities between large and small producers can be significant. Smaller farming operations are diminishing in number, while larger operations are increasing (Figure 8.1). Some see agricultural consolidation as a natural, market-driven phenomenon, others argue that the diminishment of small farm operations directly relates to the overall export-market-driven policy agenda of the federal and Ontario governments. By far the majority of sustainable farming – that is, farming that provides an income without devastating the natural environment and depleting soil nutrients – takes place below the Great Lakes; farming in the Ontario northland is virtually all small scale. The future of farming and agri-food production in northern Ontario is limited by the capacity of the land itself. Very little of the arable farmland in Ontario is actually located in the northern regions, as Figure 8.2 shows. Still, there is an active effort to reclaim heritage farmland, long since abandoned by modernizing settler populations, that sustained immigrant populations in the nineteenth and early twentieth centuries all over northern Ontario.

It is clear that the face of farming in Ontario and northern Ontario is getting younger as well. More young people than ever are returning to the land, and pressuring local authorities to follow food security and food sovereignty guidelines when purchasing food, educating in classrooms at all levels, and promoting health. In Thunder Bay the Roots to Harvest program, now in its third year, has created awareness among youth and school administrators of the importance of learning about food production and consumption at an early age. Following the lead

Figure 8.1. Farms by Class, Ontario, 1991–2001

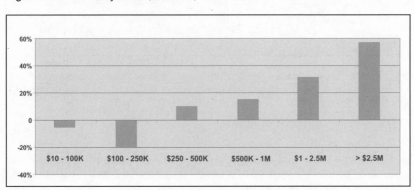

Source: Statistics Canada, Farm Financial Surveys, 1999–2001.

Figure 8.2. Prime Agricultural Lands in Ontario

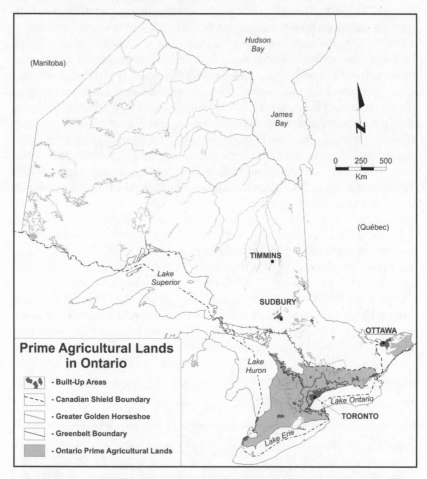

Source: John Turvey and Barb Konyi, "Ontario's Agricultural Policies, Sustainable Urban Communities, and the Greenbelt" (presentation to Post World Planners Congress – Planning for Food Seminar, Vancouver, 21 June 2006).

of school boards in California and other jurisdictions, Roots to Harvest follows a philosophy of education first, action second. Students and youth are thus encouraged to explore various food options on a daily basis, and learn how to create their own gardens. Another example is the Slow Food movement, a food security initiative emanating from Italy that focuses on re-educating consumers about the merits of growing and eating slowly, and on connecting individuals to the ground through gardening, foraging, and cooking workshops.[9]

As long as the policy community for agri-food production is dominated by the will to export, there will be two fundamentally different approaches to farming and farm income (Figure 8.3). It is imperative that the creation of agricultural policy not be dominated by this attitude if the sector is to grow into alternative forms of agri-food production. The public increasingly demands better-quality food readily available from a local source. Ontario has an opportunity to embrace the alternative and organic food movement within already-established policy structures and policy communities. To satisfy consumer demand, the policy environment will have to shift in a more natural way to include the impact of climate change, pesticide and fertilizer use, and even social determinants of health.

Agri-food Policy in Canada and Ontario:
To Export or Localize, to Feed or Profit?

Three major elements of policy form the majority of government interventions in the agriculture sector: market regulations, income stabilization, and grain transportation. The development of regulatory mechanisms for farm production is inextricably linked to the idea that farming is a mainstay of the Ontario economy. Indeed, the highly organized production of wheat, milk, and other important staples began

Figure 8.3. Average Annual Income for Ontario Farms by Source, 2001

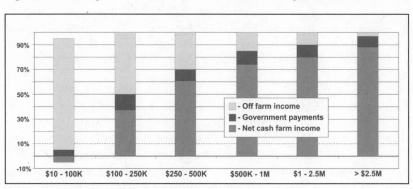

Source: Statistics Canada, Farm Financial Survey, 2001.

as early as the 1920s. Stabilizing agricultural markets was meant to produce a secure income for successful farm operations and to facilitate the more effective monitoring of the health-related elements of food production. This supply-management policy's encouragement of domestic production and administered pricing led to the creation of the Canadian Wheat Board, which was responsible for the management of wheat production for export.

Another important feature of the policy landscape is safety net policy. In 1991 an umbrella statute (the Farm Income Protection Act) created a set of guiding principles for income stabilization programs, including crop insurance, the Net Income Stabilization Account, and province-specific companion programs. Payments under crop insurance are triggered when a producer's yield falls below 70–80 per cent of the farm's average historical yield due to such production risks as drought, flood, hail, frost, excessive moisture, and insects. Province-specific companion programs are intended to complement federal programs by addressing more specific provincial and regional concerns while maintaining market neutrality. This evolution of safety net programs demonstrates the strong commitment to a system that stabilizes income fluctuations without raising incomes to an artificially high level. The aim is to be compatible with the World Trade Organization Agreement on Agriculture and, most important, to avoid a system that distorts producers' decisions.

Other Policy Initiatives

Important policy changes are also being made in other areas. For example, the federal government integrated the food safety and quality assurance activities of several departments into a new, independent Canadian Food Inspection Agency. Its mandate includes recovering a portion of its costs from users of its services. Its aim is more efficient and more effective operations and avoidance of unnecessary costs and activities.

Canada's agri-food economy traditionally has rested on the ability of farmers to produce high-quality, profitable, ready-for-export crops for a demand-driven North American and global market, and over the past thirty years agri-food policy has sought to nurture and improve farmers' ability to increase both yields and profits. Most surviving Ontario farmers now are business experts, well trained in the management of risk, the calculation of cash needs, and the analysis of the whims of a market economy. The so-called Green Revolution in agriculture that followed the Second World War set the tone for agricultural policy in Canada as in other developed nations. Funds were channelled into the development of alternative and innovative technologies for growing crops and producing livestock to feed the rest of the world, although, despite the staggering increase in global food production, much of the world's population is still undernourished.[10] In Canada, the policy direction given by a growth market strategy has led to the consolidation of production efficiencies – agri-food corporations produce foods, of diminishing nutritional value, in factories and supermarkets. It has also led to a reduction in the number of farmers in the agri-food system, due, in part, to quotas and regulation, and to a growing concern over soil degradation and environmental pollution – the "organic" agri-food movement holds a growing piece of the consumer market.

In its review of the federal government's 2003–08 Canadian Agricultural Policy Framework (APF), the principal comprehensive policy complex on agri-food in Canada, an expert panel commented that profitability remains the driving force behind entry into farming and producing practices in Canada. They cautioned, however, that profitability needed to be measured in terms other than financial profit: "other viable measures of success exist, including: a reduction in the need for ad hoc policies and programs; a stable policy environment that will encourage investment and new entrants into agriculture; premiums for Canadian food products in world markets; healthy biological systems in rural areas; and a better understanding of rural-urban issues."[11] This document marked a turn towards seeing agri-food policy in a wider context of issues and potential instruments. The motivation came from the realization that agriculture and food production policies were outwardly focused on export, not inwardly on succession planning in the industry at the farm level, and on food safety issues that caught the public's attention. The 2003 "mad cow disease" scare related to Alberta beef had caused panic among world consumers, especially in Japan and the United States, and governments began to develop policy with greater consideration of the effects of the agri-food environment on health, rural-urban relations, and food security. The APF called for five pillars of cooperation between the agri-food industry and government:

1. food safety and quality, to make Canada the world leader in producing, processing, and distributing safe and reliable food to meet the needs and preferences of consumers;

2. the environment, to help producers as resource stewards, and to respond to consumer demands regarding environmental performance;
3. science and innovation, to support sustainable development and innovation that generates profit, and to instil confidence in food safety and quality;
4. renewal, to help farm families develop skills to succeed in the knowledge-based economy; and
5. business risk management, to encourage producers to be proactive to reduce business risks.[12]

Each pillar was negotiated with the agri-food industry to create an atmosphere in which producers of all sizes could benefit from access to subsidies that would also enhance the sector's public profile. A review of the APF argued that the framework had to look at the agri-food environment as a whole, and support such farm and productions practices as collective marketing and "farmer-supported domestic policies."[13]

In announcing the successor to the APF, Growing Forward, a new multilateral agreement with the provinces, the federal government stated that agricultural productivity would be promoted through financial infrastructure spending under the government's impetus strategy. Ottawa also argued that new policy shifts would produce a "profitable and innovative agriculture, agri-food and agri-based products industry that seizes opportunities in responding to market demands and contributes to the health and well-being of Canadians."[14] This new policy direction, endorsed by all the provinces and territories, currently subsidizes increased costs in the production, transportation, and marketing of food products domestically and at the international level. Growing Forward focuses on the stabilization of the agri-food sector in a volatile economic climate. It remains to be seen if it will stem the tide of farm bankruptcies and the centralization of production that have led some to argue that Canada, like the United States and its successive corporate and export-focused farm bills, has subsidized the wrong end of the food chain at the expense of average Canadians' access to quality agri-food products.[15]

Also missing from the Growing Forward strategy is a commitment to create a comprehensive and national food policy for Canada that includes reference to the growing interest in and expectations related to the social and political movement towards greater food security and food sovereignty, inspired by the failure of the agri-food industry to produce consistently safe and locally produced and preserved food.

Actors in Agri-Food Policy in Northern Ontario

OMAFRA

By far the most significant actor in the development and implementation of agri-food policy in northern Ontario is the Ontario Ministry of Agriculture, Food and Rural Affairs (OMAFRA). A combination of specific policy issues around agricultural production and regulation, food processing and safety, and the general state of rural Ontario guides the overall approach to policy at OMAFRA. Currently its research and policy priorities include climate change, regional development, rural infrastructure, transportation, and rural labour markets, each of which affects northern Ontario, and OMAFRA has been inclusive in its efforts to hear the voices of northerners responding to proposed policy initiatives.

In addition to monitoring the effects of global and national agri-food actions, OMAFRA promotes regional development through connectivity programs such as broadband Internet expansion and improvements to transportation networks. Rapid changes in agriculture and the emergence of "new" agriculture, along with the bio-economy, food for health, and the local food movement, are having a significant impact on the sector, as well as on rural communities. This shift represents a major challenge for policy development that will require comprehensive, integrated (rural, agricultural, and urban) and flexible formation of policy priorities. Little is known about the effect of regional policies and program approaches on rural economies in Ontario, but studies supported by OMAFRA in the various agri-food subregions of northern Ontario suggest a need for stronger infrastructure for production, processing, and distribution for local food systems, and also for more innovative research on the effect of agri-food policy on First Nations.

Agri-Food Canada

Through its recently developed Growing Forward policy principles, Agri-Food Canada has developed its own response to the farm crisis in Canada. The response focuses on connecting farmers to markets, with the understanding that this will balance the goal of increased opportunities for greater expansion into foreign markets with the need to maintain protection for the interests of Canadian farmers and consumers. Growing Forward is, in essence, a stimulus package for the agri-food sector that subsidizes farm incomes, rewards business risk-management practices, and concentrates uncompromisingly on the future of agricultural production at a global level. Growing Forward delivers programs that Canadian farmers use for making business decisions, and is about stability and the future growth of the sector. AgriInvest, AgriStability, AgriRecovery, and AgriInsurance are the first programs available under Growing Forward. These will provide northern Ontario farmers with programs that are simple, responsive, predictable, and bankable. Now that the policy formulation is completed, Ontario and other levels of government are working towards developing and rolling out new programs.

FedNor

Another avenue for federal government involvement in the agri-food sector in northern Ontario is through the Northern Ontario Development Program (NODP) of the Federal Economic Development Initiative in Northern Ontario (FedNor), which promotes economic growth throughout a large and diverse geographic area stretching from the Muskoka Lakes to James Bay and from the Manitoba border to western Quebec. Program contributions are available to support projects in six areas: community economic development, innovation, information and communications technology, trade and tourism, human capital, and business financing. Also, the FedNor International Business Centre is committed to making a positive difference in the global competitiveness of northern Ontario. Working in partnership with community stakeholders and business leaders, the business centre develops and implements key strategies to strengthen links to international markets and promote greater opportunities for Northern Ontario entrepreneurs.

Grain Farmers of Ontario

Grain Farmers of Ontario (GFO) represents Ontario's 28,000 farmers who grow corn, soybeans, and wheat, and its Web site is "designed to provide vital resources to help Ontario's corn, soybean and wheat farmers make daily business decisions."[16] GFO is a merger of three separate producer associations, and its board is empowered to collect licence fees from growers in order to work collectively on their behalf in marketing-related activities. The board is financially self-supporting, and is governed by an elected, fifteen-member board of directors.

Ontario Federation of Agriculture

The Ontario Federation of Agriculture (OFA) is a farmer-led, dynamic, provincial lobby that works to represent the interests of its farm members to government. The "largest voluntary general farm organization in the country, OFA has more than 38,000 members, as well as 32 organizational members and affiliates representing most agricultural commodity groups."[17] Areas they are interested in include: agri-food research, beginning farmer programming, biotechnology, business risk management, farm income, farm labour and safety issues, farm property, food safety, nutrient management, pest management, right to farm, rural economic development, trade, transportation, water issues, and wildlife and wildlife damage.

The OFA has specifically targeted northern agri-food policy by enabling agricultural economic impact studies in Thunder Bay, Rainy River, Manitoulin Island, Sudbury, and New Liskeard. These studies have become a focal point for the regional discussion of the value of farming to local economies. In general, they have come to similar conclusions:

* northern Ontario needs a northern Ontario-first agri-food policy;
* governments at all levels need to recognize the potential for growth in this sector in northern Ontario;
* the role of First Nations communities in policy development must be regarded as essential; and
* agri-food infrastructure development, farm training for youth, increased subsidization of local agri-food operations and small-farm operations, and increased research and development should be accorded higher priority by the Ontario government.

The federation has representatives in all major farming areas of northern Ontario and affiliations with over 35 producer-oriented farming and lobby groups across the North and in the rest of Ontario. A Policy Advisory Council with 104 members maintains the OFA's connections with farmers throughout the province, and examines specific issues in depth, consults with professionals on particular topics, and develops recommendations for the board's consideration.

The Ontario Association of Agricultural Societies

The Ontario Association of Agricultural Societies, through "promotion, communication and educational activities, ... provides leadership to its members."[18] In the North, the association helps to sponsor numerous agricultural fairs in three northern districts. These public fairs help to draw attention to the value of community in farming practice and support as the year's activities are highlighted and promoted. Attendance at these fairs has been on the rise in recent years.

Farmers' Markets

Farmers' markets are organized as an alternative to corporate food, and have become the focal point for public debate about organic and local food production and how to wrestle with the exorbitant cost of fresh produce in the North. In recent years the decline in the number of markets, including in northern Ontario, has reversed, and municipalities are working actively to create space for markets that will allow local farmers to sell their produce. In northern Ontario, nine affiliated farmers' markets "challenge the overwhelming dominance of the food market by super-sized grocery chains, which often force farmers to grow specific styles of food favoured by them."[19]

The Agricultural Research Institute of Ontario

"The Agricultural Research Institute of Ontario, created by legislation in 1962, reports directly to the minister of agriculture, food and rural affairs." Its mandate includes inquiring "into programs of research with respect to agriculture, veterinary medicine and consumer studies; ... select[ing] and recommend[ing] areas of research for the betterment of agriculture, veterinary medicine and consumer studies; and ... stimulat[ing] interest in research as a means of developing in Ontario a high degree of efficiency in the production and marketing of agricultural products."[20] Membership consists of farmers, agribusiness and rural partners, and researchers, reflecting the broadly based nature of Ontario's agri-tech industry. Up to 15 members (plus one *ex officio*) from Agriculture and Agri-Food Canada are appointed by the minister of agriculture, food and rural affairs, who also appoints the director of research from the ministry.

The National Farmers Union in Ontario

The National Farmers Union in Ontario (NFU) "promotes policies that will revitalize agriculture in Ontario by strengthening family farms ... The NFU advocates alternative structures and government policies that resist corporate control of food at the local, national, and international levels. With farmers and consumers, the NFU works to encourage vibrant rural communities, environmentally sustainable practices, and the production of safe, wholesome food."[21]

The Ontario Soil and Crop Improvement Association

The Ontario Soil and Crop Improvement Association (OSCIA), with over 5,000 members, represents most commodity producing groups in Ontario. As a member-defined association, the OSCIA boasts a significant presence in all areas of agriculture. The promotion of careful and planned management of Ontario's agricultural soil is the main thrust of its operation, with sponsored cooperative research into new crops and innovative harvesting a growing concern.

The Christian Farmers Federation of Ontario

"The Christian Farmers Federation of Ontario (CFFO) is an organization with the dual purpose of enabling farmers to work out their Christian faith in their vocation as citizens and developing policy applications of the Christian faith to agriculture. The CFFO regularly develops public policies on major, selected issues affecting Ontario agriculture, and focuses on education/communication."[22]

FoodNet Ontario

FoodNet Ontario is the official Web site of the Ontario Healthy Communities Coalition. There is also the Food Security Workgroup at the Ontario Public Health Association. These electronic networks are designed to provide links among organizations involved in food security in Ontario. The networks also enable members to exchange information with each other about food security programs, policy and research activities, and along with efforts relating to community action and advocacy.

Indigenous Peoples and Food Security/Sovereignty

The position of indigenous peoples in northern Ontario regarding food security is linked specifically to their relationship with the land. In almost all traditional indigenous societies and communities, country food or traditional food was the mainstay of the local economy. With European contact came a new relationship with food, local and imported, a rise in the incidence of health-related nutritional dysfunctions such as diabetes and heart disease, and a concomitant and renewed dependency on imported food and imported medical knowledge. "Modern" food, or food created and processed at a distance, has become the norm in all indigenous communities in northern Ontario. The federal government runs a Food Mail subsidy program that gives indigenous communities increasing access to food that is acceptable under the Canada Food Rule guidelines. This, unfortunately, increases rather than decreases dependence on imported food. The future of food security and food sovereignty in First Nations communities now depends on whether or not indigenous peoples wish to return to the primary consumption of country or traditional food. Dependency on "modern" food will prove hard to break, however, as First Nations struggle on many fronts to deliver services related to basic water, sewage, and energy. In many cases food comes last as a policy area, because it is assumed that the regulatory system in northern Ontario for food protection allows access to safe, sometimes affordable, and sometimes fresh food. Policies and programs are required that not only maintain and improve the availability and accessibility of nutrient-rich, high-quality traditional foods, but also improve income levels and access to affordable, healthy market food choices, and education on methods of preparing market food. In addition, policies and programs need to provide indigenous peoples the infrastructure and education required to maintain, sustain, and develop their traditional food system, while also being sensitive to their custom of sharing.[23]

Food Security, Food Sovereignty, and
Sustainable Agri-Food Systems

In northern Ontario and elsewhere in Canada, critics argue that conservative government policies that protect the interests of corporate agri-food producers do not adequately consider the rights of the consumer.

According to Rod MacRae, a leading visionary in the movement to establish a more secure and locally driven food system,

a comprehensive food policy would create a food system in which:

- Everyone has enough food (quality and quantity) to be healthy;
- Food production, processing, and consumption are suited to the environmental, economic, technological, and cultural needs, potentials, and limits of the various regions of Canada;
- The food system is seen as providing an essential service, and food supply and quality are dependable, and they not threatened by social, political, economic, or environmental changes;
- Food is safe for those who produce, work with, and eat it, and it's safe for the environment;
- Resources (energy, water, soil, genetic resources, forests, fish, wildlife) are used efficiently (in an ecological sense) and without waste;
- The resources of the food system are distributed in a way that ensures that those who perform the most essential tasks have a decent income (in particular, people in rural communities have enough work and income to maintain or improve their life and to care for the rural environment);
- The system is flexible enough to allow people to improve and adapt it to changing conditions;
- Everyone who wants to be involved in determining how the food system works has a chance to participate;
- Opportunities are available in the food system for creative and fulfilling work and social interaction; and
- Our food system allows other countries to develop food systems that express similar values. [24]

Food security is a complex issue that necessitates coordinated networks across a broad span of policy communities, as well as cooperation among community service providers, government, and the private sector. Canada recognized the importance of food security by voting, in April 2005, in favour the "right to food resolution" of the UN Commission on Human Rights, an update of the earlier Rome Declaration on World Food Security.

A 2005 survey revealed that an estimated 3.7 million Canadians (14.7 per cent of the population) experienced food insecurity in the previous twelve months.[25] Moreover, the use of food banks continues to rise throughout Canada.[26] Development of indicators of a healthy nutrition environment and approaches to enhancing food localism (both purchasing and production) could help to counter the increasing vulnerability to food insecurity among Canadians who rely on a weakened social safety net as their main source of support. This could be achieved by developing community gardens and scaling up local sustainable food production, solving challenges in short-growing season climates, saving seed to protect local and native diversity, monitoring climate change, and maintaining and protecting traditional food sources.

Food insecurity negatively affects nutritional and physical health. There are strong associations between food insecurity and self-reported poor physical health, poor functional health, multiple chronic conditions, heart disease, diabetes, and high blood pressure. The effects of hunger are not limited to nutritional and physical health risks, as strong associations between food insecurity and depression, distress, and social isolation are evident.[27] Further, studies have noted the effects of food insecurity on one's sense of self-worth, mental health, and learning and education performance.[28] Several studies have demonstrated that hungry children are at risk of not being able to concentrate and thus of having difficulty learning, which becomes apparent in lower test scores and greater odds of repeating a grade.[29]

Ideas of food security and food sovereignty are based on developing a food system that considers a variety of factors connected to the well-being of individuals, communities, and the environment. In designing a policy that includes food security as a central feature, it is imperative that policy makers listen to and learn from the elements of the food system that are integral to the overall health of the community in a sustainable way. The Six Pillars of Food Sovereignty, developed in 2007,[30] include focusing on food for people, not for export. Food sovereignty requires that producers understand that they are intimately connected to consumers, and that access to food is a legal right. As well, food sovereignty recognizes the value of food producers as workers, families, migrants, and integral members of our communities. There is, therefore, a concomitant right to produce food. Food sovereignty means the cultivation of locovores — people who commit themselves to eating local food. Thus, the food system, by demand, focuses on providing food to the people around it and living in and through it. The food system becomes an integral part of the sustained political system. The politicization of the food system leads to more effective place-based policy alternatives that an attentive public can create and supervise. This aligns food sovereignty with local environmental practice, as well as promoting species diversity. Finally, food sovereignty logically implies the need to share knowledge, as opposed to privileging it. Under this rubric, policy development would honour nature, as opposed to exploiting it, and make the natural environment a component of personal sovereignty. The political resilience of food sovereign communities would be phenomenal, as food production would become the centrepiece for community planning mechanisms, and care for food safety would lead to care for water purity, a cautionary outside investment strategy, better school curricula that are also locally based, and so on.

Many groups in northern Ontario are working to realize a more food secure region. These include food bank associations, food action groups, and health and education officials who see the benefits of local food translating into a healthier community and economy. Their influence in policy development is local and significant; those that are grassroots movements and organizations can influence people's choices on the ground, so to speak. Their efforts are focused on developing food system analysis tools that are accessible to the average consumer, and they follow the mantra of Michael Pollan, the author of the widely read *The Omnivore's Dilemma*, who cautioned people to "eat with full consciousness of what is going into my mouth."[31] The influence of these groups on developing long-term comprehensive agri-food policy in and for northern Ontario, however, remains to be seen. Through collectives like FoodNet Ontario, Dieticians of Ontario, the Ontario Association of Food Banks, and the Ontario Federation of Agriculture, the policy voices of northerners might be heard more often, but it is still a government agency that is the prime driver of agri-food policy in northern Ontario.

In terms of policy development, food security and food sovereignty provide a nexus for issues that range from food safety to land use. As a result, the potential policy areas that affect these complex questions include food and farm regulatory policy, tax policy, land use strategic planning, food marketing boards, transportation policy, health policy, regional and municipal planning, resource policy, environmental policy, climate change, and many others. Agri-food policy development and implementation thus becomes a severely "wicked" policy problem, with multiple layers of potential policy involvement. The expansion of the policy community in this regard is so exponential that it might prove impossible to create a comprehensive set of agri- food policies. Moreover, given the international pressure to combat the effects of environmental degradation through climate change, land use, and so on, the formulation of local, provincial, and international agri-food policies is pressured by a global movement towards land reform and increased production at the same time as a peak-oil global food crisis. In both the short and the long run, agri-food policies will be largely local in nature, focusing on the immediate food needs of populations, and limited to transforming local food systems by probably less than 10 per cent of their operational capacities. In this sense food security and food sovereignty are really global policy problems that involve trans-boundaried policy sectors and trans-national actors whose impact on our daily food intake is staggering.

Conclusion: Developing a Local Agri-food Policy for Northern Ontario

> Out-migration rates of youth in North-western Ontario range from 13.7 per cent to 19.7 per cent. Further, between 2000 and 2006, this was the only region in Ontario to experience a decline in employment, losing 6,100 jobs (−5.5 per cent). This situation has deteriorated even further in the last year. Meanwhile, we import the majority of our food and (often low quality) household items, typically, through foreign-owned box store chains that usually provide low wages and little "skills training." We need to retain [and retrain] our young workers, creating a more robust local culture and economy by shifting our reliance to locally produced food and the manufacture of high quality heritage products made from locally sourced, value-added materials.
>
> – William Wilson[32]

In northern Ontario, the agri-food sector accounts for approximately $40 million in gross revenue for the region, an amount that, on the surface, pales in comparison with forestry and mining, the mainstays of the traditional northern economy. Add the fast-growing services sector, however, and a different story could emerge. If agri-food was viewed as a service provision to northern residents — if, in other words, policies encouraged northerners to feed themselves as much as possible — the contribution of the agri-food sector to the northern Ontario economy could take a potentially interesting shape. Combined with a general policy direction in governance and government-to-government relations with First Nations, then perhaps the northern economy, by feeding itself, could help relieve the stress of food insecurity and poverty in First Nations communities.

Reports of various kinds have made small, yet significant suggestions concerning the agri-food sector in northern Ontario. The encouragement of biomass fuel production and the recognition that the agri-food sector could be a significant component of northern economic self-sufficiency and sustainability are the focal points around which the Rosehart Report, for example, made recommendations for the future of the region's economic development.[33] In the northeast, agricultural feasibility studies in the Manitoulin-Sudbury-North Bay corridor and in the Cochrane and Parry Sound regions have shown the viability of a locally driven agri-food sector that grows food not for export but as an alternative to excessive and costly food imports. Community-supported agriculture, an important organic alternative to corporate agri-food in southern Ontario, is growing in popularity in the North, as are the numbers of food charters, of health authorities who are advocating a better diet for northerners and linking it to long-term health, and of advocates for community-run gardens and farmers' markets.

The pressure that is being put on northern Ontario's pockets of agri-food production could lead to one of two outcomes. It could cause a growth in the number of reclaimed homestead farmlands, now abandoned due to generational off-farm and regional out-migration. Such growth, however, would need special policy consideration from local and provincial policy actors. The other outcome could be the collapse of northern Ontario's fledgling local agri-food industry under the weight of increased expectations and obligations, and the continuing development of the factory-focused agri-food sector that people would like to avoid.

NOTES

1 See Ontario Forest Research Institute, "Non-timber Forest Products in Ontario: An Overview," Forest Research Information Paper 145 (Toronto: Queen's Printer for Ontario, 1999), available online at http://www.mnr.gov.on.ca/en/Business/OFRI/Publication/279239.html.

2 Northern Ontario Large Urban Mayors, Northwestern Ontario Municipal Association, and Federation of Northern Ontario Municipalities, "Creating Our Future: A New Vision for Northern Ontario" (n.p., 2005), i; available online at http://www.city.greatersudbury.on.ca/content/div_mayor/documents/CreatingOurFuture_march29-05.pdf.

3 R. Rosehart, *Northwestern Ontario: Preparing for Change*, Northwestern
   Ontario Economic Facilitator Report (n.p., 2008), available online at http://
   www.mndm.gov.on.ca/nordev/documents/noef/REPORT_FEB2008.
4 B. McKibben, *Deep Economy: The Wealth of Communities and the Durable
   Future* (New York: Columbia University Press, 2007). See also W. Berry,
   "The Idea of a Local Economy" (Santa Rosa, CA: Post Carbon Institute,
   2001), available online at http://www.orionmagazine.org/index.php/
   article/299/.
5 J.D. Wood, *Making Ontario: Agricultural Colonization and Landscape
   Re-creation before the Railway* (Montreal; Kingston, ON: McGill-Queen's
   University Press, 2000), 6.
6 R. Brown, "Saving Rural Ontario: Planning for the Preservation of
   Ontario's Countryside Landscape," Occasional Paper 6 (Toronto: Ryerson
   Polytechnical Institute, Department of Urban and Regional Planning,
   1981).
7 D. Sparling, "'Options' to Fix Farm Income in Ontario?" *Ontario Farmer*,
   19 September 2006, A7.
8 D. Sparling and P. Laughland, "The Two Faces of Farming" (Guelph, ON:
   Institute of Agri-Food Policy Innovation, 2006), 1.
9 M. Pollan, *The Omnivore's Dilemma* (New York: Basic Books, 2005).
10 Canada, Department of Agriculture and Agri-Food, "The Agricultural
   Policy Framework - A New Departmental Approach to Sustainable
   Development" (Ottawa, 2005), available online at http://www4.agr.gc.ca/
   AAFC-AAC/display-afficher.do?id=133614774268&lang=end.
11 APF Framework Review Panel, "Assessing Progress: Agricultural Policy
   Framework Review Panel Policy Report" (Ottawa, 2006), 18.
12 Ibid., 24.
13 Ibid., 20.
14 Canada, Agriculture Canada and Agri-Food Canada, "Governments
   announce completion of the *Growing Forward* multilateral framework,"
   press release (Quebec City, 11 July 2008), available online at http://www.
   agr.gc.ca/cb/index_e.php?s1=n&s2=2008&page=n80711.
15 Mustafa Koc et al., eds., *For Hunger-Proof Cities: Sustainable Urban Food ·
   Systems* (Ottawa: International Development Research Centre, 1999).
16 See the Grain Farmers of Ontario Web site at http://www.gfo.ca/.
17 See the Ontario Federation of Agriculture Web site at http://www.ofa.
   on.ca/.
18 See the Ontario Association of Agricultural Societies Web site at http://
   www.ontariofairs.org/cms/index.php.

19 See the Farmers' Markets Ontario Web site at http://www.farmersmarkets-ontario.com/.
20 See the Agricultural Research Institute of Ontario Web site at http://www.omafra.gov.on.ca/english/research/ario/institute.htm.
21 See the National Farmers Union – Ontario Web site at http://www.nfuontario.ca/.
22 See the Christian Farmers Federation of Ontario Web site at http://www.christianfarmers.org.
23 See Ryerson University, Centre for Studies in Food Security, "Indigenous Food Security," available online at http://www.ryerson.ca/foodsecurity/projects/indigenous/index.html.
24 R. MacRae, "Policy Failure in the Canadian Food System," in Koc et al., *For Hunger-Proof Cities*, 187–8.
25 I. Ledrou and J. Gervais, "Food Insecurity," *Health Reports* 16 (3, 2005): 47–50.
26 Canadian Association of Food Banks, "Hunger Count 2005: Time For Action" (Ottawa, 2005).
27 J. Che and J. Chen, "Food Insecurity in Canadian Households," *Health Reports* 12 (4, 2001): 11–22.
28 L. Caledron and L. Gorence, "Food Center Participants' Nutrition Knowledge and Self-perceived Quality of Diet," *Nutrition Research* 18 (3, 1998): 457–63.
29 K. Alaimo, C. Olson, and E. Frongillo, "Food Insufficiency and American School-aged Children's Cognitive, Academic, and Psychosocial Development," *Pediatrics* 108 (1, 2001): 44–53.
30 Personal correspondence with K. Kneen, Executive Director, Food Secure Canada, 9 October 2009.
31 Pollan, "Foreword," in *Omnivore's Dilemma*.
32 W. Wilson et al., "Good Life Alliance" (application to the Social Sciences and Humanities Research Council of Canada, 2009), 3.
33 Rosehart, *Northwestern Ontario*.

9 The Forgotten Industry in the Forgotten North: Tourism Developments in Northern Ontario

RHONDA L.P. KOSTER AND RAYNALD HARVEY LEMELIN

Introduction

With the exception of some farming areas around Thunder Bay, the Rainy River district, and within the Clay Belt near Timiskaming, northern Ontario can be best characterized as a landscape featuring the Canadian Shield and the Hudson Bay lowlands. It is a largely sparsely populated rural region containing vast tracts of wildlands. Most of the population is concentrated in major urban centres such as Thunder Bay, Sault Ste Marie, Sudbury, North Bay, and Timmins, with the remainder in First Nations and smaller non-Aboriginal communities, the latter mostly dependent upon primary resource-extractive industries such as mining and forestry.[1]

In this chapter we define northern Ontario as the geographic area extending from the French River-Lake Nipissing north to the shores of James Bay and Hudson Bay, and from the Manitoba border in the west to the Quebec border in the east (Figure 9.1). We can further define the region as composed of several political districts: (from west to east) Kenora – that is, north of the 50th parallel, including the Hudson Bay lowlands – Rainy River, Thunder Bay, Cochrane, Sudbury, the single-tier municipality of Greater Sudbury, Nipissing, Timiskaming, Algoma, and Manitoulin Island. Although they were considered part of Ontario's northern frontier during the nineteenth century, we exclude the Muskoka and Parry Sound districts from the discussion. The entire region is more or less accessible, the Near North by road or rail and the Far North by air or seasonal transportation routes (waterways and winter roads).

Figure 9.1

Much has been written about the development of northern Ontario and the associated trapping, forestry, mining, and other extractive activities, as well as transport and hydro-electric development, agricultural settlement, and the new economy (knowledge and technology).[2] Very little research, however, has focused on tourism and recreational initiatives, mostly emphasizing the obstacles to tourism,[3] but also bemoaning the absence of unique tourist attractions.[4] In the forgotten North,[5] tourism is often overlooked, maligned, and disregarded.[6] Yet "gentleman anglers" were visiting the area (the Nipigon River) in the nineteenth century, while steamships, trains, and, later, floatplanes brought in visitors, fishers, and hunters through the twentieth century. The completion of the two routes of the Trans-Canada Highway through northern Ontario in the early 1960s was followed by the establishment of a number of protected areas and provincial parks along these new travel corridors.

Today there are numerous opportunities for recreation and tourism in the region, including historic canoe routes, waterways, and Canadian Heritage Rivers, and a number of popular protected areas, including Killarney, Lady-Evelyn Smoothwater, Quetico, and the newly established Lake Superior National Marine Conservation Area. More recent initiatives aimed at promoting tourism in the region include the proposed Pimachiowin World Heritage Site, a trans-provincial World Heritage Site in western Ontario and eastern Manitoba, and the establishment of various cottage developments in the Kenora and Manitoulin districts. In addition, a long and continuing history of independent hunting and fishing outfitters is spread throughout the entire region. These many attractions and attributes constitute a significant economic contribution to the regional economy of northern Ontario.

Despite the opportunities for more intensive tourism development, the region's tourism potential remains embryonic. Instead, the area continues to promote and support extractive industries, with relatively limited emphasis on economic diversification. The purpose of this chapter is to examine why tourism has been a forgotten industry in northern Ontario, through a lens we term the Community Economic Development for Rural Tourism Opportunities (CED 4 RTOs) framework. We use the framework to understand and highlight tourism developments in peripheral rural communities – regions with unique characteristics that offer both tremendous opportunity and challenges to the development of tourism. The CED 4 RTOs framework is grounded on the premise that a stronger infrastructure of community networks and governance, providing the adaptive and absorptive capacity for innovative policies of economic diversification, is necessary for tourism development and planning.

We begin by providing an overview of tourism and its small but significant economic contribution to northern Ontario. We then present the theoretical basis for our CED 4 RTOs framework, which we subsequently use to provide a broad analysis of the tourism industry in the region. We illustrate how the framework can help to identify both the challenges and opportunities for tourism development, through an examination of the tourism potential the Lake Superior National Marine Conservation Area offers for the communities of the region.

Tourism in Northern Ontario

Resources-based tourism attractions provide a wide range of unique recreational opportunities to visitors to northern Ontario. These include both consumptive (such as hunting and fishing) and non-consumptive (such as canoeing) activities in a diversity of settings. Resources-based tourism can generate considerable revenue for tourist operators. It has been estimated that, in 2000, for example, "approximately 600,000 tourist nights generated over $114 million ... for operators of non-road accessible tourist sites in northern Ontario."[7] These activities are especially sought when they are complemented by remoteness, something northern Ontario has in abundance, but which is not necessarily recognized as a tourism asset. Yet remoteness is one of the most important attributes of the resources-based tourism industry, whose clients seek a range of psychological benefits, such as solitude and escape, from a trip. Remoteness, or at least the absence of roads, also assists in shielding fish and wildlife populations from most recreational hunters and anglers, while the greater abundance of fish and game in remote areas makes it easier for tourism operators to attract guests who presumably are willing to pay a premium for accessing such sites.[8]

Regional statistics on visits are difficult to come by, but a number of reports on visitation patterns in Ontario as a whole have been analysed at the regional level.[9] In 2004–05, for example, a total of 3.7 million people visited northern Ontario, but this was only about 15 per cent of Ontario's total visits. Visitors from the United States make up the bulk of the total for outdoor and pleasure tourism purposes, while visitors from elsewhere in Ontario and the rest of Canada comprise the bulk of those visiting for cultural, business, and convention purposes. Combined visitation data for person-visits to national parks, national historic sites (see Table 9.1), and provincial parks (Table 9.2) indicate that these destinations attracted more than 1.7 million visitors in the 2007–08 season. What the data do not illustrate, however, are the employment opportunities and regional economic impact associated with these protected areas. Yet tourism remains "underdeveloped, underfunded ... and undervalued" in the region,[10] despite studies identifying constraints and obstacles associated with the tourism industry, the most recent being the Ontario government's 2009 report, *Places to Grow – Better Choices, Brighter Future: Proposed Growth Plan for Northern Ontario.*[11]

Table 9.1. Visitors to National Parks and National Historic Sites, Northern Ontario, 2007–08

Sites Managed by/with Parks Canada	Number of Person-Visits
National Parks in Northern Ontario	
Pukaskwa	6,994
National Historic Sites in Northern Ontario	
Fort St Joseph	4,115
Kay-Nah-Chi-Wah-Nung* The Place of the Long Rapids	
Sault Ste Marie Canal	231,529
Total	*242,638*

*Administered by the Rainy River First Nations.
Source: Ontario, Ontario Parks, "Ontario Provincial Parks Statistics, 2008" (Peterborough, ON: Ministry of Natural Resources, 2008), available online at http://www.ontarioparks.com/statistics/2008_park_statistics.pdf.

Table 9.2. Visitors to Selected Provincial Parks, Northern Ontario, 2007–08

Provincial Park, Northeast Zone	Total Visitors	Provincial Park, Northwest Zone	Total Visitors
Lake Superior	122,864	Kakebaka Falls	283,213
Killarney	104,416	Quetico	92,758
Halfway Lake	70,495	Sleeping Giant	57,721
Pancake Bay	69,277	Rushing	56,214
Samuel de Champlain	55,473	Blue Lake	39,859
Total from selected northeast provincial parks	352,020	Total from selected northwest provincial parks	188,831
Total visitors to northeast zone	796,594	Total visitors to northwest zone	694,295

Note: Total visitors includes day-use, camper nights, and interior camper nights.
Source: Ontario, Ontario Parks, "Ontario Provincial Parks Statistics, 2008" (Peterborough, ON: Ministry of Natural Resources, 2008), available online at http://www.ontarioparks.com/statistics/2008_park_statistics.pdfhttp://www.ontarioparks.com/statistics/2008_park_statistics.pdf.

A Conceptual Framework for Understanding
Tourism in Peripheral Regions

Peripheral regions, like the forgotten North, can be defined as those located a substantive distance, both geographically and politically, from centres of major urban populations. Northern Ontario is both geographically and politically remote, having less than 10 per cent of the province's population, and more than 80 per cent of the landmass.[12] Much has been written on the resources-based history of the North, but within that literature tourism remains a forgotten industry – both for what it has contributed historically to the economy and for its capability for diversifying the region.

Among the challenges of tourism for peripheral and largely rural regions are remoteness from travel markets; lack of infrastructure; lack of economic and political control over major decisions; weak internal economic links; selective depopulation and aging societies; lack of access to human and economic capital; lack of innovation; lack of interventions by the national government; and lack of access to information.[13] These issues are often further exacerbated by distrust, lack of knowledge, lack of human capital, and governance issues. Moreover, the spatial separation of many remote tourism enterprises acts as an obstacle to successful development.[14]

In the past decade, tourism has become one of the economic diversification options often sought in peripheral regions that have been largely dependent on single resources-based industries, as those industries suffer tremendous change due to globalizing forces beyond the local community's control. One approach to diversification is community economic development (CED), which includes economic initiatives but also reaches beyond pure economic development to grasp social and environmental attributes.[15] Development strategies under CED tend to be driven from within the community from the idea through to its completion. The use of outside expertise or funding is not excluded, but these tools are sought out by the community members.[16] As a result, CED practice has led to a variety of development strategies, including tourism. Community-based tourism has its foundations in CED inasmuch as it is understood to be a bottom-up approach to tourism planning and development that meaningfully incorporates local individuals in the planning process.[17] The community-based approach is grounded in commonly held values and the transformative power of using the community's values and endogenous knowledge in constructing solutions to local problems.[18] As a result, tourism projects often have greater community support and buy-in from an inclusive list of stakeholders, and can lead to a more diversified and sustainable economy.

Although theories and models are associated with tourism development, there is limited theorization within CED, and what there is does not include any conceptual connection between CED and tourism. R.L. Koster, however, has identified three overlapping theoretical threads – institutional thickness, embeddedness, and governance – that link CED to tourism development.[19] These, along with the concept of leadership, help to identify challenges and opportunities that peripheral regions face in developing their tourism potential, which we graphically represent in Figure 9.2 and which we term a Community Economic Development for Rural Tourism Opportunities (CED 4 RTOs) framework.

Institutional thickness originated in the institutionalist movement in economic geography,[20] referring specifically to urban areas and regions within a globalizing economic environment. The theory is formulated around four factors: 1) a strong and varied institutional presence (including firms, financial institutions, chambers of commerce, economic development agencies, training agencies, economic development

Figure 9.2. A Community Economic Development for Rural Tourism Opportunities Framework

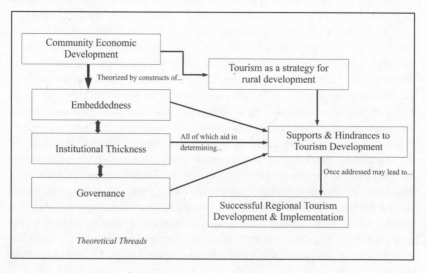

agencies, government agencies, and so on); 2) high levels of interaction among the institutions at the local level; 3) the development of well-defined structures of domination, coalition building, and collective representation to minimize sectionalism and rogue behaviour; and 4) the development of mutual awareness of and involvement in a common agenda. In the context of peripheral tourism, institutional thickness illustrates the importance of the amount and kinds of institutions in a region and how they interact to support tourism development.

Various levels of institutional thickness – community organizations, volunteers, businesses, local government, and regional participation – are identifiable in rural regions and communities, each with a role to play in the development and longevity of tourism.[21] Community organizations include chambers of commerce, credit unions, service groups, churches, other volunteer associations, and local economic development, tourism, and social development committees. These groups are crucial, as they form the basis on which tourism projects are often developed, implemented, and delivered. The level of volunteer commitment is often very high, however, with small numbers of residents often participating in a variety of capacities on numerous boards, leading to volunteer burnout and limits to innovative thinking; it can also result in advancement of individual agendas to the neglect of useful alternate ideas. The willingness and ability of businesses and individuals to work together to support development projects is indicated by the financial support and volunteer time devoted to tourism-related projects.

An important aspect of institutional thickness, as applied to peripheral locations and tourism, is the regional context within which each community operates. Municipal, business, and community leaders must work together to capitalize on the surrounding regional options in economic and community development. Networks, in the context of institutional thickness, are defined as "interconnections," meaning the connections between individual leaders in a region who are willing to exploit their shared needs to benefit the region as a whole, not just an individual community. Such leaders also must capitalize on or develop connections with external expertise and funding opportunities to build the internal capacity of the community to undertake a chosen project.

The second theoretical thread linking CED and tourism is embeddedness,[22] which refers to the fact that individuals' capacity for economic action, including undertaking development, is strongly affected by their social relationships, which also affect the way they

understand the world. There is obvious overlap between embeddedness and institutional thickness, but the connections to the culture of the
local economy go beyond it. Strategies that do not fit in the economic
culture potentially face greater challenges than those that complement
the existing economic order. Within the peripheral tourism context, this
is critically important, as residents of such areas often focus on, and
only fully understand, the economics associated with primary industries such as agriculture, mining, or forestry, while other industries,
such as tourism, are often less well understood or appreciated for their
potential. Embeddedness thus aids in understanding the success of
tourism development proposals and outcomes.

Tourism has strong links with the physical and human attributes
of place, meaning that its success is tied to both the attractions and
the participation of local people. The embeddedness of the industry
therefore is an essential element to the successful development of tourism in a place, and is made up of an understanding of the industry, a
positive attitude, and the inclusion of people in tourism development.
Community members must understand what tourism is, and believe
in its potential for their community. Connected to this is attitude – a
belief and a pride in the community – so that it becomes possible to
market the community in a way that attracts visitors. Embeddedness
in this case refers to what fits the culture, the mind-set of the residents
of the community and the surrounding region. In peripheral areas that
rely primarily on natural resources extraction, tourism is often not an
embedded industry; it is not something people readily understand or
believe money should be invested in. In contrast, resources extraction
and related industries exist in a tangible way in the psyche of peripheral areas.

The third theoretical thread is governance, a concept widely used
in academic and practitioner circles. Its use signifies a concern with
change in both the meaning and the content of government. Stoker
explains the distinction between traditional forms of government and
governance in the following manner:

> Government is used to refer to the formal institutional structure and loca-
> tion of authoritative decision-making in the modern state. The concept
> of governance is wider and directs attention to the distribution of power
> both internal and external to the state. Its focus is on the interdependence
> of governmental and non-governmental forces in meeting economic and
> social challenges. Governance is about governmental and non-governmental

organizations working together. Its concern is with how the challenge of collective action is met and the issues and tensions associated with this shift in the pattern of governing.[23]

The institutional map of local government has been transformed into a system of governance that involves a range of agencies and institutions drawn from the public, private, and voluntary sectors. Research suggests that the utility of the governance perspective is to formulate important questions regarding rural issues. In the context of tourism, the important questions to address concern the actors and institutions involved, the relationships among them, and, especially important, the role of formal governing bodies in supporting CED endeavours.[24] Because CED is understood to be a "bottom-up" strategy, it is important to examine how government policy can and does influence decisions made at a local level. Governance, a key element of our framework, brings together the constructs of institutional thickness and embeddedness in addressing a community's capacity to develop and implement effective tourism. Although all three elements include the idea of partnerships, the inclusion of governance specifically acknowledges the issue of power and its distribution (or lack of), and addresses the challenges that electoral time frames place on these partnerships, as we will discuss.

Governance elements crucial for understanding peripheral tourism development include the influence of central government programs, civic leadership, and partnerships.[25] The central characteristic of CED, as a grassroots, bottom-up approach to development, is challenged at the governance level. Does government encourage certain community responses through the types of programs and grants it offers? Many communities do try to capitalize on available grant programs, and what they undertake is influenced by the government of the time. Associated with this is civic leadership: a development program or project is only as good as the mandate of the elected leadership. Elected officials, however, have a short-term planning horizon that is based on the election cycle. If the council changes, then so can the vision for the community, and the people who deliver plans and services to the community have to "retrain" or renegotiate with the new officials. This reality has repercussions beyond simple mobilization of resources, as it means time is lost in advancing projects.

Another element of governance is the concept of partnerships, which is also connected to institutional thickness; it specifically addresses the types and numbers of committees or organizations – including economic, tourism, and social groups – that develop at arm's length from local government, but that act on behalf of local government to address a specific mandate. It is thus possible that such arm's-length organizations can make decisions and carry out projects within a long-term plan independent of, but supported by, local government. As a result, a town council is freed of some responsibilities, allowing it to focus on other areas. Part of the governance-partnership connection relates to the ways in which different levels of government provide financial (or other) support for community-based projects through various funding programs or relationships.

In addition to the three theoretical threads is the concept of leadership and its relationship to networks.[26] Effective leadership requires that leaders make connections outside their community in order to draw in people and potential industry. Such connections lead to the building of networks among communities, which, as we discuss later, is a significant challenge to the development of tourism in peripheral areas.

These theoretical threads provide a framework for understanding the development of tourism in a peripheral region, but they also point to a number of supports that such a region enjoys and the challenges it faces.[27] Table 9.3 offers a summary of these attributes and their links with the three theoretical threads. Interestingly, in many cases attributes both support and hinder tourism development. These links illustrate that, when tourism developments are chosen that are embedded in the culture of the community, and when the tourism goals are deemed achievable, attitudes are generally more positive and, as a result, the outcome of the development tends to be successful in terms of implementation and longevity. Similarly, a tourism development project or plan is likely to fail if the local government does not cooperate with or support tourism development, or where there is too much reliance on volunteers to undertake tourism planning and development, so that too few institutions are involved. In making this assertion, we are not discounting the success individual tourism businesses have had in peripheral regions; our model is concerned with tourism development and planning at the community and regional levels, not at the level of the individual business

Thus, tourism development in peripheral areas not only has to ensure local control of development, community involvement in planning, an equitable flow of benefits, and the incorporation of resident values, but

Table 9.3. Attributes that Affect Tourism Development and Their Connection to Institutional Thickness, Embeddedness, and Governance

Support for Development	Hindrance to Development	Theoretical Thread Linking Community Economic Development and Tourism
Culture of entitlement	culture of entitlement	embeddedness
	dependence on transfer payments	embeddedness
Attitude	attitude	embeddedness
Achievable goals		embeddedness
Community support	lack of supporting infrastructure for, or understanding of, tourism industry	embeddedness
Place attributes (location and facilities)	place (location and facilities)	institutional thickness
Volunteers and paid staff	volunteerism overlap and lack of paid positions	institutional thickness
Catalyst	catalyst; north–south disconnect	institutional thickness, governance
Town/city council, government	town/city council, government	governance
Government programs and funding	government programs and funding	governance
Role of policies	role of policies	governance
Leadership	leadership	governance

Source: Based on R.L. Koster, "Local Contexts for Community Economic Development Strategies: A Comparison of Rural Saskatchewan and Ontario Communities," in *Geographical Perspectives on Sustainable Rural Change*, ed. D. Winchell, D. Ramsey, R. Koster, and G. Robinson (Brandon, MB: Rural Development Institute, 2010).

also must take into account embeddedness, institutional thickness, and governance. Based on this CED framework for rural tourism development, we now turn to an examination of tourism development in northern Ontario. We suggest that, although tourism has had a long history in this region, the lack of embeddedness, institutional thickness, appropriate governance structures, and strongly networked leaders has meant that tourism is the forgotten industry of the North.

Contemporary Tourism Development:
Tourism Issues in Northern Ontario

Since the 1960s various reports have identified challenges and concerns facing the tourism industry in northern Ontario;[28] these can be contextualized largely within the previously outlined framework – namely:

- embeddedness (lack of innovation; ineffective promotion/marketing; the undervaluation of tourism relative to competing land uses; the fragmentation of the tourism industry);
- institutional thickness (weak internal economic links; access to human and economic capital; limited access to information and financing; low level of participation by First Nations); and
- governance (lack of economic and political control over major decisions; interventions by the central state; restrictive regulations; transportation issues; restrictive land use and lease policies; lack of coordination between government agencies).

The region faces additional challenges in the form of a lack of infrastructure, selective depopulation, and population aging. In the 1990s these concerns were echoed, and new ones noted, in a series of community forums conducted by a regional committee (Tourism Northwest); they found that community awareness and understanding of tourism was an issue (embeddedness), along with the lack of professional training and standards for staff and the need to improve the product base of attractions in the region (institutional thickness).[29]

Despite such frustrations, several attempts have been made to address some of the issues. A 2008 report by the Ontario Tourism Marketing Partnership Corporation outlines some of the roles and responsibilities of destination marketing organizations in the region, largely allowing them to focus on a cascade-marketing approach, whereby marketing information flows from the provincial level down to the local level.[30] Land use policies and regulations for the adventure tourism industry have recently been completed in the form of a resources-based tourism policy developed by a number of stakeholders, including various provincial ministries.[31]

Another unique feature of northern Ontario is that it is made up of districts that do not have a regional government, and therefore do not have an intermediary between the provincial government and the municipalities, as do all other regions of Ontario.[32] This presents a variety of challenges from a governance perspective when it comes to advancing economic diversification strategies, including tourism, because individual communities lack regional organizations to act on their behalf and voice their concerns.

One of the biggest challenges to tourism development in peripheral regions comes from the attitude of residents. Whether it is the creation of Crown game preserves or provincial and national parks and their associated management strategies, protected areas in northern Ontario have always been viewed by some as positive for economic diversification and by others as intrusive management tools.[33] Some of these concerns result from an economy in decline, fear of future erosion of rights and of access to Crown land, potential conflicts with local and non-local use, and distrust of provincial and federal management agencies;[34] many of these challenges point to the importance of well-developed governance structures in the region, based on highly developed networks of actors among the various institutions (institutional thickness), all working within a common context (embeddedness).

Recent research, however,[35] has demonstrated a significant shift in attitude to tourism development among local government, businesses, and recreational users in the region, as evidenced by the establishment of the Lake Superior National Marine Conservation Area along the north shore of Lake Superior. We use this example to illustrate how the CED 4 RTOs framework could help to frame the challenges and opportunities for tourism development, and possibly aid in tourism planning (see Table 9.4).

In a survey by I. Wozniczka, participants indicated increasing recognition of the value tourism brings to the region in terms of economic diversification.[36] Unlike the findings of previous surveys,[37] participants expressed a desire to open the region up to visitors, counting largely on the attractiveness of existing natural (bird watching, hiking, fishing, ice climbing, snowmobiling) and cultural (First Nations) features.[38] Participants recognized the need for infrastructure and facilities development to support the expansion of tourism, and saw such investments as setting the stage for other small businesses and operators in the region.[39] There was also an important recognition that the communities of the region needed to work together, through partnerships and collaboration, to develop the north shore of Lake Superior as a destination region. Recognition does not equal action, though, and this element is still in its infancy.

Table 9.4. Community Economic Development for Rural Tourism Opportunities Framework: Lake Superior National Marine Conservation Area Case Study

Supports for Development	Hindrances to Development	Theoretical Thread Linking Community Economic Development and Tourism
Entitlement	culture of entitlement	embeddedness
Attitude: acknowledgment of and support for the opportunities tourism may provide	attitude: not wanting to "share" natural resources with visitors; concerns about tourism-related developments (crime, crowding)	embeddedness
Achievable goals: development of tourism products based on currently available cultural and natural attributes	unachievable goals: interpretative centres in each community	embeddedness
Community support: commitment to and support for tourism projects	lack of supporting infrastructure for and understanding of tourism industry: lack of service industry knowledge and requirements; limited products	embeddedness
Place attributes (location and facilities): communities well situated with access to conservation area; beginning to develop partnerships to develop products (node specific)	place (location and distance): significant distance from large travelling populations; declining US market; limited products with limited regional connections or participation	institutional thickness
Volunteers and paid staff: each community has an economic development officer with responsibility for tourism	volunteerism overlap and lack of paid positions: overreliance on volunteers	institutional thickness
Catalyst: beginnings of community engagement (Interim Management Board)	catalyst: driven by Parks Canada	institutional thickness

(*Continued*)

Table 9.4. (*Continued*)

Supports for Development	Hindrances to Development	Theoretical Thread Linking Community Economic Development and Tourism
	north-south disjunct: concerns over local control versus "head office" control by Parks Canada in Ottawa	governance
Town/city council, government: representation on Interim Management Board	town/city council, government: lack of investment in tourism infrastructure	governance
Government programs and funding: Parks Canada investments in research and infrastructure; support through funding from various levels of government	government programs and funding	governance
Role of policies: in development through Interim Management Board	role of policies: outside conservation area, policy structure is weak at provincial level	governance
Leadership: strong community voice present on Interim Management Board; economic development officers leading development partnerships to develop tourism regionally	leadership	governance

Source: Based on Koster, "Local Contexts for Community Economic Development Strategies."

The establishment of the Lake Superior National Marine Conservation Area is viewed as a positive development in support of tourism in the region. The hope of northern Ontario residents that its establishment will provide economic benefit is based on the assumption that infrastructure and training will develop capacity and generate employment. Some concerns remain, however, with regard to protected areas management, as residents fear that decision making and economic benefits might not remain in the region, and feel that natural resources should be protected.

Such concerns point to the importance of developing positive governance relationships in the region, and the development of an Interim Management Board for the conservation area is an important step towards this goal. The mandate of the board is to work collaboratively to determine the management and development priorities of the conservation area. The board includes representation from the affected communities (including First Nations) and other stakeholder groups, thus serving multiple functions in terms of developing a strong governance structure, creating new and strengthening current networks among institutions in the region, and developing conservation area and tourism policies that could become embedded in the local culture.

Conclusion

Northern Ontario is rich in natural and cultural heritage. Its rivers, numerous protected areas – including Chapleau, the world's largest game preserve, and Polar Bear Provincial Park, Ontario's largest protected area – and unique wildlife offer much for the visitor. Developed cultural and historic sites include Fort William Historical Park, Kay-Nah-Chi-Wah-Nung, the Sault Ste Marie Canal, and Fort St Joseph. Despite such attributes and the opportunities they present for tourism development, and therefore for economic diversification, tourism in the region remains underdeveloped and undervalued.

Northern Ontario faces challenges from globalization, emigration, lower levels of education compared to the rest of the province, and a continuing dependence on primary-extractive activities such as mining and forestry, the downturn in which has left many communities in the region reeling, as they struggle to identify diversification options. There might be validity to the sense of "northern alienation" that residents feel, where the government located in southern Ontario develops policies that are meant to benefit the entire population of the province but do not address the economic or social needs of those living in the North. A case in point is the passage in 2010 of the provincial Far North Act, which protects 225,000 square kilometres, or 21 per cent of Ontario. The legislation was enacted despite the unified voice of the act's opponents, including the Chamber of Commerce of Ontario, northern communities, and First Nations, who fear the act will hinder economic development in the region.

The solutions to many of the challenges facing northern Ontario communities are local. Sudbury and North Bay illustrate how the new economy hubs in the region can be developed to address local economic concerns through tourism development. Through the development of partnerships, the city of North Bay, for example, has received nearly $1.4 million from FedNor to enhance its waterfront on Lake Nipissing, a project that, along with the creation of local employment opportunities, is also expected to beautify the downtown core and increase local access to the area.[40]

Many communities and individuals continue to benefit from the boom in resources extraction; however, the result of which is a mindset of entitlement to the benefits resulting from that sector. Consequently, economic struggles are often viewed as someone else's – namely, the government's – responsibility, which creates a cycle of dependence. Breaking that cycle will require a new mindset and a shift in philosophy – to one in which resources are used for multiple tasks, Crown land and protected areas are managed within a value-added, instead of a value-deficit, context, and individuals are empowered through a *sense d'appartenance* and of responsibility. Such a new narrative would help to inform decision and policy makers in southern Ontario about the challenges of doing business in northern Ontario. Policy would be transformed policy from a reactive process to an adaptive course of action when tourism becomes embedded in the mindset of all northerners as simply one of many solutions to the challenges the region faces, when institutional thickness and proper governance structures and relationships emerge to create a generative spiral of economic stability for the entire region, and when tourism is no longer forgotten, but respected and appropriately incorporated into regional economic strategies.

The Community Economic Development for Rural Tourism Opportunities framework provides a basis for understanding the challenges of the North and for developing strategies to create diversification and stability. When institutional thickness, embeddedness, and governance attributes are incorporated into the development strategies and relationships, they create a foundation for continuing comprehensive and deliberate action that informs community involvement by various actors and requires relationship building with outside agencies. By drawing on the capacities present in these institutions, communities are able to develop stronger governance structures that can adapt to changes that are exogenously imposed with strategies that are endogenously derived.

NOTES

1 See T.W. Dunk, "Talking about Trees: Environment and Society in Forest
   Workers' Discourse," *Canadian Review of Sociology and Anthropology*
   31 (1, 1994): 14–34; idem, *It's a Working Man's Town: Male Working-Class
   Culture*, 2nd ed. (Montreal; Kingston, ON: McGill-Queen's University
   Press, 2003); C. Southcott. "Single Industry Towns in a Post-Industrial
   Era: Northwestern Ontario as a Case Study" (Thunder Bay, ON: Lakehead
   University, Centre for Northern Studies, 2000); and idem, "Old Economy/
   New Economy Transitions and Shifts in Demographic and Industrial
   Patterns in Northern Ontario" (paper presented to the conference, Old
   Economy Regions in the New Economy, Thunder Bay, ON, 24–25 March
   2006).
2 M. Bray and E. Epp, eds., *A Vast and Magnificent Land* (Sudbury, ON:
   Laurentian University, 1984); Southcott, "Single Industry Towns"; and
   idem, "Old Economy/New Economy Transitions."
3 See M. Johnston and R.J. Payne, "Ecotourism and Regional Transformation
   in Northwestern Ontario," in *Nature-based Tourism in Peripheral Areas:
   Development or Disaster?* ed. C.M. Hall and S. Boyd (Toronto: Channel View
   Publications, 2004).
4 S. Boyd and R.W. Butler, "Definitely not Monkeys or Parrots, Probably
   Deer and Possibly Moose: Opportunities and Realities of Ecotourism in
   Northern Ontario," *Current Issues in Tourism* 2 (2–3, 1999): 123–37; T. Hinch
   and R.W. Butler, "Tourism Development Concerns in Northern and
   Eastern Ontario: A Survey of Professionals," in *Communities, Resources and
   Tourism in the North*, ed. M.E. Johnston and W. Haider (Thunder Bay, ON:
   Lakehead University, Centre for Northern Studies, 1993).
5 K. Coates and W. Morrison, *The Forgotten North: A History of Canada's
   Provincial Norths* (Toronto: Lorimer, 1992).
6 See Ipsos Reid, "Northern Ontario Research: Qualitative Branding
   Assessment," 20 April 2009.
7 L.M. Hunt, H. Wolfgang, P.C. Boxall, and J.A. Englin, "A Method for
   Estimating the Economic Contribution of Resource-based Tourism,"
   Forestry Chronicle 84 (2, 2008): 179.
8 L.M. Hunt, P. Boxall, J. Englin, and H. Wolfgang, "Forest Harvesting,
   Resource-based Tourism, and Remoteness: An Analysis of Northern
   Ontario's Sport Fishing Tourism," *Canadian Journal of Forest Research*
   35 (2, 2005): 401–9.
9 See, for example, Ontario, Ministry of Tourism, "Canadian Travellers
   Who Visited Northern Ontario: A Profile with Marketing Implications"

(Toronto: Queen's Printer for Ontario, 2007), available online at http://www.research.tourism.gov.on.ca; and idem, "Regional Tourism Profiles, 2006, International Travel Statistics (U.S. and Overseas) CD 58: Thunder Bay District" (Toronto: Queen's Printer for Ontario, 2008).

10 See Forrest Marketing + Communications, "NCIR Tourism Inventory, Survey and Gap Analysis – Phase 1," prepared for Northwestern Ontario Regional Tourism Council and Common Voice Northwest (Kakabeka Falls, ON, 2008), 8.

11 Ontario, Ministry of Energy and Infrastructure and Ministry of Northern Development, Mines and Forestry, *Places to Grow – Better Choices, Brighter Future: Proposed Growth Plan for Northern Ontario* ([Toronto]: Queen's Printer for Ontario, 2009). See also Hinch and Butler, "Tourism Development Concerns"; Johnston and Payne, "Ecotourism"; and R.J. Payne, M.E. Johnston, and D.G. Twynam, "Tourism, Sustainability and the Social Milieu in Lake Superior's North Shore and Islands," in *Tourism, Recreation and Sustainability: Linking Culture and Environment,* ed. S.F. McCool and R.N. Moisey (New York: CABI, 2001).

12 C. Southcott, *The North in Numbers: A Demographic Analysis of Social and Economic Change in Northern Ontario* (Thunder Bay, ON: Lakehead University, Centre for Northern Studies, 2006).

13 M. Hall, and S. Boyd, eds., *Nature-based Tourism in Peripheral Areas*; D.K. Müller and R. Pettersson, "Access to Sami Tourism in Northern Sweden," *Scandinavian Journal of Hospitality and Tourism* 1 (1, 2001): 5–18; and D.K. Müller and B. Jannson, eds., *Tourism in Peripheries* (New York: CABI, 2007).

14 Boyd and Butler, "Definitely not Monkeys or Parrots."

15 See D. Douglas, "Community Economic Development in Rural Canada," *Plan Canada,* 29 (2, 1989): 28–46; S. Perry and M. Lewis, *Reinventing the Local Economy: What 10 Canadian Initiatives Can Teach Us about Building Creative, Inclusive, and Sustainable Communities* (Vernon, BC: Centre for Community Enterprise, 1994); and J. Lotz, *The Lichen Factor: The Quest for Community Development in Canada* (Sydney, NS: UCCB Press, 1998).

16 See B. Ashton, "Community Readiness: Assumptions, Necessities and Destiny," in *Reshaping the Countryside: Perceptions and Processes of Rural Change,* ed. N. Walford, J. Everitt, and D. Napton (New York: CABI, 1999); C. Bryant, "Community Development and Changing Rural Employment in Canada," in *Contemporary Rural Systems in Transitions,* vol. II, *Economy and Society,* ed. I. Bowler, C. Bryant, and M. Nellis (London: CABI International, 1992); Douglas, "Community Economic Development in Rural Canada"; F. Dykeman, "Developing an Understanding of Entrepreneurial and Sustainable Rural Communities," in *Entrepreneurial and Sustainable Rural Communities,* ed. F. Dykeman (Sackville, NB:

Mount Allison University, Rural and Small Town Research and Studies Programme, 1990); A. Gill, "Competitive Tensions in Community Tourism Development," in Walford, Everitt, and Napton, *Reshaping the Countryside*; and D. Voth, "Evaluation for Community Development," in *Community Development in Perspective*, ed. J. Christenson and J. Robinson (Ames: Iowa State University, 1989).

17 See S. Beeton, "The Case Study in Tourism Research: A Multi-method Case Study Approach," in *Tourism Research Methods*, ed. B. Ritchie, P. Burns, and C. Palmer (Cambridge, MA: CABI Publishing, 2005); K. Blackstock, "A Critical Look at Community Based Tourism," *Community Development Journal* 40 (1, 2005): 39–49; M.C. Hall, *Tourism Planning: Policies, Processes, and Relationships* (Englewood Cliffs, NJ: Prentice Hall, 2000); P. Murphy, *Tourism: A Community Approach* (New York: Methuen, 1985); D. Reid, *Tourism, Globalization and Development: Responsible Tourism Planning* (London: Pluto Press, 2003); and C. Tosun, "Expected Nature of Community Participation in Tourism Development," *Tourism Management* 27 (3, 2006): 493–504.

18 G.H. Stankey, S.F. McCool, R.N. Clark, and P.J. Brown, "Institutional and Organizational Challenges to Managing Natural Resources for Recreation: A Social Learning Model," in *Leisure Studies: Prospects for the Twenty-first Century*, ed. E.L. Jackson and T.L. Burton (State College, PA: Venture Publishing, 1999).

19 R.L. Koster, "Mural-based Tourism as a Strategy for Rural Community Economic Development," in *Advances in Culture, Tourism, and Hospitality Research*, ed. A. Woodside (Boston: Emerald Group, 2008).

20 For further discussion on this theory, see A. Amin, "Moving On: Institutionalism in Economic Geography," *Environment and Planning* 33 (4, 2001): 1237–41; A. Amin and N. Thrift, "Globalization, Institutional Thickness and the Local Economy," in *Managing Cities: The New Urban Context*, ed. P. Healey et al. (Chichester, UK: John Wiley and Sons, 1995).

21 Koster, "Mural-based tourism."

22 G. Day, "Working with the Grain? Towards Sustainable Rural and Community Development," *Journal of Rural Studies* 14 (1, 1998): 89–105; M. Granovetter, "Economic Action and Social Structure: The Problem of Embeddedness," *American Journal of Sociology* 91 (3, 1985): 481–510; and A. Sayer and R. Walker, *The New Social Economy: Reworking the Division of Labour* (Oxford: Blackwell, 1992).

23 G. Stoker, "Public-Private Partnerships and Urban Governance," in *Partners in Urban Governance: European and American Experience*, ed. G. Stoker (London: Macmillan, 1997), 10; emphasis added.

24 Ibid.

25 Koster, "Mural-based tourism."
26 Ibid.; and idem, "Local Contexts for Community Economic Development
    Strategies: A Comparison of Rural Saskatchewan and Ontario
    Communities," in *Geographical Perspectives on Sustainable Rural Change*,
    ed. D. Winchell, D. Ramsey, R. Koster, and G. Robinson (Brandon, MB:
    Rural Development Institute, 2010).
27 Koster, "Local Contexts."
28 In particular, see Hinch and Butler, "Tourism Development Concerns."
    See also Forrest Marketing + Communications, "NCIR Tourism Inventory";
    R. Maddock and E. Dickson, "Tourism Northwest: A Regional Tourism
    Development Framework," in *Shaping Tomorrow's North: The Role of Tourism
    and Recreation*, ed. M.E. Johnston, D. Twynam, and W. Haider (Thunder
    Bay, ON: Lakehead University, Centre for Northern Studies, 1998);
    R. Rosehart, *Northwestern Ontario: Preparing for Change*, Northwestern
    Ontario Economic Facilitator Report (n.p., 2008), available online at http://
    www.mndm.gov.on.ca/nordev/documents/noef/REPORT_FEB2008; and
    M. Westlake and Forrest Marketing + Communications, "North of Superior
    Tourism Association Strategic Business and Marketing Plan 2009–2011,"
    prepared for North of Superior Tourism Association (2008).
29 Maddock and Dickson, "Tourism Northwest."
30 Forrest Marketing + Communications, "NCIR Tourism Inventory."
31 Ontario, Ministry of Natural Resources, "Resource Based Tourism
    Policy" (Toronto, n.d.), available online at http://www.mnr.gov.on.ca/
    stdprodconsume/groups/lr/@mnr/@forests/documents/document/197111.
    pdf .
32 Southcott, *North in Numbers*.
33 J. Cartwright, "Environmental Groups, Ontario's Lands for Life Process
    and the Forest Accord," *Environmental Politics* 12 (2, 2003): 115–32;
    P. Cormier, H. Pelletier, H. Lemelin, R. Koster, and K. Metansinine,
    "Foresight through Hindsight: The Establishment of the Lake Superior
    National Marine Conservation Area in Northern Ontario, a Decade in
    Overview" (presented to *Canadian Parks for Tomorrow: 40th Anniversary
    Conference*, Calgary, 2008); R.H. Lemelin, "Understanding Mukadae
    Makwa (Black Bear): Black Bear-Human Interactions in Northwestern
    Ontario," in *Transitions in Marginal Zones in the Age of Globalization: Case
    Studies from the North and South*, ed. T. Dunk (Thunder Bay, ON: Lakehead
    University, Centre for Northern Studies, 2010).
34 Lemelin, "Understanding Mukadae Makwa (Black Bear)."
35 For further studies conducted in the conservation area, see R.H. Lemelin,
    R. Koster, K. Metansinine, H. Pelletier, and I. Wozniczka, "Voyages to

Kitchi Gami: The Lake Superior National Marine Conservation Area and Regional Tourism Opportunities in Canada's First National Marine Conservation Area," *Tourism in Marine Environments, Special Issue on Tourism in the Great Lakes* 6 (2–3, 2010): 101–18; and K. Metansinine, R. Koster, and R.H. Lemelin, "Developing Experiential Tourism in the Lake Helen Region: A Foundational Document" (report prepared for Parks Canada, 2009).

36 I. Wozniczka, "Exploring Opportunities and Constraints Associated with Protected Areas in Northern Ontario" (MES thesis, Lakehead University, 2008).

37 See R. Foster, T. Socha, and T. Potter, "Survey of Attitudes for the National Marine Conservation Area Proposal on Lake Superior Survey" (Thunder Bay, ON: Northern Bioscience Ecological Consulting, 2000); and R.J. Payne, M.E. Johnston, and D.G. Twynam, "Tourism and Sustainability in Northern Ontario," in *Tourism and Sustainable Development: Monitoring, Planning, Managing*, 2nd ed., ed. J.G. Nelson, R. Butler, and G. Wall (Waterloo, ON: University of Waterloo, Department of Geography, 1999).

38 Metansinine, Koster, and Lemelin, "Developing Experiential Tourism."

39 Wozniczka, "Exploring Opportunities."

40 Canada, Federal Economic Development Initiative in Northern Ontario, http://waterfrontfriends.heritagenorthbay.ca/index.php?module=blog& action=view&page=5.

10 Forest Tenure Systems for Development and Underdevelopment

DAVID ROBINSON

Nations tolerably well advanced as to skill, dexterity, and judgment in the application of labour have followed very different plans in the general conduct or direction of it: and those plans have not all been equally favourable to the greatness of its produce

– Adam Smith

Introduction

Development is stalled in northern Ontario. The amount of labour required to harvest and process timber continues to decline. Population in much of the region is falling. In retrospect there was an astonishing failure in the second half of the twentieth century to convert an enormous natural resource base into the foundation for sustainable economic development.

Some of the most respected and prominent forestry economists in Canada have written that the forest tenure system is one of the fundamental causes of the underdevelopment of Canada's forestry regions. In 1998 Haley and Luckert pointed out that "the Crown tenure system, designed to attract capital to liquidate a stock of old-growth timber and establish an efficient timber-processing industry, is ill-equipped to meet today's challenges."[1] In 2006 a paper prepared for the British Columbia Forum on Forest Economics and Policy observed that "there is increasing agreement in BC that the provincial forest tenure system no longer provides the economic and social benefits it was designed to deliver and is a root cause of the forest industry's failure to maintain its competitive positioning in the global economy. The need for reform is clear."[2]

It is unlikely that the existing tenure system is even capable of producing social and economic development in northern Ontario. Concentration of resource ownership, similar to the regime we have, is historically associated with underdevelopment. The regional resource most suited to creating a base for diversification of the economy is allocated and managed in a manner that obstructs economic diversification. Patterns of investment and human capital accumulation associated with the current tenure system do not support the creation of small businesses. Outside control of resources systematically destabilizes communities and inhibits the development of the human capital needed for development. The challenge for regional leaders and provincial legislators is to understand how the current system inhibits development, and then to identify a politically feasible alternative that is capable of promoting development.

I begin with a brief description of the current tenure regime. I then go on to examine major problems with the current Crown forest tenure system. The catalogue of problems draws heavily on a presentation by forestry analyst Marty Luckert to the 2009 Conference of the Ontario Professional Foresters Association.[3] To his list I add a set of problems relating to human and economic development that are generally left out of the discussion of forest policy. I then offer a basic model of community forests, and argue that community forestry could solve 25 of the 32 most important problems with the current regime. Finally, I consider the prospects for change in an inefficient but entrenched regime.

Forest Tenure

Tenure is a general term used to refer to control of land, forests, or other resources. Resources tenure is a fundamental social relationship that shapes the organization of production, the distribution of benefits, and the pattern of economic and social development.[4] Not surprisingly, the way forest resources have been made available to timber enterprises has always been at the centre of the debate on forest policy in Canada.[5]

In Ontario tenure in Crown forests is granted through statutorily based agreements whereby the Crown transfers rights to harvest timber or manage forest lands to another party while retaining title to the land. The current practice of transferring tenure to privately owned corporations is somewhat loosely referred to as "corporate tenure," and the practice of transferring rights to harvest timber or manage forest lands to a corporation owned by the population of a region as "community tenure."[6] The emerging practice in British Columbia of transferring rights to a locally controlled organization constituted under the Societies Act but not to all the people of the region is "social forestry" in this context, while tenure held by one or more First Nations is considered community tenure.

Existing tenure arrangements are part of a complex and well-entrenched set of institutions that tend to reproduce themselves. As Druska points out,[7] Crown ownership of forest land, the sale of timber from Crown land, and a dependence on timber sale for public revenue were enshrined in the Crown Timber Act of 1849. The basic features, in fact, were in place by 1837, when the rights to resources on Crown lands and to the revenues generated from them passed to the British colonies, beginning with New Brunswick.

Northern Ontario forests are administered under the Crown Forest Sustainability Act. Although the act also applies in southern Ontario, Crown land is concentrated in northern Ontario, and land there is owned primarily by the Crown. Lands and forests in southern Ontario are largely privately owned.

On 24 June 2009, Premier Dalton McGuinty announced the realignment of forestry from the Ministry of Natural Resources (MNR) to the Ministry of Northern Development and Mines, creating the Ministry of Northern Development, Mines and Forestry (MNDMF). The formal realignment took place on 3 September 2009. Responsibility for the major natural resources in northern Ontario other than water is now under a single minister responsible for economic development.

Places to Grow – Better Choices, Brighter Futures: Proposed Growth Plan for Northern Ontario, released in October 2009 by MNDMF and the Ministry of Energy and Infrastructure, speaks of "reforming its forest tenure and pricing system to allow for broader access to fibre and to support a more diversified forest sector that is responsive to changing economic needs," and promises to "introduce a new forest tenure and pricing system to provide more equitable access to forest resources."[8] The document provided no details and no rationale for reform. I therefore present a rationale for the changes here.

The Problems

The basic source of problems with the current tenure system is simply that, "[m]arket/private interests do not always coincide with public interests" (problem **1** of 32 that I identify, indicated in boldface type in the order in which they are mentioned). The contradiction takes a variety of specific forms. To prevent infringements on the public interest, harvest licences are set about with a thicket of regulations. Regulations designed to deal with the primary contradiction impose both regulatory (2) and transactions costs (3), reduce profitability (4), reduce flexibility (5), and are costly to administer (6).

Partial Rights

The most dramatic restriction is on the extent of tenure rights. No Canadian government extensively transfers rights to non-timber forest resources to the private sector.[9] Provinces transfer only specific harvesting rights, and only for a limited time. Comprehensive rights lead a rights holder to pay attention to the effect of his actions on the entire range of outputs. Allocating partial rights, however, creates a situation in which agents are economically disconnected from the consequences of at least some of their actions (7). Decisions made by an agent with partial rights are unlikely to be economically efficient (8).

Building a road on a steep slope to harvest wood, for example, might degrade a stream that is crucial to a tourism operator. Since the harvester gains no benefit from the stream, he is unlikely to count any recreational losses as costs. The costs are external, in the language of economics. A road used by hunters, on the other hand, generates a positive externality that the harvester does not count in his planning. Projects that generate positive externalities might not be undertaken because the net benefit for the rights holder is smaller than the social benefit. The opportunity to exploit positive externalities is often lost simply because the cost of getting an agreement that provides gains for all participants might be too high.

A forest ecology is a strongly interlinked system, and interactions are almost unavoidable. A forest economy is also strongly interlinked. A model with only two goods can be used to illustrate some of the problems inherent in a strongly interlinked system and to show how assigning comprehensive or partial rights affects the outcomes.

The right to harvest wood is one part of the comprehensive bundle of rights held by the province. The right to "harvest" recreational services is another part of that bundle. A Sustainable Forest Licence provides the right to harvest only the wood. Figure 10.1 shows the possible combinations of wood and recreation for a hypothetical forest.[10] The curve is a special case of a production possibilities frontier, a concept introduced in most first-year economics courses. It shows the maximum quantity

Figure 10.1. A Multi-Product, Multi-interest Forest

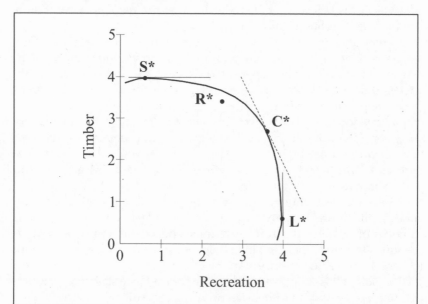

of wood for any given quantity of recreational services. Points below the curve are feasible but inefficient. Let us call the curve a "forest possibilities frontier" (FPF).

The generally negative slope of the FPF expresses the notion that, as the amount of wood taken increases, the recreational value of the forest will decline. The problem is to choose the right mix of these interconnected outputs. The right mix, of course, depends on who you are. The holder of a Sustainable Forest Licence with rights just to the wood would choose S*, while a tourism operator would choose L*. A regulator might choose R*, attempting to take the interests of both sides into consideration. R* is closer to S* than to L* in the illustration, reflecting an assumption about the relative power of the two interest groups. The theory of regulatory capture suggests that groups or individuals with a high-stakes interest in the outcome of policy or regulatory decisions can be expected to focus their resources and energy to gain the policy outcomes they prefer, while members of the public, each with only a tiny individual stake in the outcome, will ignore it altogether **(9)**. In this case R* is below the FPF, reflecting that the regulatory solution is unlikely to be economically efficient.

Harvey and Hillier attribute the failure of the current system to "the tenuous relationship between community, resource planner/decision-maker, and resource developer (that) creates a rift between community development and resource management."[11] One way to solve the problem is to privatize the forest. If the forestry firm also owned the rights to the recreational services, it would select an efficient point somewhere between S* and L*, such as C*. The point would depend on whether timber prices were high or low. Higher prices would lead the firm to produce more wood, while low wood prices and a rising interest in forest base recreation would lead to lower wood production and more emphasis on recreational uses. Market prices can be represented by lines in the figure. A zero market price for recreation would appear as a horizontal line, and a zero price for wood would appear as a vertical line. The profit-maximizing choice for a producer leads to a point where the price line is tangent to the FPF.

The point C* is "supported" by a line with a fairly steep slope, representing a relatively high relative price for recreational services. Given exactly those prices, a firm with comprehensive rights would choose C*. If it happened that C* were ideal from the point of view of society at large, privatization would result in a market solution that was also the ideal solution from the point of view of society at large.

Whether the global market for timber and recreation reliably sets prices that support C* is in doubt, of course. Market solutions work when markets are "complete" **(10)**, meaning that all the relevant values are fully represented in the price system. Aboriginal claims are not currently supported by purchasing power, and there are no markets for the environmental services provided by forests **(11)**. Climate change introduces inter-temporal considerations that markets have so far failed to incorporate **(12)**. And, of course, the squirrels have yet to convert their land claims to market power, so their interests cannot automatically appear in the price system **(13)**. As the number of claims on the forest increases, the problem becomes more complex and, in fact, less amenable to market solutions through privatization **(14)**.

Community control of forests might provide a way to capture the benefits of a grant of comprehensive rights. Local communities include individuals whose livelihoods depend on harvesting forests and others who depend on a variety of forest-based activities. Local communities directly benefit from many of the environmental services that are natural consequences of the presence of the forests around them. The community is the natural instrument for aggregating the interests of the local stakeholders. In Figure 10.1 the community might choose C*. C* is on the FPF, which is possible because local participants have more information than the regulators, and are motivated to use local knowledge to get as much benefit as possible from the resource. The interests of the people of Ontario might not be quite the same as those of the community,[12] but C* is likely to be a better approximation of the public interest than S* or R*.

The Management Regime

The principle of sustained yield is part of the thinking of a regulatory regime responding to partial rights and incomplete markets. Sustained yield is entirely about timber production. Non-timber resources are treated as harvesting constraints, rather than joint products to be optimized **(15)**. Luckert suggests that trying indirectly to maintain the conditions for non-timber forest products by putting restrictions on wood harvests makes less sense than having direct performance requirements for the non-timber products.[13] The allocation of limited rights results in placing relatively arbitrary constraints on wood harvest to achieve goals in other domains. In any case, tenure arrangements that suited the sustainable yield paradigm, Luckert argues, are not suited to a newer regime that mimics natural processes, conserves diversity, and supports varying degrees of multiple uses.[14]

With limited harvesting rights, the shape of the future forest is driven by current volume requirements **(16)**. The allowable cut effect (ACE), for example, is the increase in today's average annual allowable cut attributable to expected future increases in yields.[15] The ACE gives an incentive to plant faster-growing trees on land subject to an average allowable cut (AAC) to benefit from the immediate increase in the AAC that results. The ACE has been the major instrument for encouraging voluntary private investment in silviculture on Crown land, according to Luckert and Haley, although not a successful one.[16] Zhang and Pearse similarly report that the form of tenure influences the reforestation rate, with more secure and comprehensive tenure being associated with more complete reforestation.[17] The general principle is the assignment of rights, and the associated harvest constraint may shape tomorrow's forest.

The problem of regulating partial rights introduces additional rigidities into the management regime. Changing the sustainability targets for wildlife requires changing regulations for wood harvest because the licensee does not have economic incentives for performance with respect to wildlife **(17)**. Furthermore, it is argued, the effort to stabilize the harvest of a single class of forest product might gradually destabilize the ecological system, as Holling shows **(18)**.[18]

Because jobs are a goal of policy, the regulatory regime imposes additional conditions on the harvesters. The Sustainable Forest Act includes a "use it or lose it" provision that might force production when market conditions would suggest stopping it **(19)**.[19] Forests that are economically marginal are most likely to be subject to this provision.

Another class of problems that arise as a result of the conflict between the interests of private harvesters and those of the public appears as distortions in the industrial structure. Appurtenancy and processing requirements are the most obvious example. Timber processing or processing requirements require licensees to process the timber they harvest under the licence, or an equivalent volume, at facilities they own. Such provisions are intended to ensure that at least some processing of logs occurs in the harvest region.

Under appurtenancy, in particular, a central feature of the Canadian policy regime, a licensee is required to construct, modify, or maintain a timber-processing facility. Forestry firms are thus forced to become vertically integrated **(20)**. Former chief forester of Ontario Ken Armson has suggested[20] that much of the problem with the province's forestry sector has its roots in the tight link between forest tenure and the ownership of mills.[21] Sociologist Pat Marchak observes that "[t]hese corporations have subsequently held enormous power to influence government action because their bargaining position is so strong" **(21)**.[22] According to Jessica Clogg, Staff Counsel for West Coast Environmental Law, "this strength is based on public and government fears that the corporation may simply exit the economy, with devastating impacts on forest-dependent communities, forest workers, and government revenue."[23] Marchak argues that, "once captured in this way, governments are rarely able to extricate themselves from the long-term obligations they have incurred through the granting of land or harvesting rights. They provide further subsidies, reduce tax obligations, and create new incentives to keep the industry operating in their territories. The system becomes self-perpetuating."[24]

Trade Issues

One point of friction in the softwood lumber dispute with the United States is that the administratively set price of wood to Ontario suppliers is thought to be lower than the market would justify, and that there is an implicit subsidy in the administered charges the province sets. As a result, Canadian producers have faced a series of countervailing tariffs **(22)**. In response, British Columbia, New Brunswick, and Quebec have instituted auction markets for part of the wood supply as a mechanism for setting the administered price. It is not yet clear that these concessions will eliminate the perception that the Canadian forestry companies are effectively subsidized.

Disincentives for Social and Economic Development

The natural path of development in a resources-rich area is to accumulate the proceeds of resources extraction as the basis of development of more advanced industry. This is not a contentious statement: it has been the consensus theory of development in Canada since Harold Innis promulgated the Staples Thesis.[25] It was the rationale for the creation of the Alberta Heritage fund and for the far more successful Norwegian sovereign fund that was built up with oil revenue.

Papageorgiou and Turnbull point out that the specific form of property rights in a region affects the pace and pattern of the region's economic development.[26] Property rights generally arise in conjunction with the technology of production. In agriculture, for example, crops that require large-scale production, such as sugar and cotton, support plantation-style agriculture. Plantation systems, however, have created some of the world's most inequitable societies, and rarely support rapid development. Other crops, such as coffee, rice and wheat, can be produced economically on a relatively small scale, and tend to create entrepreneurial societies based on small-holdings. Such societies, including that of southern Ontario, provide opportunities for extensive economic growth.[27]

In northern Ontario public policy favours both large-scale land holdings and large-scale production. One of the most consistent complaints about the existing tenure system and policy regime is that they make it difficult for local producers to gain access to the local wood supply **(23)**, even when it is not used by the holder of a Sustainable

Forest Licence. The result is that small businesses based on the forest resources are inhibited, and the process of developing new skills and new products required for economic and social development is blocked. Restricting access to the wood supply inhibits entrepreneurship and innovation **(24)**, and prevents economic diversification **(25)**. By inhibiting the development of human capital, it impoverishes the entire nation **(26)**. By preventing economic diversification, the tenure system produces communities that are too small to provide amenities **(27)**, too limited to retain young people **(28)** or to attract professionals **(29)**, and too narrowly based to survive changing economic conditions **(30)**.

The fact that the current tenure system fails to develop human and social capital is its most profoundly harmful feature. Other things being equal, a tenure system that involves more people in decision making is a better system. Responsibility is fundamental to the development of human capacity. Involving people is costly, however. It requires taking time, sharing information and, ultimately, developing expertise and decision making skills. For a forestry company there might be advantages to public participation, but in most cases public participation is a cost **(31)**. Modern management is designed to economize on intelligence and attention **(32)** precisely because they are among the most valuable and costly resources a company can have. For the community these costs are investments in both correct decisions and human development, and thus similar to educational expenditures.

Community Forestry

It is easy to make the case that the current tenure system is inefficient and cannot support strong economic or social development in northern Ontario. It is more interesting to try to identify alternatives. Community forestry is the obvious and most attractive candidate.

According to Duinker et al.,[28] policy inquiries repeatedly find that forest-dependent communities ought to have a stronger role in determining their relations with the surrounding forests. Lawson, Levy, and Sandberg[29] find that the case for real local control in forest policy, particularly for those at the short end of labour shedding "efficiencies" and monopoly control, has always been strong. Examples abound of robust systems and institutions where resources rights are held by a community and where those directly involved have successfully managed complex resource systems over long periods.[30]

There is, however, no widely accepted definition of a community forest, and there are no large-scale models in Canada. Experiments in British Columbia make it clear that community control of forests on a small scale is feasible and politically acceptable. The success of the management regime for the Algonquin forest and the unusually high level of community representation in the Nipissing and the French-Severn forests show that community-oriented forestry is feasible for large areas. The existing variety of forms and sizes provides little more than suggestions about what a general community forestry regime would look like applied across northern Ontario.

Since we are interested in alternatives capable of replacing a system that has failed, and not in marginal experiments, we need to imagine a version of community forestry that could be extended to the entire northern Ontario forest system. I therefore define a community forest as follows:

Community forest: *a forest that provides the economic basis of a community, and for which tenure is held under some form of local democracy.*

The requirement that a community forest provide the economic basis of community forces us to think at the appropriate scale. The requirement that tenure be held under some form of local democracy provides the link to the objective most commonly used to define community forestry management for the benefit of the community. Intentions are rarely useful markers in scientific definitions, so a definition in terms of institutional structure is preferable to one that relies on objectives. Making tenure holding the central element in the definition allows for a variety of management arrangements and forestry practices.

An Alternative Model

It is helpful to have at least a plausible structure in mind. The simplest model is forest tenure held indefinitely by the municipal government, managed by a municipal corporation capable of exactly reproducing the current harvest pattern and wood allocations. This is an important observation. It implies that initial arrangements might be designed to minimize disruptions while opening new possibilities. The current system cannot achieve many of the objectives that community forests might pursue, but in principle community forests could do anything the current regime does.

In this model of community forestry, Crown forests would remain under public ownership, but management would be increasingly decentralized. The minister would retain the final say about forest management plans. Nothing would prevent the ministry from continuing its current efforts to reduce transaction costs and remove rigidities in the wood-allocation process.[31]

To create community forests, the minister might invite municipalities, with the assistance of MNDMF, to create "community forest corporations." The corporations would accept existing commitments, and maintain existing wood flows for a specified period. Initially they would operate under existing forest management plans and, as now, changes would be reviewed by the minister. The corporations almost certainly would hire the foresters that created the current management plan, and the previous holders of a Sustainable Forest Licence would be relieved of the burden. The forestry management system would continue to be funded out of revenues. The Forest Renewal Fund would continue as at present. The minister might require the formation of local consultative committees to ensure that mill owners, loggers, and other stakeholders are systematically consulted.

Understood this way, the introduction of community forestry would not be disruptive. There would be a gradual change of management, allowing a gradual revision of forest management practice and development policy. The most important innovation would be for the Crown to transfer management functions and forest revenues to the community forest corporations. The Crown would be responsible for research, for setting general performance standards, for auditing, and for functions best performed centrally. Other responsibilities, including land use management, planning reforestation, harvesting, and the sale of forest products would be the responsibility of the corporations. The Crown Forest Sustainability Act already gives the minister the authority to institute a system of community forests along these lines.

37. (1) The Minister may, subject to the Public Lands Act and to the provisions of a license under section 26, sell, lease, grant or otherwise dispose of land that is subject to a forest resource license.

(3) A sale, lease, grant or other disposition of land under this section terminates the licence in respect of the land and terminates all rights of the licensee in respect of forest resources on the land. 1994, c. 25, s. 37 (3).

The act appears to say that the minister can terminate all Sustainable Forest Licences, and grant the land to the municipalities. If so, it is technically possible to move to a regime of community forestry very rapidly, although a measured process would be much better.

Community Forestry as a Solution

At this point we should consider whether community forestry solves many of the problems associated with the current tenure regimes, and whether it would encourage regional development.

1. The current tenure system does not give owners a stake in the future of the forest because the tenure period is too short.

Community forestry gives decision making power to agents with a stake in the long-term health and productivity of the forest. Communities are not mobile in the same way that firms are, and therefore have a long-term interest in the location and productivity of the forests. Families in northern communities prefer to imagine their children staying in or returning to the community. If a community corporation held tenure, the forest would belong in a significant way to the local population, and would be part of the legacy of the individuals in the community. Community members would be more attached to the forest, and would be drawn to the principles of sustainable stewardship because of their long-term interest in it.

Some might argue that the time horizon of citizens of smaller communities is not infinite, but it is clearly longer than that of the typical corporation. It is almost certainly longer than the horizon of most politicians and public sector managers.

2. Partial rights: the current tenure system allocates the rights to various forest products to different agents, making integrated management difficult.

Because community forestry is a form of public ownership, it would be politically acceptable to transfer complete rights to community forest corporations. Since local communities physically bring together almost the complete range of interests in the lands and forests around them, rights and interests then would largely coincide. Even if the rights to various "products" were vested in varying degrees in different local people, the rights holders would all be members of the same community, with multiple ties and redundant opportunities to interact.

Transactions costs generally would be lower and individual payoffs higher than in a large, centralized organization.

Under a comprehensive system of community forest corporations, communities necessarily would band together to produce harvest and renewal plans, develop shared roads, manage log markets, and let harvest contracts. Such collaboration would reduce the risk of producers' playing them off against one another.

3. *The boom-bust cycle: by limiting diversification, the current tenure system subjects forest communities to exaggerated business cycles.*

Community forestry would stabilize employment by encouraging diversification, more intensive forestry (which would require more labour), stabilization planning, and the cyclical shift of workers from harvesting to silviculture.

4. *Barriers to entry: the current tenure system creates large barriers to entry for small firms.*

A system of community forest corporations would solve the problem of barriers to entry by new firms by having strong incentives to encourage local businesses. Tax revenue does not interest the owner of a mill or the holder of a Sustainable Forest Licence, but it certainly matters to a community. The incentive structure of community forestry would favour local economic growth, and, since municipal revenues are correlated with provincial revenue from income and sales taxes, it would promote projects that contribute to provincial revenue.

5. *Low value added: the current tenure system discourages value-added production.*

As a community organization, a community forest would have strong incentives to help create local value-added businesses. It would be able to share risk effectively and find ways to reduce the costs of business start-ups.

6. *Barriers to human capital: forestry firms have little incentive to invest in the development of human capital.*

Firms in northern Ontario have little incentive to invest in people who often move on to other jobs. Under a system of community forestry, human capital would be more likely to stay in the community, providing economic stability and a foundation for diversification. Even if young people leave, those who remain have some stake in their success and likely would be willing to invest in their development.

7. Economizing on brains: the current tenure system provides an incentive to minimize management's use of intelligence.

Unfortunately, economizing on intelligence reduces the capacity to exploit local resources and opportunities. Community forestry, by contrast, would involve more members of the community and provide opportunities for developing skills and knowledge, thereby bringing to bear more local talent and knowledge than the current system can.

8. Land use conflict: the current tenure system makes it difficult to resolve conflicts among housing, agriculture, logging, and recreation.

Most land use issues are already dealt with at the municipal level. Community forest corporations, as democratic and inclusive organizations operating at the municipal level, would be able to resolve many of the conflicts among users. Decision makers, in general, would have the right incentives, as well as local knowledge.

9. Inefficient wood allocation: unlike a market system, the current tenure system fails to allocate wood to its highest-value use.

Community forestry would provide a natural transition to market allocation. More important, perhaps, since markets remain incomplete, the democratic process of community forestry likely would identify uses at the local level leading to economic and human development that might not have been considered under corporate tenure.

10. Rigidity: the current rigid tenure system inhibits efficient reallocation of forest land to higher uses, and limits the products tenure holders may extract.

Rigidity arises from centralized control and the need to regulate actors with partial rights and short time horizons. Assigning authority to community forest corporations would empower them to develop specific policies for specific areas. Local rules can vary, and evolve much more easily, than those applying to the entire province. Decentralized decision making would lead to experimentation, innovation, and improved processes – community forestry would "let a hundred flowers blossom."

11. Lack of local revenue: the current tenure system
leaves industry out of northern communities' tax base.

A serious problem for northern development is that northern communities largely rely on property tax for their revenue, unlike in southern Ontario, where municipalities typically have industrial properties as part of their tax base. Under community forestry, the rights to forest revenue and the responsibility for collecting renewal funds could be transferred to the local community corporations, which would then give northern communities a strengthened revenue base.

12. Misuse of biomass: the current tenure system
generally allocates biomass inefficiently.

It is more efficient economically to use biomass locally than to use it to produce power for export. Under the current tenure system, however, local communities, which do not have the rights to the resources, are unable to attract the capital and expertise to manage local biomass projects.

13. Annual allowable cuts: the current tenure system is structured
around an increasingly outdated and clumsy harvest system.

Community forestry would eliminate the need for annual allowable cuts at the provincial level. The province would simply download the responsibility to community forest corporations, whose local knowledge and flexibility would contribute to improved harvest planning.

14. Appurtenancy: the current tenure system ties forest
management and harvesting to mills.

Appurtenancy, which links the right to harvest timber to an obligation to provide local employment and economic benefits, imposes costs on the sawmill industry and enforces an inflexible vertical integration. Community forestry would eliminate the need for appurtenancy requirements at the provincial level. Each community would be responsible for managing its portion of the forest to create as much local wealth as possible. As designated owners of the resource, community forest corporations would have the right to sell to mills or to local users or enter into joint ventures that committed wood to new mills or processors.

15. Stumpage fees: the current system employs a clumsy, partial pricing system for public resources.

Under community forestry there would be no need for provincial stumpage fees, which are simply a mechanism for setting a price when selling public property. Community forest corporations necessarily would set prices to maximize the return to the community for given demand conditions. Northerners would be much more likely to derive full value from the forest resource than the province does under the current centralized system.

16. Lack of a price system: the current tenure system lacks a market that sets prices, and so requires an administrative process to value wood.

Community forestry would create a natural foundation for a pricing system in northern Ontario. A key feature of an effective market is a reasonably large number of buyers and sellers; in the United States, for example, extensive private forests create the basis for market prices.[32] By creating a large number of local community forests, and ensuring that the communities receive the revenues from sales, community forestry would create a competitive situation. Community forests, in general, would be smaller than those exploited by current holders of Sustainable Forest Licences. Not all community forest corporations would own mills, but they certainly would want to develop effective log markets and a market structure that generate prices efficiently. It would not be necessary for communities to auction all of their wood supply, only that they be free to market as much of it as they wished.

17. Countervailing tariffs: the current system of stumpage fees exposes Ontario to charges of selling below market value and to the imposition of countervailing tariffs.

A decentralized market of private log-supplying communities with complete rights would undermine the arguments in the United States to impose countervailing tariffs on forest products from Ontario.

18. *Price instability: the use-it-or-lose-it rule keeps volume high
even when prices fall, resulting in larger price swings.*

Community forestry would stabilize timber prices and markets by
reducing harvests in the face of lower prices. Ideally, local corporations would simply move labour to other tasks, including silvicultural
work.

19. *Lack of private woodlots: the current system restricts
private operators' access to wood and markets.*

Private woodlots are generally more productive than lots exploited by
holders of Sustainable Forest Licences. Community forestry would
support private lots for their contribution to the local economy and
to municipal revenues, which, in turn, would raise productivity
and increase economic stability.

20. *Political shackles: under the current tenure system, the sector's
difficulties are entirely the responsibility of the provincial government.*

Community forestry would let Queen's Park download political problems related to the northern Ontario forestry industry, thus decentral-
izing the political risk of innovation.

21. *Resentment of First Nations claims: the current tenure
system worsens divisions among northern Ontarians.*

Northern Ontario's First Nations claim the right to control local forest
resources and use them for economic development. Under community
forestry, this right would extend to all northern communities, which
would give First Nations and non-Aboriginal northerners opportunities to collaborate politically and economically and thus help to allay
resentment of Aboriginal land claims.

22. *The friendless intensive forest: the current tenure
system makes intensive forestry a political orphan.*

Intensive forestry is attractive for many reasons. It reduces the area
mills require to obtain the wood they process and transportation costs
for both mills and workers. It maximizes carbon capture, and increases

measured land productivity. Nonetheless, intensive forestry is seen as politically unacceptable since only forest companies are thought to gain from it. Community forestry, however, would have a strong incentive to promote intensive forestry, under the banners of community control and environmental responsibility, opening the door to improved management and more viable communities.

23. *Mistrust of industry: northern Ontarians are increasingly suspicious of the concessions and subsidies bestowed on private firms to influence their behaviour.*

It likely would be easier to regulate a community forest corporation than a large private holder of a Sustainable Forest Licence. Financial incentives to community organizations would be politically more acceptable than subsidies to private firms.

24. *Misallocated risk: the current tenure system forces companies to take on responsibility for workers during periods of low demand, buffering some changes while exposing the system to firm failure and more violent collapse.*

Community forestry would make communities the frontline bearers of risk, but would also give them the tools for dealing with risk. Communities could manage and reduce risk by diversifying, saving, and investing wisely. As well, by creating a risk-bearing public, community forestry would reduce the tendency to politicize the business cycle.

Summary

I have made 24 strong claims about the advantages of community forestry. Each claim arises from considering a specific and widely recognized problem with the current tenure system. Each is plausible, and each can be supported by both theoretical and historical argument. It is essential to understand that none of the 24 claims can be lightly dismissed – they represent the real challenge to any reform proposals for Canadian forestry.

The principal advantage of community forestry is its incentive structure, which would promote both responsible stewardship and economic development. As a result, community forestry likely would produce more wealth, human capital, jobs, value added, secondary and tertiary economic development, research, carbon sequestration, and forest diversity, and it would also support more people and create more attractive and liveable communities.

Conclusions

There is no doubt that the current forest tenure regime in northern Ontario yields suboptimal outcomes. Descended from seventeenth-century colonial relations, it works strongly against human and economic development in northern Ontario's communities, and it has lost the confidence of both the producers and the people of the region. Simple application of standard economic analysis shows that community forestry could solve, at least partially, the system's three main failures: to produce sustainable economic development; to develop the capacities of northern Ontarians; and to attract investment in either the forest itself or value-added products. Finding a path to a potentially superior system, however, would be a challenge at many levels. Ostrom, Gardner, and Walker[33] describe such a situation as a "policy dilemma": the heart of the dilemma in this case is that tenure, policy, and management regimes interact to resist change. Howlett[34] describes a tenure regime as a long-lasting pattern of legal rights, a policy regime as a long-lasting pattern of decision makers and decisions, and a forest management regime as a period during which the same set of principles for managing the forests is applied by the same institutions.

Once a regime is established, the same actors, institutions, and governing ideas tend to dominate policy making for extended periods. The resulting policies are variations on a theme determined by the ruling ideas and interest of the participants. Policies, players, and ideas together support one another to form a self-reproducing system. Tenure holders use earnings from the existing system to defend the system that gives them those earnings. The fact that administered systems generally have few players makes it easy for tenure holders and managers to collaborate explicitly and tacitly to suppress competition.

Despite its well-known failings and the presence of a considerably more attractive alternative, the current tenure/policy/management regime is likely to survive. Community forestry, if it appears at all in the next policy document, probably would be limited to a few "pilot projects," which likely would have little more effect than those of the 1990s. Tenure regimes can be extremely resilient.

NOTES

1 D. Haley and M. Luckert, "Tenures as Economic Instruments for Achieving Objectives of Public Forest Policy in British Columbia," in *The Wealth of Forests: Markets, Regulation and Sustainable Forestry*, ed. C. Tollensen (Vancouver: University of British Columbia Press, 1998), 147.

2 D. Haley and H. Nelson, "BC's Forest Tenure System in a Changing World: Challenges and Opportunities," Synthesis Paper 06-01, Executive Summary (Vancouver: BC Forum on Forest Economics and Policy, 2006), available online at http://conservation-economics.com/pdf_pubs/synth_paper/SP0601_Forest_Tenure_System.pdf.

3 M. Luckert, "Considering Privatization in Canada's Forest Tenures" (paper presented to the Ontario Professional Foresters Association conference, "Whose Forest Is It Anyway? The Role of Tenure, Pricing and Ownership in the Future of Ontario's Forests," Sudbury, ON, 23 April 2009).

4 E. Ostrom and H. Nagrenda, "Insights on Linking Forests, Trees and People from the Air, on the Ground and in the Laboratory," *Proceedings of the National Academy of Sciences of the United States of America* 103 (51, 2006): 19224–31.

5 D. Zhang and P.H. Pearse, "The Influence of the Form of Tenure on Reforestation in British Columbia," *Forest Ecology and Management* 98 (3, 1997): 239–50.

6 The term is convenient and conventional, but not particularly precise. Strictly speaking, municipal tenure and cooperative tenure are also corporate tenure – corporations and societies are individuals under the law, and tenure can be held only by an individual.

7 K. Druska, *Canada's Forests: A History* (Montreal; Kingston, ON: McGill-Queen's University Press, 2003).

8 Ontario, Ministry of Energy and Infrastructure and Ministry of Northern Development, Mines and Forestry, *Places to Grow – Better Choices, Brighter Future: Proposed Growth Plan for Northern Ontario* ([Toronto]: Queen's Printer for Ontario, 2009), 14.

9 Haley and Luckert, "Tenures as Economic Instruments."

10 The analysis here is based on D. Robinson, "The Elementary Economics of Forest Tenure," Discussion Paper 07-01 (Sudbury, ON: Institute for Northern Ontario Research and Development, August 2007).

11 S. Harvey and B. Hillier, "Community Forestry in Ontario," *Forestry Chronicle* 70 (6, 1994): 725–50.

12 M. Luckert, "Are Community Forests the Key to Sustainable Forest
    Management? Some Economic Considerations," *Forestry Chronicle*
    75 (5, 1999): 789.
13 Luckert, "Considering Privatization in Canada's Forest Tenures."
14 Luckert, "Are Community Forests the Key."
15 M. Luckert and D. Haley, "The Allowable Cut Effect as a Policy Instrument
    in Canadian Forestry," *Canadian Journal of Forest Resources* 25 (1995):
    1821–9.
16 Ibid.
17 Zhang and Pearse, "Influence of the Form of Tenure."
18 C.S. Holling, "Resilience and Stability of Ecological Systems," *Annual
    Review of Ecology and Systems* 4 (1973): 1–23; see also idem, "The Resilience
    of Terrestrial Ecosystems: Local Surprise and Global Change," in
    Sustainable Development of the Biosphere, ed. W.E. Clark and R.E. Munn
    (Cambridge: Cambridge University Press, 1986).
19 In practice these requirements are often waived, as is the requirement that
    companies pay the stumpage fees they owe when mills close. Ad hoc flex-
    ibility may be a virtue, but its exercise is an indicator that the regulatory
    system is poorly adjusted and, perhaps, fragile.
20 K. Armson, "Issue #1: Forest Land Tenure," *Forestry Chronicle* 79 (2, 2003):
    177–8.
21 A similar point is made by Haley and Nelson, "BC's Forest Tenure
    System"; and Luckert, "Considering Privatization in Canada's Forest
    Tenures."
22 P. Marchak, *Falldown: Forest Policy in British Columbia*. (Vancouver: David
    Suzuki Foundation, 1999).
23 J. Clogg, "Tenure Background Paper" (presented to the Kootenay
    Conference on Forest Alternatives, Nelson, BC, 4–6 November 1999),
    8, available online at http://www.for.gov.bc.ca/hfd/library/documents/
    bib96990.pdf.
24 Marchak, *Falldown*.
25 See H. Innis, *The Fur Trade in Canada: An Introduction to Canadian Economic
    History*, rev. ed. (Toronto: University of Toronto Press, 1977).
26 C. Papageorgiou and G.K. Turnbull, "Economic Development and
    Property Rights: Time Limits on Land Ownership," *Economic Development
    Quarterly* 19 (3, 2003): 271–83.
27 J. Frieden, *Global Capitalism: Its Fall and Rise in the Twentieth Century*
    (New York: W.W. Norton, 2006).
28 P. Duinker, P.W. Metakala, F. Cheng, and L. Bouthillier, "Community
    Forests in Canada: An Overview," *Forestry Chronicle* 70 (6, 1994): 131–5.

29 J. Lawson, M. Levy, and L.A. Sandberg, "Perpetual Revenues and the Delights of the Primitive: Change, Continuity and Forest Policy Regimes in Ontario," in *Canadian Forest Policy: Adapting to Change*, ed. M. Howlett (Toronto: University of Toronto Press, 2001), 302.

30 This is the argument of Elinor Ostrom in *Governing the Commons: The Evolution of Institutions for Collective Action* (New York: Cambridge University Press, 1990). See also E. Ostrom, "Designing Complexity to Govern Complexity," in *Property Rights and the Environment*, ed. S. Hanna and M. Munasinghe (Washington, DC: Beijer International Institute of Ecological Economics and the World Bank, 1995).

31 The so-called cooperative Sustainable Forest Licence is intended to reduce management costs and improve allocation.

32 The highest-value use might not be reflected in the market price: consider the value of allocating a small stream of wood to a new business. Furthermore, markets are incomplete – there is no market for environmental services, for example – and therefore market allocations cannot be assumed to be efficient.

33 E. Ostrom, R. Gardner, and J. Walker, *Rules, Games and Common-Pool Resources* (Ann Arbor: University of Michigan Press, 1994).

34 M. Howlett, "Introduction: Policy Regimes and Policy Change in the Canadian Forest Sector," in Howlett, *Canadian Forest Policy*, 5–6.

11 Conclusion

BOB SEGSWORTH AND CHARLES CONTEH

We are tough, we are tenacious and we are tired of watching our rich potential diminished and flowed [*sic*] elsewhere, taking opportunity and our youth along with it.

—Rick Bartolucci, Minister of Northern Development
and Mines, 10 June 2004[1]

[W]e are ensuring that Northern Ontario will excel in this knowledge-based economy ... Together, we will continue to open doors and build futures for a prosperous Northern Ontario.

—Tony Clement, Minister Responsible for
FedNor, 19 March 2010[2]

[I]f we do not change the way we make decisions in and for northern Ontario, we are doomed to catastrophic economic failure that will be self-induced, and which has already taken root ... [N]orthern Ontario is an exploited third world economy, which has not benefited from the resources and wealth it has created and suffers from the politically expedient and unbecoming welfare state mentality that brought forth Growthnot and FedNot in the first place.

—Michael Atkins, 4 August 2009[3]

Many of the chapters in this collection were first presented at a workshop at Laurentian University in the fall of 2009 where the authors, discussants, and participants examined the economic development of northern Ontario. As with many discussions that take place in marginal regions, those present were united by their sense of community and shared identity. The book began with basic questions: can we demonstrate that – as is widely believed in northern Ontario – the region's economic development has not kept pace with that in other parts of the province and the country? If we are correct in identifying this problem of underdevelopment, what causes it, and what should be done about it?

The empirical question of whether we can demonstrate that the economic development of northern Ontario has not kept pace has been answered unequivocally. Segsworth, looking at a variety of measures of economic activity in Chapter 4, concludes that every single one indicates that "[t]he economy of northern Ontario has performed far less well than that of the province as a whole since the early 1980s." A stable or growing population promotes, and is promoted by, economic growth. Southcott, in Chapter 2, paints a picture of population decline in the region, with the proportion of people over age sixty-five increasing among those who remain. The major exception is the growing First Nations population, whose largest demographic group is under age fifteen.

After this basic consensus, however, the authors have chosen different paths, ultimately pursuing one of two approaches to the questions of what causes economic underdevelopment and what should be done about it. The first approach, which we can refer to as *governance*, deals with how policy is made. One main problem is that no forum or vehicle exists for making regional policy that reflects regional interests. Because the federal and Ontario governments have their own political and jurisdictional priorities, the two have not cooperated in or coordinated their programs except in limited, formal, or superficial ways, as evidenced in the war of words between the Minister Responsible for FedNor, Tony Clement, and Ontario's Minister of Northern Development and Mines, Rick Bartolucci. In a press release issued on 7 January 2009, Bartolucci claimed to be "steadfast in his view that the federal government is no friend to Sudbury or local economic development projects like [Sudbury's proposed Centre for Excellence in Mining Innovation] – one that fully fits the criteria of FedNor and has international implications in terms of long-term economic possibilities."[4] Clement responded by stating that "the proposal required a huge investment that would have killed many other worthy projects. After careful consideration and due diligence, I concluded Northern Ontario would be better off by making a number of strategic investments, rather than by putting all of our eggs in one basket."[5]

In this process, moreover, representatives of municipalities and local communities lack agency – too often treated as grant recipients than as partners in policy development. The decisions of the Harper and

McGuinty governments in May 2009 each to give $5.5 million to help the University of Toronto build an Innovation Centre for the Canadian Mining Industry amply testify to this absence of an active northern Ontario role in provincial and federal economic development policy making. It is a problem primarily of vertical dimension: federal, provincial, local.

Economic development in northern Ontario also has problems, however, of horizontal dimension. Some it shares with all regions: how to coordinate policies and actions of both public and private sector actors in a wide range of fields. Some challenges are on a bigger scale than those in other regions, such as how to cooperate more closely with growing First Nations communities that are increasingly important to the region's economic future. Other horizontal problems are substantively different in northern Ontario, because transportation and communication are more difficult and because large areas have no municipal structure at all. In an April 2007 position paper, the Northern Ontario Large Urban Mayors group noted that about 65 per cent of the region's population resides in five major centres "separated by large distances requiring long travel times between them."[6] The mayors point out that lower assessment bases and larger geographic areas to serve than their southern Ontario counterparts contribute to higher costs for northern Ontario communities. They go on to say that they face increased costs to serve the mining companies, even though, in some cases, the companies "escape municipal taxation because their assets are either underground or outside municipal boundaries."[7]

Theoretical work, such as the multi-actor governance principles advanced in the Introduction and by Conteh in Chapter 3, offers new ways to think about how the policy making process could be adjusted to improve economic development policy in northern Ontario. It demonstrates the potential of local organizations and their impact when they design initiatives to which they and their communities are strongly committed. Madahbee (Chapter 5), for example, shows that First Nations communities, with the appropriate support, can develop and sustain successful economic development and growth strategies. In Chapter 9, Koster and Lemelin explain the unfulfilled potential of tourism when the appropriate governance arrangements and policy instruments are, on the other hand, withheld. West (Chapter 8) claims that national and provincial agri-food policies have not benefited the North. Interestingly, he suggests that northern Ontario municipal organizations, working with the Association of Municipalities of Ontario, should lobby Queen's Park for a northern Ontario-made agri-food policy for the region.

While the first approach, governance, focuses on conflicts among policy makers, the lack of a regional forum, and implementation problems, the second approach, *sustainability*, focuses on the absence of sustainable development in northern Ontario. The authors who take this approach see wealth-extraction policies as a primary cause of underdevelopment in general, and abrogation of treaty rights as a cause of underdevelopment for First Nations communities. The recognition of Aboriginal rights in the 1982 Constitution Act, court decisions upholding treaty rights, the legislated duty to consult and accommodate the interests of First Nations, and the establishment of Aboriginal financial institutions have all contributed to the progress First Nations are making in their efforts to create (or recreate) self-sustaining communities throughout northern Ontario.

To create sustainable communities among the non-Aboriginal population, major changes would have to be made in the wealth-extraction policies that Ontario governments put in place as long as a century ago. The wealth might be in our region, but it does not stay. As Robinson argues in Chapter 7 about mining, "[t]he most striking feature of northern Ontario's development is that the region retains little of the wealth generated from its mineral resources." The problem, Robinson says, is not the lack of policy infrastructure or conflict between federal and provincial policy makers; rather, "[t]he province simply has not *attempted* to achieve sustainable regional development in the North" [emphasis added]. For many communities, such as Elliot Lake, mining has ended, but the town remains. What, then, of new mineral discoveries? Who is making the decisions about the workforce, about the town site, about where the wealth will go?

Robinson also makes a compelling case for a change in the forest tenure system, arguing that the current system is inconsistent with (and even antithetical to) the broader goal of sustainable development in northern Ontario. The existing forestry regime perpetuates economic dependency and stifles economic diversification, because it creates disincentives for community entrepreneurial and social initiatives. The alternative tenure system, the community forest, appears to offer many advantages, and could be introduced through small-scale pilot projects in both Aboriginal and non-Aboriginal communities. Such an innovation offers several opportunities for community development and for research.

One way of thinking about the subject of sustainable economic development in northern Ontario is to ask, simply, who benefits from the current policies? Beaulieu argues, in Chapter 6, that northern Ontario has been an internal colony, exploited to serve the interests of southern Ontario. Robinson's discussion that northern Ontario should be viewed as a periphery or hinterland that serves the interests of the metropolis to the south follows logically from a reading of his argument that the interests of the communities of northern Ontario are not well served by provincial policy makers in their forest tenure policies. The 2007 Northern Ontario Large Urban Mayors paper claims that the "2005 GDP of Northern Ontario was roughly $24.2 billion, surpassing the respective GDPs of Prince Edward Island, New Brunswick and Newfoundland and Labrador and all three of the territories combined."[8] Despite wealth "that has reliably contributed to provincial and federal wealth for more than one hundred years,"[9] northern Ontario is increasingly a have-not region of Canada.

Several lessons can be drawn from the discussions of economic development policy governance in the region. First, policy governance, it seems, lacks a regional policy infrastructure to enhance the relevance, coherence, and legitimacy of development policy intervention. The discussions in some of the chapters amount to compelling critiques of the ways the existing governing infrastructure of policy formulation and implementation follows an outdated model, one suited for managing a dependent staples economy, but not a self-sustaining, diversified knowledge economy. The lack of regional structures of policy governance, it seems, is the most blatant institutional lacuna in northern Ontario, one that ensures that the area remains no more than a geographical construct.

A second lesson that can be drawn from the preceding chapters is that the nature of the partnership among public agencies, the private sector, and community groups is such that it could benefit from the more horizontal management or governance models that are inclusive of non-state actors. Central to these three issues is the need for networks of social capital, an entrepreneurial attitude to the surrounding ecosystem, and an appreciation for institutional mechanisms of coordinated decision making and implementation. An illustration of this need can be found in West's example in Chapter 8 that the current land tenure regime is inconsistent with the overarching goal of entrepreneurial development in northern Ontario. The inconsistency perpetuates economic dependency and stifles economic diversification by acting as a disincentive for community entrepreneurial and social initiatives, West argues. Policy interventions through capital investment programs could make only cosmetic differences (or simple gestures) unless the most central aspects of production – natural resources, in particular – are equitably distributed and accessible to entrepreneurs. "Land," in the context of West's usage, represents a general sense of natural resources and their use.

A third lesson is that improvements in intergovernmental policy coordination could change regional economic development in northern Ontario from tactical to strategic policy intervention. A tactical approach is a classic case of intergovernmental political rivalry and contestation, as each agency, representing a certain level government, narrowly focuses on maximizing program outputs, often to the exclusion of other agencies operating similar programs. A tactical approach tends to be rich in short-term projects, but bankrupt in policies supporting them. A strategic approach, on the other hand, focuses on longer-term policy forecasting and coordinated programs among the various agencies involved. Such an approach could reduce program duplication, fragmentation, and misdirected spending. As the various levels of government integrate their activities, their organizational motivation for cooperation grows, and policy processes and outcomes become truly regional.

Another lesson that can be extrapolated from the foregoing chapters is the need for an awareness of the keen challenges of overcoming geographical and racial distances to forge concerted community action within and across each of the five subregions of northern Ontario. Such transformations, it seems, require a convincing message from higher policy and institutional levers that concerted community initiatives can become the force and arena of policy action in the region.

By examining the capacity, relevance, and integrity of existing institutions in light of current exogenous or strategic challenges facing economic development in Ontario's North, this book has endeavoured to foster discussion about the activities of the provincial and federal governments in the region. Northern Ontarians, including First Nations, increasingly call for more citizen mobilization and engagement in issues affecting economic development in their region. Yet the institutions and mechanisms of economic policy development and governance have hardly been true to rhetoric about participatory government. By revealing weaknesses in the present relationships among governments, the business community, and other interested community groups, we have sought – we believe successfully – ways to strengthen the capacity of policy partners for more meaningful engagement in northern Ontario.

NOTES

1 Rick Bartolucci, "Speaking Notes, Minister of Northern Development and Mines, The Northern Prosperity Plan," Sudbury, ON, 10 June 2004.
2 Canada, Industry Canada, Federal Economic Development Initiative in Northern Ontario, "Meet the Minister Responsible for FedNor," 19 March 2010, available online at http://www.ic.gc.ca/eic/site/fednor-fednor.nsf/eng/fn02571.html, accessed 7 August 2010.
3 M. Atkins, "How Societies Choose to Fail or Succeed," Northern Life, 4 August 2009, available online at http://www.northernlife.ca/displayArticle.aspx?id=21605, accessed 12 November 2009.
4 Rick Bartolucci, "Tony Clement Continues Playing 'Hide and Seek' with Sudburians," Press Release, 7 January 2009, available online at http://www.rickbartolucci.com/pressreleases.aspx?id=64, accessed 16 February 2010.
5 Bill Bradley, "Tony Clement Counters Bartolucci Attack," Northern Life, 9 January 2009, available online at http://www.northernlife.ca/news/local-News/2009/clement090109013.aspx, accessed 16 February 2010.
6 Northern Ontario Large Urban Mayors, "Northern Lights: Strategic Investments in Ontario's Greatest Asset" (n.p., 2007), 2, available online at http://www.cityofnorthbay.ca/cityhall/otm/photos/nolum.pdf.
7 Ibid., 3.
8 Ibid., 2.
9 Ibid., 1.

Contributors

Michel S. Beaulieu is chair and associate professor in the Department of History, director of the Centre for Northern Studies, chair of the Interdisciplinary Programs in Northern Studies Committee, and adjunct professor of philosophy at Lakehead University.

Charles Conteh is graduate program director and associate professor of public policy and management in the Department of Political Science at Brock University. His research and teaching interests are in the areas of Canadian and comparative public policy, public management, and political economy. He investigates how local, regional, and national economies are reinventing themselves in the face of seismic global economic changes.

Rhonda L.P. Koster is currently the director of the School of Outdoor Recreation, Parks and Tourism at Lakehead University. Her research focuses on the contribution of tourism towards rural sustainability, with expertise in the areas of determinants of success in rural tourism planning; building capacity for tourism development with First Nations communities; experiential tourism development; the role of Appreciative Inquiry in tourism development; gateway communities and protected areas; rural tourism in the Canadian urban fringe; and frameworks for evaluating tourism as a community economic development endeavour.

Raynald Harvey Lemelin is the research chair in Parks and Protected Areas and associate professor at the School of Outdoor Recreation,

Parks and Tourism, Lakehead University, and the Lakehead University's representative on the Interim Management Board of the Lake Superior National Marine Conservation Area. His research interests are the human dimensions of parks and protected areas management, Aboriginal tourism, and wildlife tourism.

Dawn Madahbee is general manager of Waubetek Business Development Corporation and a member of the Executive Committee of the National Aboriginal Economic Development Board. She is a former chair of the Northern Ontario Development Corporation, and sits on several federal and provincial economic advisory committees.

David Robinson is an associate professor in the Department of Economics at Laurentian University and director of the Institute of Northern Ontario Research and Development. He is also co-author of a book on game theory and writes a regular column on northern policy issues.

Bob Segsworth is professor of political science at Laurentian University where he teaches courses in public administration and public policy. His research focuses on program evaluation policy and practice in the government of Canada.

Chris Southcott is a professor in the Department of Sociology at Lakehead University and chair of the Research Outreach Program at the University of the Arctic.

Doug West is an associate professor in the Department of Political Science and Interdisciplinary Studies at Lakehead University in Orillia, Ontario.

The Institute of Public Administration of Canada Series
in Public Management and Governance